METRICS FOR SOFTWARE CONCEPTUAL MODELS

METRICS FOR
SOFTWARE
CONCEPTUAL
MODELS

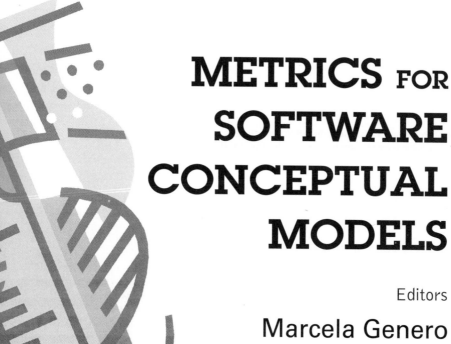

Editors

Marcela Genero
Mario Piattini
Coral Calero
University of Castilla–La Mancha, Spain

ICP Imperial College Press

Published by

Imperial College Press
57 Shelton Street
Covent Garden
London WC2H 9HE

Distributed by

World Scientific Publishing Co. Pte. Ltd.
5 Toh Tuck Link, Singapore 596224
USA office: 27 Warren Street, Suite 401-402, Hackensack, NJ 07601
UK office: 57 Shelton Street, Covent Garden, London WC2H 9HE

British Library Cataloguing-in-Publication Data
A catalogue record for this book is available from the British Library.

METRICS FOR SOFTWARE CONCEPTUAL MODELS

ISBN   1-86094-497-3

Typeset by Stallion Press
Email: sales@stallionpress.com

Printed in Singapore.

Dedicated with admiration and warmth to Isidro Ramos,
with whom the authors have had the pleasure to work.

CONTENTS

Preface ix

Chapter 1
Towards a Framework for Conceptual Modelling Quality 1
Mario Piattini, Marcela Genero, Geert Poels and Jim Nelson

Chapter 2
A Proposal of a Measure of Completeness
for Conceptual Models 19
Oscar Dieste, Marcela Genero, Natalia Juristo
and Ana M. Moreno

Chapter 3
Metrics for Use Cases: A Survey of Current Proposals 59
Beatriz Bernárdez, Amador Durán and Marcela Genero

Chapter 4
Defining and Validating Metrics for UML Class Diagrams 99
Marcela Genero, Geert Poels, Esperanza Manso
and Mario Piattini

Chapter 5
Measuring OCL Expressions: An Approach Based
on Cognitive Techniques 161
Luis Reynoso, Marcela Genero and Mario Piattini

Chapter 6
Metrics for Datawarehouses Conceptual Models   207
*Manuel Serrano, Coral Calero, Juan Trujillo, Sergio Luján
and Mario Piattini*

Chapter 7
Metrics for UML Statechart Diagrams   237
José Antonio Cruz-Lemus, Marcela Genero and Mario Piattini

Chapter 8
Metrics for Software Process Models   273
Félix García, Francisco Ruiz and Mario Piattini

Index   311

PREFACE

Nowadays, the idea that "measuring quality is the key to developing high-quality software systems", is gaining relevance. Moreover, it is widely recognised that the key to obtaining better quality software systems is to measure the quality characteristics of early artefacts, produced at the conceptual modelling phase.

Even though conceptual modelling represents only a part of the overall software system development effort its impact on the final result is probably greater than any other phase. As a result, conceptual modelling has become a key task in the early phases of IS life cycle. Proof of this is that modern approaches towards object-oriented system development, like OPEN, Catalysis and Rational Unified Process, include conceptual modelling as a relevant early task. Moreover, the OMG Model Driven Architecture emphasizes the role of conceptual models in the development of object-oriented systems.

Additionally, as experience has proven, problems in artefacts produced in the initial stages of system development propagate to artefacts produced in later stages, where they are much more costly to identify and correct. Therefore, the quality of conceptual models must be evaluated (and improved where necessary), and the effort expended on improving it is likely to pay off many times over in later phases. Thus, improving the quality of conceptual models represents a major step towards the quality improvement of software system development.

Furthermore, quality has been identified as one of the main topics in current conceptual modelling research.

In practice, evaluation of the quality of conceptual models occurs in an *ad hoc* manner, if at all. There are generally no accepted guidelines for evaluating the quality of conceptual models, and little agreement even among experts as to what makes a "good" model. However, for software system design to evolve from an art to a science, we need to find ways to formally evaluate models rather than solely rely on the judgement of the designer. Thus, there is a need for metrics that can be applied at the conceptual modelling phase.

Since the seventies, software engineers have been putting forward huge quantities of metrics for software products, processes and resources. Almost all of them are, unfortunately, focused on programs or detailed design characteristics, and do not pay any special attention to conceptual modelling. Since the mid-nineties, however, the need for metrics for conceptual modelling has emerged. This corroborates the fact that in comparison to the concept of quality in software engineering — the concept of conceptual modelling quality is poorly understood.

This book provides an overview of the most relevant existing proposals of metrics for conceptual models, covering conceptual models for both products and processes.

The book is structured into 9 chapters. Chapter 1 provides a comprehensive framework to understand conceptual modelling quality research. Chapter 2 provides a measure for conceptual model completeness called "fitness", which indicates how well matched a conceptual model is to a given domain. Chapter 3 provides a thorough state-of-the-art of metrics for use cases, covering use case metrics for project estimation, some metrics as indicators of the requirements engineering process, some metrics to evaluate the modifiability of requirements specification and some heuristics which can be used to identify use cases that potentially can have defects. Chapter 4 examines the most relevant proposals of structural properties of UML class diagrams, such as size, complexity, coupling, etc. Moreover, Chapter 4 proposes and validates a new set of metrics for measuring the structural complexity of UML class diagrams based on the use of UML relationships. Chapter 5 proposes, in a methodological way, a set of metrics for measuring structural properties of OCL expressions, considering those OCL concepts which involve the use of two cognitive techniques — "chunking" and "tracing". Chapter 6 presents a set of metrics for conceptual models for datawarehouses specified using an extension of UML. Chapter 7 deals with quality aspects of behavioural diagrams, especially focusing on metrics for the structural complexity of UML statechart diagrams. Finally, Chapter 8 introduces some metrics for process models.

Space limitations prevented us from giving a more in-depth treatment to each topic, or from including other ones. Readers who wish for further information should refer to the references of each chapter.

The book aims at senior undergraduates and graduates, to complement their software engineering courses. Researchers, PhD students, analysts, designers, software engineers, and those responsible for quality and auditing may also find an overview of these topics interesting and useful for their job.

Acknowledgements

This book compiles works of different authors who have contributed with their knowledge and experience in specific conceptual modelling quality areas. Very special thanks go to all of them for their patience and collaboration.

We would like to thank Imperial College Press, especially Gabriella Frescura, Laurent Chaminade, and Steven Patt for their support during the preparation of the book.

Marcela Genero
Mario Piattini
Coral Calero
October 2004

ABOUT THE EDITORS

MARCELA GENERO

She is an assistant professor in the Department of Computer Science at the University of Castilla-La Mancha, Ciudad Real, Spain. She received her MSc degree in computer science from the Department of Computer Science at the University of South, Argentine in 1989 and her PhD from the University of Castilla-La Mancha, Ciudad Real, Spain, in 2002. Her research interests are advanced database design, software metrics, conceptual data models quality, and database quality. She has published several papers in prestigious conferences and journals such as *CAiSE, E/R, OOIS, METRICS, ISESE, SEKE, Journal of Systems and Software, International Journal of Software Engineering and Knowledge Engineering, Information and Software Technology, Software Quality Journal*, etc. She is the co-editor of the book *Information and Database Quality*, 2002, Kluwer Academic Publishers, USA.

MARIO PIATTINI

He has an MSc and PhD in computer science from the Politechnical University of Madrid and is a Certified Information System Auditor Manager by ISACA (Information System Audit and Control Association). He is a professor in the Department of Computer Science at the University of Castilla-La Mancha, in Ciudad Real, Spain. Author of several books and papers on databases, software engineering and information systems, he leads the ALARCOS research group in the Department of Computer Science at the University of Castilla-La Mancha, in Ciudad Real, Spain.

His research interests are advanced database design, database quality, software metrics, software maintenance and security in information systems. He has co-edited several books, *Advanced Databases: Technology and Design*, 2000, Artech House, UK; *Auditing Information Systems*, Idea Group Publishing, 2000, USA; *Information and Database Quality*, 2002, Kluwer Academic Publishers, USA, etc.

CORAL CALERO

She is an associate professor in the Department of Computer Science at the University of Castilla-La Mancha, Ciudad Real, Spain. She received her MS degree in computer science from the Deparment of Computer Science at the University of Seville, Seville, Spain, in 1996, and her PhD at the University of Castilla-La Mancha, Ciudad Real, Spain. Her research interests are database quality, metrics for advanced databases, formal verification and empirical validation of software metrics. She has published several papers on information systems, software quality, information software and technology, IEE software, etc and co-edited the book *Information and Database Quality*, 2002, Kluwer Academic Publishers, USA.

ABOUT THE AUTHORS

BEATRIZ BERNÁRDEZ

Beatriz is an assistant professor in the Department of Computer Science at the University of Seville, Spain. She received her MS degree in Computer Science from the University of Seville in 1998. Her research interests are requirements engineering, quality requirements, engineering software measurement and software process improvement. She has published several papers in conferences such as WER, JISBD, etc.

JOSÉ ANTONIO CRUZ-LEMUS

José Antonio is an assistant professor in the Department of Computer Science at the University of Castilla-La Mancha, Spain. He received his MS degree in Computer Science at the University of Castilla-La Mancha in 2003. He is also a PhD student at the same university. His research interests are metamodelling using UML, metrics for UML models, etc.

OSCAR DIESTE

Dr. Oscar Dieste is an assistant professor with the School of Computing at the Universidad Complutense de Madrid, Spain. Dr Dieste has a BS and a PhD in computing. He has been a guest editor of the *International Journal of Software Engineering and Knowledge Engineering*, and reviewer of journals such as *IEEE Computer* or *IEEE Software*.

AMADOR DURÁN

Amador received his MS degree in computer science in 1993 and his PhD in computer science in 2000, both from the University of Seville, Spain. He has been an assistant professor in the Department of Computer Languages and Systems at the University of Seville since 1994. His current research interests are requirements engineering, software development process modelling, conceptual modelling, software engineering for web applications and empirical software engineering. He has published several papers in requirements engineering conferences, such as RE, WER, etc.

FÉLIX GARCÍA

Félix has an MSc degree in computer science from the University of Castilla-La Mancha, Spain and is an assistant professor at the same university. He is a member of the Alarcos Research Group, specializing in information systems, databases and software engineering. He is the author of several papers related to software process modelling and measurement. His research interests are software processes and software measurement.

NATALIA JURISTO

Dr. Natalia Juristo is a professor of software engineering with the School of Computing at the Universidad Politecnica de Madrid, Spain. Since 1992, she is the Director of the MSc in Software Engineering. Dr. Juristo has a BS and a PhD in computing. She was a fellow of the European Centre for Nuclear Research (CERN) in Switzerland in 1988, and a member of staff of the European Space Agency (ESA) in Italy in 1989 and 1990. During 1992, she was a resident affiliate of the Software Engineering Institute at Carnegie Mellon University. She was program chair for SEKE97 and general chair for SEKE01 and SNPD02. Professor Juristo has been a key speaker for CSEET03. She has been a guest editor of special issues in several journals, including the *Journal of Software and Systems, Data and Knowledge Engineering* and the *International Journal of Software Engineering and Knowledge Engineering*. Dr Juristo has been a member of several editorial boards, including *IEEE Software* and the *Journal of Empirical Software Engineering*. She is a senior member of IEEE.

SERGIO LUJÁN-MORA

He is a lecturer in the Computer Science School at the University of Alicante, Spain. He received a BS in 1997 and a Master in computer science in 1998 from the University of Alicante. Currently, he is a doctoral student in the Department of Language and Information Systems being supervised by Dr Juan Trujillo. His research spans the fields of multidimensional databases, data warehouses, OLAP techniques, database conceptual modelling and object oriented design and methodologies, web engineering and web programming. He is author of several national journal papers and papers presented in international conferences such as ER, UML and WAIM.

ESPERANZA MANSO

She has a MSc in science (statistic) from Valladolid University, and is a lecturer in the Department of Computer Science of the same university. She is doing her PhD in empirical software engineering. She has several papers in prestigious conferences such as CAiSE, OOIS, METRICS, etc. She was co-author of the book "Medición par la gestión en Ingeniería del Software", 2000 RAMA, Spain. Her research interests are empirical validation of software metrics and models, reuse, software metrics and software quality.

ANA Mª MORENO

Dr. Ana Mª Moreno is an associate professor with the School of Computing at the Universidad Politecnica de Madrid. Dr Moreno has a BS and PhD in computing. Since 2001, she has been Director of the MSc in Software Engineering. Dr Moreno has been visiting scholar at the Vrije Unviersiteit (Amsterdam, The Netherlands) and visiting professor at the Unviersity of Colorado at Colorado Springs (USA). She was program chair for NLDB'01 and SNPD'02 and general chair for CSEET03. She has been a guest editor of special issues in several journals including *Data & Knowledge Engineering* and *International Journal of Software Engineering and Knowledge Engineering*; and reviewer journals like *ACM Computing Reviews, IEEE Transactions on Software Engineering, IEEE Computer* or *IEEE Software*. In 2001, she published a book, *Basics on Software Engineering Experimentation*.

JIM NELSON

Jim Nelson is an assistant professor of accounting and management information systems at The Ohio State University. He received his BS in

Computer Science from California Polytechnic State University, San Luis Obispo, and his MS and PhD in Information Systems from the University of Colorado, Boulder. His research interests include developing theoretically grounded models and metrics for evaluating business processes, investigating the problems people have shifting to emerging technologies, and determining the business value of information technology. Jim generally teaches the more technical courses in information systems including object oriented technology, systems analysis and design, database theory and practice, and business data communications.

GEERT POELS

He is a lecturer in the Department of Management Information, Operations Management, and Technology Policy of the Faculty of Economics and Business Administration at Ghent University and guest professor in the Center for Industrial Management of the Catholic University of Leuven. He holds a Master Degree in business engineering (1991) from the Limburg Business School and a Master Degree in computer science (1993) and PhD in applied economics (1999) from the Catholic University of Leuven. His research interests include theoretical foundations of software measurement, metrics for event-based models, OO software metrics, conceptual model quality, accounting system data models and ontologies, and functional size measurement. From 1999 till 2001, he was the Program Chair of the FESMA series of conferences on software measurement. Since 1996, he has co-organized workshops on OO software metrics, business software component identification, quantitative approaches in OO software engineering, and conceptual modelling quality at the OT, ECOOP and ER conferences. He has published papers in *IEEE Transactions on Software Engineering and Information and Software Technology*, and presented at conferences such as CAiSE, ER, and OOIS.

LUIS REYNOSO

Luis is an assistant professor at the National University of Comahue, Neuquen, Argentina. He received his MSc degree in computer science from the National University of South Argentine in 1993. He also obtained a Magister in computer science at the same university in 2003. He was a fellow in the International Institute of Software Technology, one of the

Research and Training Centres of the United Nations University, researching on a project about object-oriented design patterns. He has published papers in several international conferences. His research interests are focused on object-oriented metrics and the combination of formal and informal methods applied to software engineering.

FRANCISCO RUIZ

He obtained his PhD in computer science from the University of Castilla-La Mancha (UCLM) and MSc in Chemistry-Physics from the University Complutense de Madrid. He is a full time associate professor in the Department of Computer Science at UCLM in Ciudad Real (Spain). He was Dean of the Faculty of Computer Science between 1993 and 2000. Previously, he was a Computer Services Director in the aforementioned university (1985–1989) and he has also worked in private companies as an analyst programmer and project manager. His current research interests include software process technology and modelling, software maintenance, methodologies for software project planning and managing, and advance database modelling. In the past, other work topics have included GIS (geographical information systems), educational software systems, and deductive databases. He has written eight books and fourteen chapters on the aforementioned topics and has published ninety papers in magazines, congresses and conferences. He belongs to several scientific and professional associations — ACM, IEEE-CS, ISO JTC1/SC7, EASST.

MANUEL SERRANO

Manuel Serrano received his MSc and Technical degree in computer science from the University of Castilla-La Mancha. Nowadays, he is developing his PhD at UCLM. He is an assistant professor in the Department of Computer Science at the University of Castilla-La Mancha University in Ciudad Real. He is a member of the Alarcos Research Group, in the same university, specialising in information systems, databases and software engineering. He is the secretary of the ATI (Computer Technicians Asociation) group in Castilla — La Mancha. His research interests are datawarehouse quality and metrics, and software quality.

JUAN TRUJILLO

He is an associate professor in the Computer Science School at the University of Alicante, Spain. He received his PhD in computer science from the University of Alicante (Spain) in 2001. His research interests include database modelling, conceptual design of data warehouses, multidimensional databases, OLAP, and object-oriented analysis and design with UML. He has published papers in international conferences and journals such as ER, UML, ADBIS, WAIM and *IEEE Computer*. He is a Program Committee member of several workshops and conferences such as ER, DOLAP, DSE, ICIS and SCI.

Chapter 1

TOWARDS A FRAMEWORK FOR CONCEPTUAL MODELLING QUALITY

MARIO PIATTINI[*,a], MARCELA GENERO[*,b],
GEERT POELS[†] and JIM NELSON[‡]

*Department of Computer Science, University of Castilla-La Mancha
Paseo de la Universidad, 4, 13071, Ciudad Real, Spain
[a]mario.piattini@uclm.es
[b]marcela.genero@uclm.es

†Department of Management Information, Operations Management,
and Technology Policy
Faculty of Economics and Business Administration
Ghent University, Hoveniersberg 24, 9000 Gent, Belgium
geert.poels@UGent.be

‡Department of Accounting and MIS, Fisher College of Business
The Ohio State University, 2100 Neil Avenue, Columbus, Ohio, USA
nelson_j@cob.osu.edu

1. Introduction

Information technology has become a relevant part of our daily life, and it will be the cornerstone for technology infrastructure of our society in the near future. Central to this cornerstone is the process of conceptual modelling (Chen et al., 1999).

1

Conceptual models[1] are the outcome of conceptual modelling and provide the link between the user's needs and the software solution that meets them. Conceptual models are no longer only for databases. From its genesis in data modelling, the field of conceptual modelling has broadened to include behavioural constructs. The advent of technologies such as object orientation, workflow systems, and so forth has placed greater emphasis on the need to model behavioural aspects of information systems (IS) in addition to static aspects (Liddle et al., 1997).

Historically, researchers first proposed desirable properties or criteria that conceptual models must fulfil to be considered "good" models (Batini et al., 1992; Reingruber and Gregory, 1994; Boman et al., 1997). These lists are mostly unstructured, use imprecise definitions, often overlap and properties of models are often confused with language and method properties (Lindland et al., 1994). So, in the mid-nineties more rigorous frameworks were been proposed which attempt to address quality in a much more systematic way (Lindland et al., 1994; Moody and Shanks, 1994; Moody et al., 1998; Krogstie et al., 1995; Schuette and Rotthowe, 1998), but most of them lack the quantitative assessment of conceptual model quality. More recently, different authors have proposed metrics for conceptual models in order to evaluate such properties both subjectively and objectively (Moody, 1998; Genero et al., 2000, 2001b).

However, the notion of quality of conceptual models is yet not well understood (Krogstie, 1998). The proposed quality frameworks and metrics have different objectives such as improving readability, predicting maintainability, evaluating simplicity, assuring completeness, and so on. There does not seem to exist a comprehensive view on quality in conceptual modelling. Therefore, it is difficult to build a solid body of knowledge about the work done in conceptual modelling quality.

---

[1]Terminology in this area is a bit confusing, in fact, for Falkenberg et al. (1998) the model is actually a "purposely abstracted, clear, precise and unambiguous conception". Meanwhile the model denotation is a "precise and unambiguously representation of a model, in some appropriate formal or semi-formal language". For several authors, including ISO (1987), the conceptual schema is "a consistent collection of sentences expressing the necessary propositions that hold for a universe of discourse". In this book, we will use conceptual model and conceptual schema indistinctively.

An additional problem in generalising the results of conceptual modelling quality is that the studies are performed on conceptual models for different kinds of application systems. For example, a UML class model could be used to model application programs, databases, datawarehouses, web applications, pervasive IS, ubiquitous application systems, and so on. Any effort to categorise research in conceptual modelling quality must therefore explicitly consider the application domain that is used within the research context.

There are a number of different existing proposals that address the issue of conceptual modelling quality. This paper presents a framework for organising these proposals into a number of interesting and useful dimensions. In the next section, we present the different dimensions which can be used to classify quality in conceptual modelling, based on a three-dimensional framework first used to classify contributions in the *First International Workshop on Conceptual Modelling Quality* (IWCMQ) (Poels et al., 2002).

2. Dimensions in Conceptual Modelling Quality

Quality is a multidimensional concept. In order to analyse conceptual modelling quality in detail, we propose to distinguish seven different dimensions. In fact, we can analyse the different proposals on conceptual modelling quality considering:

- The *type of quality*, i.e. the correspondence level between the different elements participating in conceptual modelling (stakeholders, languages, models, etc.).
- The *object of study*, i.e. the focus of the research (e.g. process, language, model).
- The *research goal*, i.e. what is the aim of the proposal (e.g. understanding, improving, etc.).
- The *quality characteristic* (e.g. maintainability, completeness, etc.).
- The *context of study*, i.e. the area in which the conceptual model is used (e.g. databases, web information systems, object-oriented programs, etc.).
- The followed *research method* (e.g. experiments, surveys, literature analysis, etc.).

- The *type of proposal* proposed for improving, assuring, etc. conceptual modelling quality (e.g. methodologies, patterns, metrics, etc.).

2.1. *Types of quality*

The "type of quality" classification scheme in this paper is based on two main works:

- Krogstie (1998), which is based on the works done by Lindland et al. (1994), Krogstie et al. (1995) and Pohl (1994).
- Nelson et al. (2001), which is an extension of Krogstie (1995).

Krogstie (1998) proposed a set-theoretic approach defining quality as the correspondence between different sets (see Fig. 1):

- Language extension (L): the set of all statements that are possible to make according the vocabulary and syntax of the modelling languages used.
- Modelling Domain (D): the set of all statements, which can be stated about the situation at hand.
- Model Externalisation (M): the set of all statements in someone's model of part of the perceived reality written in a language. According to the ISO (1987), it corresponds to the term "model denotation".

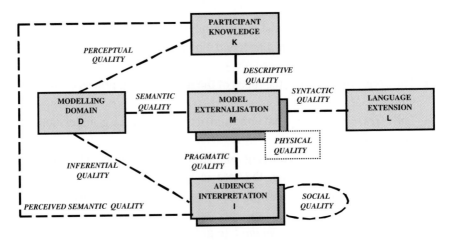

Fig. 1. Different types of conceptual modelling quality.

- Participant Knowledge (K): the relevant explicit knowledge of a member of the audience.
- Audience[2] Interpretation (I): the set of all the statements, which the audience thinks that an externalised model consists of.

The types of quality are defined as a level of correspondence between these sets. Krogstie (1998) distinguishes fives types of quality (see Fig. 1):

- *Physical quality*: Refers to how well the model corresponds to participant knowledge. The basic quality features on the physical level are externalisation, that the participant has been externalised by the use of a conceptual modelling language, and internaliseability, that the externalised model is persistent and available.
- *Syntactic quality* refers to how well the model corresponds to the language.
- *Semantic quality* refers to how well the model corresponds to the domain. There exists two semantic goals; *validity* which means that all statements made in the model are correct and relevant to the domain and *completeness* which means that the model contains all the statements which would be correct and relevant about the domain. These goals are made more applicable by introducing the notion of feasibility. Feasible validity means there is no invalid statement that is cost efficient to remove from the model. Feasible completeness means that there is no statements in the domain, but not in the model, that is cost efficient to include in the model.
- *Perceived semantic quality* is the similar correspondence between the audience interpretation of a model and their knowledge of the domain. Whereas the primary goal for semantic quality is a correspondence between the externalised model and the domain as indicated above, this correspondence can neither be established or checked directly (Krogstie, 1998). To build a model, one has to go through the participant knowledge regarding the domain, and to check the model, one has to compare with the audience interpretation of the externalised model (Krogstie, 1998). Hence, what we observe at quality control is not the

---

[2]The Audience is the union of the set of individual, organisational and technical (tools) actors who need to relate to the models being developed (Krogstie, 1998).

actual semantic quality based on comparisons of the two imperfect interpretations (Krogstie, 1998).

- *Pragmatic quality* refers to how well the model corresponds to its audience interpretation. Feasibility is also defined for pragmatic quality.
- *Social quality* refers to the agreement among participant interpretations.

The proposal of Krogstie (1998) was extended by Nelson et al. (2001) to include two types of quality that cover the earliest stages of modelling (see Fig. 1):

- *Perceptual quality*: That refers to how well the actors within the domain of interest understand that domain.
- *Descriptive quality*: The ability of the modeller to elicit a description of that domain.

And one type that gives an overall assessment of model quality:

- *Inferential quality*: Which refers to how well the conceptual model as understood by the audience matches the original domain.

These nine types of quality form the first dimension of the framework we propose for conceptual modelling quality.

2.2. Object of study

Another useful dimension is the object of the study. Quality research can focus on any (or all) of the three modelling elements (see Fig. 2). The first is the process of creating the model. In general, the quality of the modelling process is directly proportional to the quality of the model produced by the process (Nelson et al., 2001). In general, modelling process quality has been disregarded. However, as Moody et al. (1998) and Maier (2001) remarked, if the modelling process is of high quality, there is a greater chance of obtaining higher quality conceptual models.

The second element is the modelling language that is used in the modelling process to produce the conceptual model. The existing languages can be classified as classic — E/R (Chen, 1976) and its extensions (Elmasri and Navathe, 2002; Teory, 1990; Talheim, 2000), DFD (Yourdon, 1989), or object-oriented — nowadays, mainly UML (Booch et al., 1998) and OML

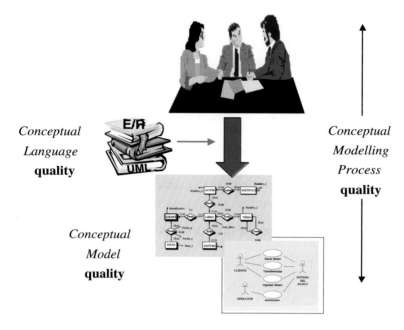

Fig. 2. Objects of study in conceptual modelling.

(Firesmith et al., 1998). Traditionally, different comparisons between modelling languages has been performed (Batra et al., 1990; Kim and March,
1995; Rossi and Brinkkemper, 1996; etc) and workshops as the *Evaluation
of Modelling Methods in Systems Analysis and Design* (EMMSAD) are
mainly focused on modelling language issues.

The third element is the conceptual model itself, which usually consists
of a diagram and a complementary textual description. Traditionally, conceptual models could describe static (information), functional or dynamic
aspects of information systems. Conceptual models could also focus on process and business (Curtis et al., 1992) and IS architectural aspects or even
goals of organisations. Recently, with the diffusion of web-based systems,
navigational, interactive, and other conceptual models are used. Conceptual
models have been introduced even in other areas, such as account data
models (McCarthy, 1982).

Forums like the *International Conference on Conceptual Modelling*
(*ER*) and specially its *International Workshop on Conceptual Modelling
Quality* (*IWCMQ*), *International Conference on Advanced Information*

Systems Engineering (CAiSE) and its *International Workshop on Requirements Engineering Foundations for Software Quality (REFSQ)*, *The Requirements Engineering Conference (RE)*, or the *International Conference on UML* deal with conceptual model quality issues.

2.3. *Goal*

The third conceptual model quality dimension is the research goal. There are several goals, in fact every researcher or organisation pursuit its own goals. In general, we can distinguish five different goals — understanding, measuring, evaluating, assuring, and improving conceptual model quality:

- Research into *understanding* quality seeks to define the various dimensions of quality.
- *Measuring* quality examines the scales that can be used to determine quality and how to apply those dimensions against conceptual models.
- Research that *evaluates* quality explores the correlation between the quality measurements and real-world experiences with the model. For example, how various measurements correlate with model understanding, model maintenance, and so on.
- Quality *assurance* research examines how to ensure that the process that produces the conceptual model actually does produce a quality model.
- Finally, the research into *improving* quality examines how to make conceptual modelling quality better.

2.4. *Quality characteristic*

Quality characteristics depend on the object of study and are therefore very diverse.

For conceptual modelling process one could be interested in analysing the typical quality characteristics of software processes, such as those defined in CMM (SEI, 1995), SPICE (ISO, 1998) or CMMi (SEI, 2002) models — capability, maturity, stability, etc.

Considering both the modelling language and the conceptual model as software products, we could follow the ISO 9126 standard ("Software Product Evaluation-Quality Characteristics and Guidelines for their Use" and its characteristics (Functionality, Efficiency, Maintainability, Portability, Usability and Reliability)) and all their subcharacteristics (ISO, 2001).

There are, however, more specific quality characteristics defined for modelling languages by different authors, for example, Krogstie (1998) considers:

- Domain appropriateness, ability of the modelling language to capture the domain.
- Comprehensibility appropriateness, how easily the modelling language could be learned, used, and understood by the participants of the modelling effort.
- Executability appropriateness, to what extent the language is formalised to enable execution, simulations, etc.
- Knowledge externalisability appropriateness, how relevant knowledge of the domain may be articulated in the language.

Regarding conceptual model quality, if we consider a conceptual model as a software requirement specification, we could apply the quality properties defined by Davis et al. (1993) or the International Standard ISO 830 (IEEE, 1998). However, several proposals exists in this area:

- ISO (1987): conceptualisation principle and 100 percent principle.
- Batini et al. (1990): completeness, correctness, minimality, expressiveness, readability, self-explanation, extensibility, and normality.
- Reingruber and Gregory (1994): Conceptual correctness, conceptual completeness, syntactic correctness, syntactic completeness, and enterprise awareness.
- Boman et al. (1997): Ease of understanding, semantic correctness, stability, completeness, and conceptual focus.
- Moody and Shanks (1994) and Moody et al. (1998): completeness, integrity, flexibility, understandability, correctness, simplicity, integration, and implementability.
- Olivé (2000): Completeness, correctness, principle of conceptualisation (design independent conceptual schema), syntactically valid, simplicity, ease of understanding, and stability (flexibility, extensibility, modifiability).
- Marjomaa (2002) defines the conceptualisation principle, the 100 Percent principle, the formalisation principle, the semiotic principle, the correspondence condition for knowledge representation, the

Sperber–Wilson principle of relevance, the invariance principle, the principle of contextuality, and the principle of partiality.

2.5. *Context of study*

In order to totally characterise conceptual model quality issues, we think it is very important to specify in what context quality proposals are made. In this sense, traditionally, conceptual models are conceived for management IS, specifically for design application programs and databases. Also, real-time IS and embedded software were designed using special extended conceptual models.

More recently, new methodologies are proposed for developing other kind of software using conceptual models, like datawarehouses, web applications, pervasive IS, etc.

2.6. *Research method*

Nowadays, in Software Engineering (SE) it is very important to increase the level of rigor in research and more importance is given to follow research methods, which could provide a scientific basis to findings (Fenton et al., 1994; Zelkowitz and Wallace, 1995; Zelkowitz and Wallace, 2002).

Additionally to research methods used traditionally in SE such as literature analysis, concept implementation, mathematical proof or simulation; more qualitative methods are being adopted from the humanistic areas (Seaman, 1999), such as action research (Avison et al., 2000).

Also, since the last years, methods used in experimental sciences are gaining importance in our area, giving raise to the so-called Empirical Software Engineering. In fact, (laboratory) experiments, case studies, surveys, or meta-analysis are basic to create evidence-based knowledge (Fenton and Pfleeger, 1997; Juristo and Moreno, 2001, 2003; Kitchenham et al., 2002; Pfleeger and Kitchenham, 2001; Wohlin et al., 2000). Other research methods used in SE can be found in Glass et al. (2002) but they have not been applied, at least in our knowledge, in conceptual model quality research.

2.7. *Type of proposal*

Finally, we can classify researches depending on the type of proposal proposed to deal with conceptual modelling quality. As we have already

Table 1. Summary of quality classification dimensions.

Type of quality ∈ {perceptual, descriptive, physical, syntactic, semantic, perceived semantic, pragmatic, social, inferential}

Object of study ∈ {process, language, model}

Research goal ∈ {understanding, measuring/assessing, assuring, evaluating, improving}

Quality characteristic ∈ {completeness, consistency, simplicity, maintainability, flexibility, understandability, stability, etc.}

Context of study ∈ {management IS (MIS), application programs, databases, datawarehouses, web applications, ubiquitous application systems, pervasive IS, real-time IS, embedded software, business processes, accounting systems, workflow systems, etc.}

Research method ∈ {literature analysis, concept implementation, mathematical proof, simulation, meta-analysis, action research, (laboratory) experiments, case studies or surveys}

Type of proposal ∈ {list of characteristics, frameworks, metrics, languages, heuristics, tools, patterns, refactorings, schema transformations, reference models, other techniques}

---

presented, quality in conceptual modelling started with "lists of characteristics", followed by "quality frameworks", and more recently also "metrics". But there are other proposals for improving the quality of conceptual models — several proposals to extend existing modelling languages or creating new ones, model transformations (Assenova and Johannesson, 1996; Reingruber and Gregory, 1994; Batini et al., 1992), modelling heuristics (Sindre and Krogstie, 1995), tools (Matulevicius and Strašunskas, 2002), patterns (Coad, 1992; Fowler, 1996), refactoring (Fowler, 2000), reference models (Misic and Zhao, 2000; Poels et al., 2001) and other techniques.

In Table 1, we summarise the seven dimensions and some of their possible alternatives.

3. Classification of Book Contributions

In this section, we classify the nine chapters of this book along the dimensions proposed in the previous section (See Table 2.).

Table 2. Classification of book chapters contributions to conceptual modelling quality research.

Ch.	Type of quality	Object of study	Research goal	Quality characteristic	Context of study	Research method	Type of proposal
1	all	all	understanding	all	all	literature analysis	framework
2	pragmatic	language	measuring evaluating	completeness	all	experiments	metric
3	pragmatic	Model (requirement specifications — use cases)	measuring evaluating improving	modifiability fault-proneness	all	literature analysis	metrics heuristics prediction models
4	pragmatic	Model (UML class diagrams)	measuring evaluating	understandability analyzability modifiability	all	literature analysis experiments mathematical proof	metrics prediction model
5	pragmatic	Model (conceptual datawarehouses models)	measuring evaluating	understandability modifiability	Datawarehouses application systems	literature analysis mathematical proof experiments	metrics
6	pragmatic	Model (OCL expressions)	measuring evaluating	understandability	all	mathematical proof	metrics
7	pragmatic	Model (UML statechart diagrams)	measuring evaluating	understandability	all	literature analysis mathematical proof experiments	metrics
8	pragmatic	Model (process models)	measuring evaluating	understandability analyzability modifiability	all	mathematical proof experiments	metrics

4. Conclusions

As an early stage activity, conceptual modelling plays a crucial role in software, database, web development, etc. Therefore, the success of systems development strongly depends on conceptual modelling quality.

Current research on conceptual modelling quality is disperse and very difficult to evaluate and integrate, because of the lack of a systematic framework. In this chapter, we have elaborated a first proposal in this sense, and used it to classify the chapters of this book. We hope this classification helps to better understand the different contributions in this book.

The framework that is proposed must be further refined and validated. In order to achieve a better framework and to provide a more comprehensive aid to the users (analysts, designers, quality managers, etc.) concerned about conceptual modelling quality, we are in the process of classifying most of the relevant literature in this area using the proposed framework. We have not finished yet, but we anticipate that some conclusions can be derived from this kind of analysis, for example that (1) quality aspects of the conceptual modelling process has been largely disregarded, (2) most of the researchers focus on pragmatic and syntactic types of quality, (3) little work has been done towards measuring, evaluating and assuring the quality of conceptual representations of behaviour, activities, processes, etc., (4) more scientific validation is needed.

This kind of study could help to identify major opportunities for future research in conceptual modelling quality. There are clearly areas identified by our framework that have been studied fairly heavily, but there are also areas of conceptual modelling quality that have received little attention. Addressing these areas will perhaps lead to better quality models, thus leading to higher quality software engineering projects.

Acknowledgements

This research is part of the DOLMEN (TIC 2000-1673-C06-06) and the CALDEA (TIC 2000-1673-C06-06) projects, financed by Subdirección General de Proyectos de Investigación, Ministerio de Ciencia y Tecnología (Spain).

References

Avison, D., Lau, F., Myers, M. and Nielsen, A. (1999). Action Research. *Communications of the ACM*, Vol. 42, No. 1, pp. 94–97.

Assenova, P. and Johanneson, P. (1996). Improving quality in conceptual modelling by the use of schema transformations. *Proceedings of 15th International Conference of Conceptual modelling (ER '96)*, Cotbus, Germany, pp. 277–291.

Batini, C., Ceri, S. and Navathe, S. (1992). *Conceptual Database Design. An Entity Relationship Approach*. Benjamin Cummings Publishing Company.

Batra, D., Hoffer, J.A. and Bostrom, R.P. (1990). A Comparison of User Performance Between the Relational and the Extended Entity Relationship Models in the Discovery Phase of Database Design. *Communications of the ACM*, Vol. 33, No. 2, pp. 26–139.

Boehm, B. (1981). *Software Engineering Economics*. Prentice-Hall.

Boman, M., et al. (1997). *Conceptual Modelling*. Prentice Hall.

Booch, G., Rumbaugh, J. and Jacobson, I. (1998). *The Unified Modelling Language User Guide*. Addison-Wesley.

Chen P. (1976). The Entity-Relationship Model: Toward a Unified View of Data. *ACM Transactions on Database Systems,* Vol. 1, No. 1, pp. 9–37.

Chen, P., Thalheim, B. and Wong, L. (1999). Future Directions of Conceptual Modelling. *Conceptual Modelling: Current Issues and Future Directions*. Eds. Chen, P., Akoka, J., Kangassalo, H. and Thalheim, B., *Lecture Notes in Computer Science 1565*, pp. 258–271.

Coad, P. (1992). Object-Oriented Patterns. *Communications of the ACM*, Vol. 35, No. 9, pp. 152–159.

Curtis, B., Keller, M.I. and Over, J. (1992). Process Modelling. *Communications of ACM,* Vol. 35, No. 9.

Davis, A.M., Overmeyer, S., Jordan, K., Caruso, J., Dandashi, F., Din, A., Kincaid, G., Ledeboer, G., Reynolds, P., Sitaram, P., Ta, A. and Theofanos, M. (1993). Identifying and Measuring Quality in a Software Requirements Specification. *Proceedings of the 1st International Software Metrics Symposium*, pp. 141–152.

Elmasri, R. and Navathe, S. (2001). *Fundamentals of Database Systems*, 3rd edition. Addison Wesley.

Falkenberg, E.D., Hesse, W., Lindgreen, P., Nilsson, B.E., Han, J.L., Rolland, C., Stamper, R.K., Van Assche, F.J.M., Verrijn-Stuart, A.A. and Voss, K. (1998). *A Framework of Information System Concepts*. The Frisco Report. IFIP.

Fenton, N., Pfleeger, S.L. and Glass, R.L. (1994). Science and Substance: A Challenge to Software Engineers. *IEEE Software*, Vol. 11, No. 4, pp. 86–95.

Fenton, N. and Pfleeger, S. (1997). *Software Metrics: A Rigorous Approach*, 2nd edition. London, Chapman & Hall.

Firesmith, D., Henderson-Sellers, B. and Graham, I. (1998). *The Open Modelling Language (OML) Reference Manual*. SIGS Book, Cambridge University Press.

Fowler, M. (1996). *Analysis Patterns: Reusable Object Models*. Addison-Wesley.

Fowler, M. (2000). *Refactoring — Improving the Existing Code*. Addison-Wesley.

Genero, M., Piattini, M. and Calero, C. (2000). Early Measures For UML class diagrams. *L'Objet,* Vol. 6, No. 4, Hermes Science Publications, pp. 489–515.

Glass, R.L., Vessey, I. and Ramesh, V. (2002). Research in Software Engineering: An Analysis of the Literature. *Information and Software Technology*, Vol. 44, pp. 491–506.

IEEE (1998). *IEEE Recommended Practice for Software Requirements Specifications*. IEEE Std. 830. The Institute of Electrical and Electronics Engineers, Inc., USA.

ISO (1987). *Information Processing Systems — Concepts and Terminology for the Conceptual Schema and the Information Base*. Technical Report 9007, Switzerland.

ISO (1998). *A Reference Model for Processes and Process Capability*, ISO IEC 15504 TR2:1998, part 2. ISO/IEC JTC1/SC7, Switzerland.

ISO (2001). Software Product Evaluation-Quality Characteristics and Guidelines for their Use, ISO/IEC Standard 9126, Switzerland.

Juristo, N. and Moreno, A. (2001). *Basics of Software Engineering Experimentation*. Kluwer Academic Publishers.

Juristo, N. and Moreno, A. (2003). *Lecture Notes on Empirical Software Engineering*, Vol. 12, New Jersey, World Scientific.

Kim, Y.-G. and March, S.T. (1995). Comparing Data Modelling Formalisms. *Communications of the ACM*, Vol. 38, No. 6, pp. 103–115.

Kitchenham, B., Pfleeger, S., Pickard, L., Jones, P., Hoaglin, D., El Emam, K. and Rosenberg, J. (2002). Preliminary Guidelines for Empirical Research in Software Engineering. *IEEE Transactions on Software Engineering*, Vol. 28, No. 8, pp. 721–734.

Krogstie, J. (1998). Integrating the Understanding of Quality in Requirements Specification and Conceptual Modelling. *ACM SIGSOFT Software Engineering Notes*, Vol. 23, No. 1, pp. 86–91.

Krogstie, J., Lindland, O.I. and Sindre, G. (1995). Towards a Deeper Understanding of Quality in Requirements Engineering. *Lecture Notes in Computer Science*, 932, *Proceedings of the 7th International Conference on Advanced Information Systems Engineering (CAiSE'95)*, Jyvaskyla, Finland, June 12–16, 1995, Springer, Berlin, pp. 82–95.

Liddle, S., Stephen, W. and Woodfield, S. (1999). A Summary of the ER '97 Workshop on Behavioural Modelling. *Conceptual Modelling: Current Issues and Future Directions*. Eds. Chen, P., Akoka, J., Kangassalo, H. and Thalheim, B., *Lecture Notes in Computer Science 1565*, pp. 258–271.

Lindland, O.I., Sindre, G. and Solvberg, A. (1994). Understanding Quality in Conceptual Modelling. *IEEE Software*, Vol. 11, No. 2, pp. 42–49.

Maier, R. (2001). Organizational Concepts and Measures for the Evaluation of Data Modelling. *Developing Quality Complex Databases Systems: Practices, Techniques and Technologies*. Ed. Becker S., Idea Group Publishing, pp. 1–27.

Marjomaa, E. (2002). Necessary Conditions for High Quality Conceptual Schemata: Two Wicked Problems. *Journal of Conceptual Modelling*, Vol. 27, December.

Matulevicius, R. and Strašunskas, D. (2002). Evaluation Framework of Requirements Engineering Tools for Verification and Validation. International Workshop on Conceptual Modelling Quality (IWCMQ '02). *Lecture Notes in Computer Science*, Springer-Verlag.

McCarthy, W.E. (1982). The REA Accounting Model: A Generalized Framework for Accounting Systems in a Shared Data Environment. *The Accounting Review*, Vol. 57, No. 3, pp. 554–578.

Misic, V. and Zhao, J. (2000). Evaluating the Quality of Reference Models. *19th International Conference on Conceptual Modelling (ER '2000). Lecture Notes in Computer Science 1920*, Salt Lake City, USA, October, pp. 484–498.

Moody, D. (1998). Metrics For Evaluating the Quality of Entity Relationship Models. *Proceedings of the 17th International Conference on Conceptual Modelling (ER '98)*, Singapore, pp. 213–225.

Moody, L. and Shanks, G. (1994). What Makes A Good Data Model? Evaluating the Quality of Entity Relationships Models. *Proceedings of the 13th International Conference on Conceptual Modelling (ER '94)*, Manchester, England, pp. 94–111.

Moody, L., Shanks, G. and Darke, P. (1998). Improving the Quality of Entity Relationship Models — Experience in Research and Practice. *Proceedings of the

17th International Conference on Conceptual Modelling (ER '98), Singapore, pp. 255–276.

Nelson, H.J., Monarchi, D.E. and Nelson, K.M. (2001). Ensuring the "Goodness" of a Conceptual Representation. *Proceedings of the 4th European Conference on Software Measurement and ICT Control (FESMA'01)*, Heidelberg, Germany.

Olivé, A. (2000). An Introduction to Conceptual Modelling of Information Systems. *In Chapter 2: Advanced Database Technology and Design*, Eds. Piattini, M. and Díaz, O., Artech House, pp. 25–57.

Pfleeger, S.A. and Kitchenham, B.A. (2001). Principles of Survey Research. *Software Engineering Notes*, 2001, Vol. 26, No. 6, pp. 16–18.

Poels, G., Dedene, G. and Viaene, S. (2001). A Quantitative Assessement of the Complexity of Static Concetual Schemata for Reference Types of Front-Office. *Proceedings of the 5th International Workshop Quantitative Approaches in Object-Oriented Software Engineering (QAOOSE 2001)*, pp. 47–58.

Poels, G., Nelson, J., Genero, M. and Piattini, M. (2002). Quality in Conceptual Modelling — New Research Directions. *International Workshop on Conceptual Modelling Quality (IWCMQ 2002)*, Tampere, Finland, *Lecture Notes in Computer Science (LCNS) 2784*, Springer–Verlag (to appear).

Pohl, K. (1994). The Three Dimensions of Requirements Engineering: A Framework and its Applications. *Information Systems*, Vol. 19, pp. 243–258.

Reingruber, M. and Gregory, W. (1994). *The Data Modelling Handbook. A Best-Practice Approach to Building Quality Data Models.* John Wiley & Sons, Inc.

Rossi, M. and Brinkkemper, S. (1996). Complexity Metrics for Systems Development Methods and Techniques. *Information Systems*, Vol. 21, No. 2, pp. 209–227.

Schuette, R., and Rotthowe, T. (1998). The Guidelines of Modelling — An Approach to Enhance the Quality in Information Models. *Proceedings of the 17th International Conference on Conceptual Modelling (ER '98)*, Singapore, pp. 240–254.

Seaman, C.B. (1999). Qualitative Methods in Empirical Studies of Software Engineering. *IEEE Transactions on Software Engineering*, Vol. 25, No. 4, pp. 557–572.

SEI (1995). *The Capability Maturity Model: Guidelines for Improving the Software Process*, 1995. Software Engineering Institute (SEI). In http://www.sei.cmu.edu/cmm/cmm.html

SEI (2002). *Capability Maturity Model Integration (CMMI^{SM})*, version 1.1. Software Engineering Institute (SEI). March 2002. In http://www.sei.cmu/cmmi/cmmi.html.

Teorey, T. (1990). *Database Modelling and Design: The Entity-Relationship Approach*. Morgan Kaufmann.

Thalheim, B. (2000). *Entity-Relationship Modelling*. Springer-Verlag.

Wohlin, C., Runeson, P., Höst, M., Ohlson, M., Regnell, B. and Wesslen, A. (2000). *Experimentation in Software Engineering: An Introduction*. Kluwer Academic Publishers.

Yourdon, E. (1989). *Modern Structured Analysis*. Englewood Cliffs, NJ: Prentice-Hall.

Zelkowitz, M. and Wallace, D. (1995). Experimental Validation in Software Engineering. *Information and Software Technology*, Vol. 39, pp. 735–743.

Zelkowitz, M. and Wallace, D. (2002). Experimental Validation of New Software Technology. *In Lecture Notes on Empirical Software Engineering*, Eds. Juristo, N. and Moreno, A., World Scientific, Singapore, pp. 229–263.

Chapter 2

A PROPOSAL OF A MEASURE OF COMPLETENESS FOR CONCEPTUAL MODELS

OSCAR DIESTE*, MARCELA GENERO[†],
NATALIA JURISTO[‡,a] and ANA M. MORENO[‡,b]

Departamento de Sistemas Informáticos y Programación
Universidad Complutense de Madrid
28040 – Ciudad Universitaria-Madrid, Spain
odiestet@fdi.ucm.es

[†]*Alarcos Research Group*
Department of Computer Science
University of Castilla-La Mancha
Paseo de la Universidad 4 – 13071 – Ciudad Real, Spain
marcela.genero@uclm.es

[‡]*School of Computing*
Technical University of Madrid – 28660 – Boadilla del Monte
Madrid, Spain
[a]*natalia@fi.upm.es*
[b]*ammoreno@fi.upm.es*

1. Introduction

All software development methods use one or more conceptual models (CM). CMs provide the material support for recording and communicating all the relevant aspects of the problem domain (Motschnig-Pitrik, 1993; Borgida, 1991; Beringer, 1994; Loucopoulos and Karakostas, 1995) that should be taken into account to undertake the future implementation of a software system.

Each CM has a set of constructs, such as processes, classes, relationships, states, etc, from which the model derives its expressive possibilities (Dieste et al., 2000). During the use of CMs in practice, each construct is instantiated with the aspects of the problem domain to which it bears a formal resemblance, that is, each particular construct has a more or less well-defined semantics that determines what things or events it can represent. For example, given a domain consisting of a university and the problem of developing an automated enrolment system, aspects like students, subjects, etc, are perceived as sets composed of elements with common properties, by means of which they can be assigned to the entity (or class) construct of models such as the entity-relationship or class diagrams.

The constraints imposed by the semantics of the constructs therefore limit the expressive capabilities of each CM. That is, CMs act like a filter of the problem domain, where only a subset of the important aspects of the domain are recorded, others are minimised and any aspects that cannot be expressed by the constructs proper to the CM in question are concealed. Consequently, any one domain model is only a partial representation of the domain, because of this CM-induced filtering effect.

In simple or familiar domains, where the analysts themselves can cover all the important aspects of the problem to be solved, the fact that CMs are only partial representations does not put the development at risk, because the analysts can make up for the shortcomings of the CMs (Curtis et al., 1988). However, as software systems become more complex and the problem domain moves further away from knowledge familiar to developers, CMs become crucial, since they help to represent the problem to be solved (McGregor and Korson, 1990; Bonfatti and Monari, 1994; Høydalsvik and Sindre, 1993). Any constraint on the content of the CMs brings with it the risk of omitting information that is important for future implementation, which can detract from the quality of the final software product (Maier, 1996).

As CMs can only partially represent a domain, an important question to be cleared up is what part and how much of the problem domain a CM can represent. This question, termed model completeness is addressed as part of the evaluation of CM quality and a range of proposals have been put forward in the literature. These proposals cannot, however, assess how well suited a CM is for a given problem in a specific domain. In this chapter, we propose a new approach that can output a quantitative value, termed fitness, which indicates how well matched a CM is to a given domain.

For this purpose, we will adhere to the following outline. Section 2 offers a review of the literature on CM quality and specifies the limitations of the proposals made. Section 3 proposes and details a new completeness measure. Section 4 is given over to describing how the soundness of the proposed fitness measure was validated. To close the chapter, Sec. 5 sets out our conclusions.

2. Conceptual Model Completeness

The literature includes several proposals for assessing CM quality. The formality of these proposals varies, ranging from property lists, such as (Batini et al., 1992; Boman et al., 1997; Reingruber and Gregory, 1994), through frameworks (Lindland et al.,1994; Krogstie et al., 1995; Schuette and Rotthowe, 1998) to more or less formalised metrics (Kesh, 1995; Moody et al., 1998; Piattini et al., 2000). These proposals interpret CM quality as the achievement of given objectives or, alternatively, the extent to which the CMs comprise a series of properties, such as correctness, maintainability, extendibility, etc. Although there is no unanimous agreement on what particular properties determine model quality (Lindland et al., 1994), completeness is typically among the properties covered by most proposals.

Completeness is denoted as the extent to which a CM matches the problem domain it represents. Completeness is, therefore, a measure of the match between a given domain, described as a set of *a priori* unknown sentences D and an instance of a CM, described as another set of sentences M, as shown in Fig. 1. This model is said to be complete if $D \backslash M = \emptyset$. In absolute terms, of course, completeness is an ideal, and all that can be achieved in practice is a given degree of completeness or feasible completeness. Feasible completeness is defined as $D \backslash M = S \neq \emptyset$, and is greater the lower $\#S$ is (Lindland et al., 1994).

The contents of M and D need to be identified to determine the completeness of a model. The sentences in M are acquired, as shown in Fig. 1, by modelling the domain. It is trickier, however, to get the sentences that make up D. Therefore, (Kesh, 1995), for example, suggests establishing

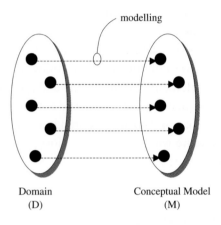

Fig. 1. Match between D and M for determining completeness.

completeness by obviating the set D and having domain users assess the completeness of M subjectively instead of comparing D and M, whereas (Moody et al., 1998) interprets D as a set of user requirements, which means that D and M are compared indirectly. The procedure for identifying the constituent sentences of sets M and D brings to light a series of complications as regards to determining completeness. Firstly, to determine the completeness of a CM, an instance of a model needs to be defined before its completeness can be assessed, that is, M is a concrete conceptualisation of a domain D. Now, because of the filtering effect of the constructs used, a CM can only represent a fraction of the problem domain, which means that it is not feasible to consider completeness as $D \backslash M = \emptyset$ or even as $D \backslash M = S \neq \emptyset$, as foreseeably $\#D \gg \#M$.

Secondly, the definitions of completeness and feasible completeness only make sense if the scope of the sentences of D is restricted. Indeed, the above definitions appear to assume that D and M are closely related, that is, they venture that total completeness is possible and, therefore, all the important aspects of the domain (that is, D) can be recorded in the CM. Therefore, $\#D = \#M$, and any divergence should be put down to deficiencies in the modelling process and/or to the analyst's expertise and not to intrinsic properties of the actual model. Consequently, the definitions of completeness and feasible completeness do not really refer to a match between the domain and the CM; they apply to a match between the

aspects of the domain that can be described in the CM used and a particular instance of this CM, as shown in Fig. 2. That is, we should really be
talking about potential or conditional completeness, insofar as completeness is determined with respect to only a fraction D of the domain and not
with regard to the totality D' of the domain. For example, given any domain
that contains interesting dynamic and logical aspects, an entity-relationship
model could never be complete, unless these dynamic or logical aspects
were obviated to determine completeness.

Apart from the aforesaid limitations, the procedure for determining the
content of the set D, even considering only the fraction of the domain that
can be represented in a given CM (what is termed conditional completeness), is not without its problems either. The most important problem is
that the procedure for determining the sentences in D is not systematic.
As already mentioned, the procedures proposed for the purpose identify
the content of D indirectly, either by means of a subjective assessment
(Kesh, 1995) or by resorting to alternative elements that are reckoned to

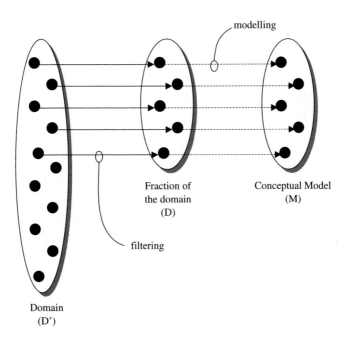

Fig. 2. Match between D', D and M for determining completeness.

represent the domain, such as user requirements (Moody et al., 1998). The final result is that the sentences that form D are never acquired explicitly and, therefore, the set $S = D \backslash M$ is undefined. This means that completeness represents at most a qualitative value (poor, fairly, very…) that divides and graduates the continuum of possible completeness.

After analysing these shortcomings, we can say that the CM quality frameworks and metrics have not satisfactorily solved the problem of determining completeness. Therefore, the definition of completeness needs to be refined, and the right procedures for determining the completeness values of the CM as quantitatively and objectively as possible have to be established. In this respect, the next section proposes a new approach for determining completeness.

3. Proposal of a New Conceptual Model Completeness Measure

As mentioned above, the chief difficulties involved in defining the property of completeness are: (1) determining the propositions and sentences in D; (2) the filtering effect caused by the CMs and (3) the need to have an instance of a model M of the domain D in advance. We have developed an approach that can palliate the above-mentioned difficulties. This approach has the following characteristics:

- It can identify the most relevant aspects of a domain using a generic CM (GCM). Precisely, because it is generic, this GCM can prevent the filtering effect caused by the more classical CMs, such as the class diagram or the data flow diagram, thus allowing all the information on a domain to be recorded.
- A concrete instance of a CM is not needed for the domain in question. On the contrary, it is sufficient to consider the semantic and syntactic features of the CMs (that is, the constructs and their possible combinations) to determine the completeness of each CM.

These two characteristics can avert the above-mentioned difficulties. The aim of the first step of the proposed approach is to output a domain model using the GCM, which can record all the important aspects of the problem. After the GCM has been developed, the second step involves a process by means of which the GCM is compared with different CMs. This process of comparison is based on the semantic and syntactic features of the constructs of CMs, such as the class diagram or the data flow diagram, and not on an instance of a particular domain model. The final result of the aforesaid process of comparison is an association between particular aspects of the problem domain and the constructs (such as processes, classes, relationships, etc.) of the traditional CMs. In the third step, this association between the domain aspects and the traditional CM constructs outputs a measure of completeness, which is called fitness. The fitness measure is a quantitative value that is defined as the quotient of the number of sentences that can be expressed by a particular CM and the total number of interesting sentences of the problem domain recorded in the GCM.

The following sections describe the three steps of the proposed approach in more detail. Section 3.1 describes the proposed GCM and how it is used in domain modelling. Section 3.2 explains the way in which the semantic and syntactic features of the CM can be exploited to compare the concept map with the traditional CMs. Finally, Sec. 3.3 describes how to output the quantitative fitness value for the different CMs.

3.1. *Step 1: Domain modelling using a generic conceptual model*

As mentioned above, to determine the fitness of a CM for any domain, all the relevant aspects of this domain have to be identified and recorded, irrespective of whether they are static, dynamic or logical. For the purposes of identification, the domain needs to be explored or analysed, which implies a conceptualisation process and, foreseeably, a modelling process. However, all CMs categorise problem domain information, as they employ constructs with a well-defined meaning. This means that, during modelling, problem domain information is filtered according to the viewpoint permitted by the CM in use.

So, for example, suppose we were to capture the information *"Invoices are created when customers place orders"* in a CM. If we were to record this information in a class diagram, as shown in Fig. 3(a), or a data flow diagram, as shown in Fig. 3(b), the final result would be that only the domain aspects that each conceptual model is capable of recording would be considered during analysis. Specifically, in Fig. 3(a), information related to the

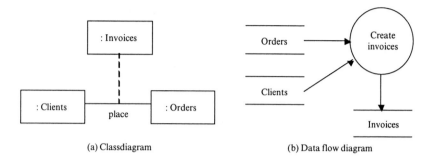

(a) Classdiagram   (b) Data flow diagram

Fig. 3. Information represented by means of a class diagram and a data flow diagram for the sentence "Invoices are created when customers place orders".

apparent causality between "place orders" and "invoices" (the phrase "are created when" has been lost, and this has been replaced by an association class, rewriting the problem in static code. In Fig. 3(b), on the other hand, the relationship between customer and orders is lost, and the information gathered is transcribed functionally, which, ultimately, merely indicates that the invoices are generated on the basis of orders and customers. The real danger lurks, however, in the fact that, ultimately, neither of the CMs shown in Fig. 3 is incorrect. On the contrary, the two models represent, constrained by their expressive power, some aspects of the problem domain, obviating any that they cannot represent.

Consequently, CMs are not suited for describing all the important aspects required for future development process, because they filter the problem domain information they record. Therefore, alternative models need to be used that can record any relevant aspect, irrespective of its class, and without it being filtered by the representation constraints of the model in use.

The model proposed in this chapter, which has been called concepts map, has such a representation capability. The concepts map was inspired by the conceptual maps, derived from the work of Ausubel on Learning Theory and Psychology, later formalised by (Novak and Gowin, 1984). From the viewpoint of form, concept maps bear some resemblance to semantic nets, insofar as they can both describe concepts and associations, as shown in Fig. 4. The limitations to representation capability are originated by the finiteness of the constructs used by the CMs (like, for example, classes, relationships, processes, etc.), as well as by the strict semantics (that is, the

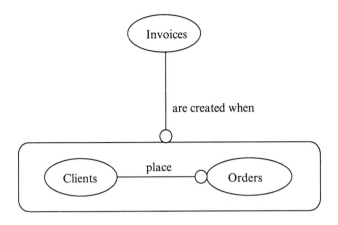

Fig. 4. Example of a concept map.

ascription of a given construct to a specific aspect of the problem domain), and the concept map sidesteps the above limitations to achieve a limitless representation capability. In particular, the concepts map minimises the number of constructs and, additionally, ascribes no semantics or particular meaning to them. They can be used and interpreted freely by each individual analyst and they are, therefore, intrinsically ambiguous. Additionally, concept maps can be used to build combinations of concepts and associations (called *propositions*) of varying complexity, with an expressiveness approximating natural language. Finally, concept maps can be structured hierarchically, similarly, albeit founded on different theoretical principles, to data flow diagram hierarchies (Dieste, 2003).

The intrinsic ambiguity of the concepts map allows modelling of the problem domain without any class of conceptual or computational restriction such as those imposed by the traditional CMs. Although it may appear, at first glance, that ambiguity and conceptual modelling are incompatible terms (van Griethuysen, 1982) the use of ambiguity allows categorisation at the end of the problem analysis, that is, when all the relevant information is available. This view of modelling is vaguely similar to the approach proposed by other authors, such as (Ceri, 1983) and (Kopand and Mayr, 1998), who also use formally simple intermediate representation formalisms to record the problem domain information before moving on to more formal representation schemas like CMs.

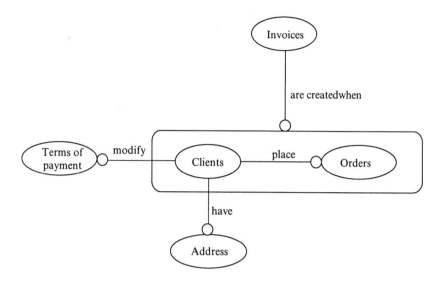

Fig. 5. Concept map recording new information.

By way of an example, there is no constraint demanding that "clients should be interpreted as a class or as an external entity or that "place" should be considered as a relationship or as a process in the concepts map shown in Fig. 4. Indeed, the concept map encourages analysts to interpret the information gathered when and how they like. This means that if the analyst detects more static or dynamic information about, for example, the clients ("clients have an address", "clients modify terms of payment"), this information can be added to the concept map directly, as shown in Fig. 5, without having to decide what particular information can be represented and thus averting the filtering caused by CMs.

As it can represent all the problem domain aspects, avoiding the selective filtering of information, the concept map can record all or the vast majority of the relevant aspects of the domain.

3.2. Step 2: Comparison of the concept map with traditional conceptual models

The concept map, as mentioned above, can record the important elements of the problem generically, that is, without strictly categorising these elements because the constructs (concepts, associations and propositions) of the concepts map are intrinsically ambiguous.

Our goal, however, is to determine the completeness, which has been termed fitness of the traditional CMs, such as the class diagram or data flow diagram. Modelling the problem domain using the concept map does not, *per se*, give this measure, as there is no association between the domain information recorded in the concept map and the traditional CMs.

Additionally, the features of the traditional CMs are just the opposite to the concept map, that is, these CMs strictly categorise the elements of the problem domain because they use a set of constructs with well-defined semantics, which rules out direct comparison. The characteristics of the concept map and the CMs are, therefore, diametrically opposed. For this reason, to be able to compare and match the concept map to the CMs, that is, the problem domain information (recorded in the concept map) to the CM, the theoretical fundamentals of the two representations need to be approximated or assimilated. As the main difference between the concept map and the CMs lies in the ambiguity/strict semantics dichotomy, the best alternative for establishing a relationship between the two models is to remove the ambiguity from the concept map and give it a well-defined meaning, closer to the formulation of the traditional CMs. This process of disambiguation has been termed interpretation.

To interpret the concept map, a given interpretation has to be ascribed to each concept and association in the concept map, that is, the intrinsic ambiguity of these constructs needs to be removed. Additionally, as the objective is to assimilate the concept map to traditional CMs, the best strategy for removing ambiguity is to assign, to each concept and association, the real-life aspect to which it refers from the viewpoint of the traditional CMs (classes, relationships, processes, states, etc.).

Refer, for example, to the concept map shown in Fig. 4. The information recorded in this concepts map refers to real-life "things", like clients, orders or invoices, as well as to relationships (place) and actions (are created when). It is relatively easy to understand the concepts and associations of the concepts map in this manner, as, ultimately, this interpretation is coherent with the typical reasoning of any analyst. Palpable proof of this was given earlier, as, at the end of the day, the class diagram shown in Fig. 3(a) and the data flow diagram illustrated in Fig. 3(b) do no other than reflect this interpretation of the problem domain used as an example. This interpretation of the concepts and associations in the concepts map illustrated in Fig. 4 means that these constructs can be labelled as shown in Fig. 6.

When the concepts map has been interpreted, the different concepts and associations have a well-defined meaning, that is:

- There are clients, orders and invoices in the problem domain.
- There is a static relationship between clients and orders.
- There is a dynamic relationship between clients, orders and invoices.

Indeed, the concept map can be rewritten using, for example, a class diagram, as shown in Fig. 7(a), and a data flow diagram, as shown in Fig. 7(b). It is simply a matter of considering the concepts and associations of the concept map, which after interpretation, have been labelled with constructs compatible with the desired CM. Thus, for example, in the concept map shown in Fig. 6, the association "are created when" has been interpreted as a process. As class diagrams (obviating the concept of method, closer to

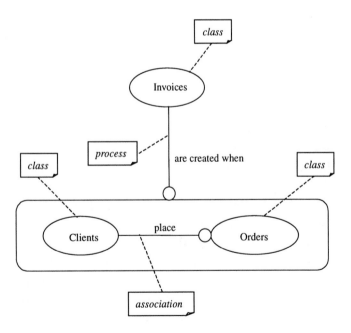

Fig. 6. Example of the concept map after interpretation.

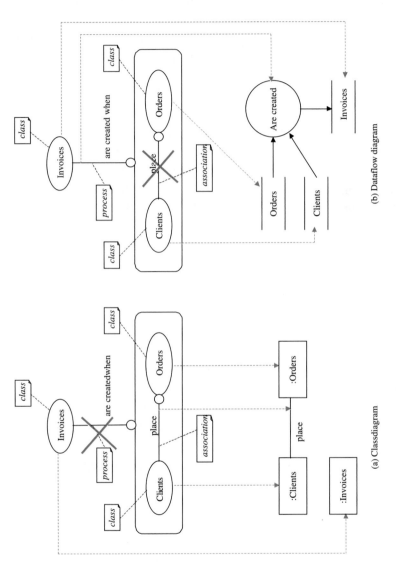

(a) Classdiagram

(b) Dataflow diagram

Fig. 7. Conceptual models derived from the interpreted concepts map.

software design than domain modelling) cannot represent processes, this association cannot be included in this CM. On the other hand, data flow diagrams cannot represent relationships or associations between entities or classes and, therefore, the association "place" cannot materialise in this CM. Apart from this, the other concepts and associations can be transferred immediately both to the class diagram and the data flow diagram.

The above example shows that interpretation is a reasonable procedure for disambiguating the concept map, as the CMs in Figs. 7(a) and 7(b) are very similar to the conceptual models of Figs. 3(a) and (b). However, gratuitously ascribing a meaning to each concept and association in the concepts map results in a subjective interpretation that may, therefore, be biased (for example, many concepts could be arbitrarily interpreted as classes, converting the concepts map into a substitute class diagram or, alternatively, the associations could be interpreted as processes, misrepresenting the concepts map and turning it into a data flow diagram).

It is more reasonable, therefore, that any interpretation procedure should follow some objective rules to reduce or remove analyst subjectivity. These rules can be identified by considering that the result of any interpretation should be the constructs of the different CMs. Accordingly, the interpretation should involve comparing and matching the concepts and associations of the concepts map to the different expressions that can be formed in the different CMs.

It is simpler to use a representation formalism that we have termed descriptive dictionary for the above matching process. The descriptive dictionary is a tabular representation formalism that can be derived from the concepts map using a systematic set of transformation rules (Dieste, 2003). Essentially, these rules can be used to rewrite each proposition in the concepts map as a tuple (association, concept1, concept2), as shown in Table 1.

A formalised procedure of interpretation, which employs a set of interpretation tables as shown in Table 2, has been defined on the basis of the descriptive dictionary. The procedure and the interpretation tables are founded on a requirements representation formalism proposed by (Davis, Jordan and Nakajima, 1997), although it has been profoundly restructured and adapted to be used to interpret the concept map and the descriptive dictionary. This formalism, termed canonical model was initially designed

Table 1. Descriptive dictionary.

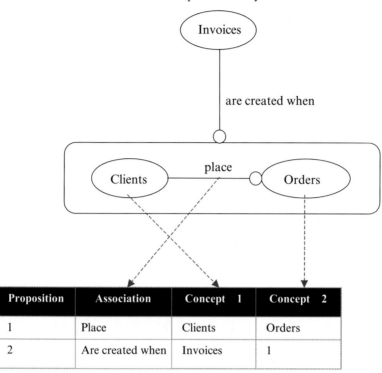

Proposition	Association	Concept 1	Concept 2
1	Place	Clients	Orders
2	Are created when	Invoices	1

to integrate the information recorded in a variety of conceptual models during requirements specification. The canonical model has a set of building blocks (called elements and links) for this purpose, which can be used to represent the information contained in a wide range of conceptual models.

The interpretation procedure involves matching the concepts and associations from the descriptive dictionary to canonical model elements and links. This matching procedure is carried out algorithmically following a set of predefined steps, that is, the interpretation procedure is largely independent of the analyst who is using it. Total independence is out of the question in some situations, however. This applies when two or more canonical model elements or links can be assigned to any given concept or association of the descriptive dictionary. This occurs typically at the start of interpretation, when hardly any concepts or associations have been interpreted and, therefore, the number of possible concept-element and

Table 2. Possible combinations between elements and links.

	entity [repl]	entity [notrepl]	process	predicate	transition	message	constraint	value	statespace
entity [repl]	Spec subs pof rel activate								
entity [notrepl]	spec pof rel bel activate	spec pof rel activate							
process	pof sends receives	pof sends receives -activate	spec pof activate						
predicate	operand	operand	-stimulate	operand					
transition	stimulus response	stimulus response	stimulus response	stimulus response	stimulus response				
message	-sends -receives	-sends -receives	-sends -receives	-operand	-stimulus -response	Pof			
constraint	-operand	-operand	-pof	-operand	-stimulus -response	-operand	operand		
value	pof	pof	affect -sends -receives pof	-operand	-stimulus -response	-operand	-operand	spec pof	
statespace	pof	Pof	-sends -receives pof	-operand	-stimulus -response	-operand	-operand	hval	Pof

association-link combinations is very high. In this case, it is the analyst who has to decide, depending on his or her knowledge of the domain problem, which particular interpretation is best suited. As the interpretation procedure advances, the number of possible matches falls and, therefore, the analyst is required to intervene less often or not at all.

For example, suppose we have the proposition "clients place orders", recorded in the descriptive dictionary shown in Table 1. As this is the first proposition of the descriptive dictionary to be interpreted, analyst intervention will be required, because there are a lot of possible matches. The analyst should select one of all the possible combinations, which matches what the analyst believes the concepts in the problem domain mean. As it is quite clear that "clients" and "orders" are collections of elements that have the same characteristics in the problem domain, the best interpretation would be to match "customers" and "orders" to the element entity[repl] (whose meaning, within the canonical model, is "entity that has several instances in the problem domain"). Finally, it follows from Table 2 that there are several alternative combinations, that is, links between two elements of the type entity[repl]. Therefore, a plausible match should likewise be selected. Of the possible links (spec, subs, pof, rel, activate), the closest to the meaning of the association "place" is rel, as "place" appears to reflect a static relationship between the entities "clients" and "orders". Accordingly, the finally result of the match would be as shown in Fig. 8.

Table 2 can be used to interpret concepts and associations, although separate tables should be used to interpret propositions (such as, for example, proposition 2 in the descriptive dictionary, shown in Table 1 "Invoices are created when clients place orders" (Dieste, 2003). A fragment of these tables is shown in Fig. 9, and their full version is attached as Annex A. Proposition 2 should also be interpreted by the analyst, as the interpretation of a single proposition is not usually sufficient to exclude the possibility of multiple matches. As illustrated in Fig. 9, however, the number of possible matches falls as the matching procedure progresses. Indeed, there are only three possible matches for proposition 2: to consider "Invoices" as an entity[repl], an entity[notrepl] or a process (due to a specific rule of the interpretation procedure, it is the association "are created when" that could be considered as a process") (Dieste, 2003). Note that the range of the possible matches mentioned above is fully coincident with the way in which

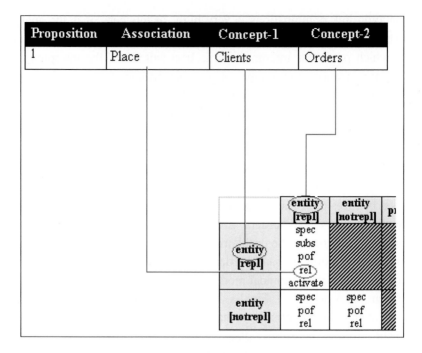

Fig. 8. Match for the proposition "Clients place orders".

the conceptual models, shown in Fig. 3, allowing the information on the problem domain to be recorded: considering "Invoice" as a class or entity, and "are created when" as a relationship or process. This is because the interpretation tables cover all the possible expressions that can be recorded by the CMs and, therefore, all these expressions are considered during interpretation, where only the one that is best suited to the problem domain is finally selected.

After interpretation, the descriptive dictionary would be labelled with the selected elements and links, as shown in Table 3. We have decided to interpret "are created when" as a process, which is why proposition 2 has been divided into two subpropositions. This is because, unlike the relationships in a class diagram or entity-relationship model, which are binary (and are described, therefore, using just two elements and a link), the processes have at least one input and one output, which means that more than two elements and links are required for description (Dieste, 2003).

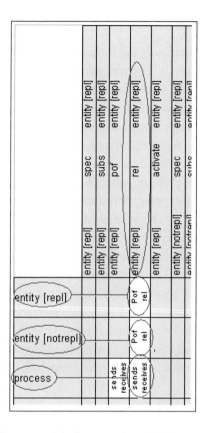

Fig. 9. Fragment of the interpretation table for propositions.

Table 3. Descriptive dictionary after interpretation.

Proposition	Association	Concept – 1	Concept – 2
1	**Rel:** Place	**Entity[repl]:** Clients	**Entity[repl]:** Orders
2–1	**Process:** Are created when	**Receives:**	1
2–2	**Process:** Are created when	**Sends:**	**Entity[repl]:** Invoices

Note that the interpreted descriptive dictionary, which is shown in Table 3, reads exactly like the naive interpretation, which was proposed by way of an example in Fig. 6. Specifically, propositions 2–1 and 2–2 describe the generation of invoices, whereas proposition 1 describes the relationship between clients and orders.

3.3. Calculating fitness

Once the descriptive dictionary has been completely interpreted, CM fitness can be determined directly. For this purpose, we have defined the fitness of a CM (for the problem domain modelled in the concepts map) as the number of aspects that this CM is capable of expressing about the problem. The above-mentioned calculation is done using the interpreted descriptive dictionary to which as many columns as conceptual models whose fitness is to be calculated are added, as shown in Table 4.

A mark is made in each cell where a proposition and a CM intersect if the CM in question can express the proposition. For example, proposition 1, "Clients place orders" can be expressed in a class diagram, which means that the intersection between proposition 1 and the above-mentioned model would be marked, as shown in Table 4. However, fitness cannot be determined as subjectively as described above, as it is not always so obvious which proposition can be expressed by which model. Therefore, a series of tables, which have been called identificative tables, are used to assign propositions to models, one of which is shown in Table 5. The identificative tables list the CMs that can express a given element-link-element combination. There is an identificative table for every link in the canonical model (Dieste, 2003).

The identificative tables are very easy to use. For each proposition, such as:

Rel: Place   **Entity[repl]**: Clients   **Entity[repl]**: Orders

Table 4. Descriptive dictionary prepared for fitness calculation.

Proposition	Association	Concept – 1	Concept – 2	Data flow diagram	Class diagram
1	**Rel**: Place	**Entity[repl]**: Clients	**Entity[repl]**: Orders		X
2–1	**Process**: Are created when	**Receives**:	1		
2–2	**Process**: Are created when	**Sends**:	**Entity[repl]**: Invoices		
Total					

	entity [repl]	entity [notrepl]	process	predicate	transition	message	constraint	value	statespace
entity [repl]	CD ER								
entity [notrepl]	CD ER	CD ER							
process									
predicate									
transition									
message									
constraint									
value									
statespace									

Table 5. Identificative table for the link rel.

Table 6. Fragment of the identificative table for the link receives.

	spec entity [repl]	subs entity [repl]	pof entity [repl]	rel entity [repl]	activate entity [repl]	spec entity [repl]
entity [repl]						
entity [notrepl]						
process			DFD DFDTR	DFD DFDTR		

we refer to the table for the link (in this case, the link **Rel**) and we locate the cell indicated by the elements (in this case, **Entity[repl]** and **Entity[repl]**). Two CMs appear in this cell: CD (class diagram) and ER (entity-relationship). This means that the proposition considered can be expressed by either of these models.

Other tables should be used for propositions 2–1 and 2–2, as the links are different. For example, Fig. 9 shows part of the identificative table for the link receives, which can identify the conceptual models that express proposition 2–1. (The full version of the table is shown in Annex *B*.) As illustrated, this proposition can be expressed using a DFD (data flow diagram) and a DFD/RT (Ward's data flow diagram/real time).

Table 7. Descriptive dictionary after having calculated fitness.

Proposition	Association	Concept – 1	Concept – 2	Data flow diagram	Class diagram
1	**Rel:** Place	**Entity[repl]:** Clients	**Entity[repl]:** Orders		X
2–1	**Process:** Are created when	**Receives:**	1	X	
2–2	**Process:** Are created when	**Sends:**	**Entity[repl]:** Invoices	X	
Total				2/3 (66%)	1/3 (33%)

Using the above-mentioned identificative tables (as well as an additional table for the link sends, which is attached as Annex *B*), the propositions assigned to the CM would be as shown in Table 7.

After assigning the different propositions to the conceptual models, the fitness can be calculated directly. Adding up the marks made in each column, we get the number of propositions that each model is capable of expressing. The resulting value, whether expressed in absolute terms or as a percentage of the total number of propositions in the interpreted descriptive dictionary, is the fitness value of each conceptual model to the problem under analysis. So, the data flow diagram is better than the CM for modelling the problem illustrated in Table 7, as it has a fitness of 66%, that is, it can express 2/3 of the descriptive dictionary propositions.

4. Validation of the Proposed Fitness Measure

The proposed fitness measure has been validated in practice. The validation involved using the proposed fitness measure in a series of test cases to check whether this measure was able to identify the best suited CM in each case.

Each test case was designed so that one CM was better for modelling the problem than the others in terms of representation capability. The test cases were designed by a group of experts who solved all the test cases using all the CMs accounted for in the validation, and which are detailed later. These experts assessed the instances of the models constructed and identified, which CM was best suited for each test case.

Identifying the best suited CM for a test case is, of course, not equivalent to determining the fitness of this model. That is, the fitness measure provides a quantitative value that indicates how well a CM matches a given domain, whereas the validation described above involves identifying the CM with the greatest fitness value. As there is no other quantitative measure of fitness/completeness apart from the one proposed here, an alternative validation that could verify the accuracy of the fitness measure is inconceivable for want of an appropriate yardstick. It is, however, possible to identify, albeit subjectively, the best CM for a test case and determine whether it matches the one predicted by the fitness measure. The more cases in which the prediction is correct, the greater the confidence in the fitness measure.

The set of CMs for selection included the data flow diagram (DFD), the class diagram (CD), the entity-relationship diagram (ER), the state transition diagram (STD) and the statechart (SCT). The differences between the class diagram and the entity-relationship diagram, on the one hand, and the state transition diagram and the statechart, on the other, were not taken into account for the purposes of generating and consolidating the results. The reason is that both the class diagram and the statechart contain (that is, have a representation capability at least equal to) the entity-relationship and state transition diagram, respectively. Therefore, it is very difficult to get a test case design that is able to distinguish between the two model types, and their compulsory distinction would not raise the reliability of the results output.

There were six test cases. All the test cases could be modelled using several of the CMs mentioned above (logically, any domain, no matter how small, can be modelled to a greater or lesser extent from different viewpoints). In three of the cases, one of the CMs had a broader representation capability than the others (specifically, the DFD was the best model for one case, the CD/ER for another and the STD/SCT for a third). In the other three cases, possible combinations of CMs were tried out to design cases where two CMs were equally suited and, consequently, either could be selected (DFD + CD/ER, DFD + STD/SCT and CD/ER + STD/SCT). These test cases were introduced for the reason that the "simple" cases, that is, cases that have a CM that is clearly better suited than the others, appeared at first glance to be too biased, that is, clearly conveyed which CM was the fittest. On the other hand, the "mixed" cases, that is, the cases where more than one CM is suited, were formulated in a much closer fashion to real cases and, therefore, the best suited CMs were less clearly appreciable. However, the results actually generated in practice were surprising, as will be discussed later. Three groups of subjects participated in the validation: a first group, formed by 5 people, with a profile of professionals with years of experience in industry; a second group formed by 18 undergraduate and postgraduate students, and, finally, a third group formed by 3 students specifically trained to use the proposed approach to calculate the fitness of the models. The use of the first two groups was not strictly necessary to determine the soundness of the fitness measure (it would have been sufficient for this purpose to verify whether the proposed approach correctly identifies the best suited CM for each test case, as provided by the panel of experts). However, the subjective determination of the best suited CM by the first two groups will make it possible to determine, also, whether the proposed approach is more effective than the reasoning of potential analysts.

Although it is not absolutely objective, the outlined validation schema can assess the soundness of the proposed approach. Indeed, the subjective assessment of CM completeness has been used as a metric in the literature (Kesh, 1995), which means that comparing the performance of a series of subjects with the result output by means of the proposed approach can provide an estimate of the effectiveness of the approach. Additionally, it is difficult to come up with more objective validation alternatives, insofar as there are hardly any measures of completeness available in the literature, and the ones that are available have no associated objective measurement.

The practical implementation of the validation schema described above produced the results shown in Fig. 10 and tabulated in Annex *C*. Two aspects are particularly prominent:

- The proposed approach identified the best suited CM provided by the panel of experts in all the test cases.
- The effectiveness of the subjects was around 80%, whereas the proposed approach has an effectiveness of 100%, improving on the subjective judgement of the participating subjects.

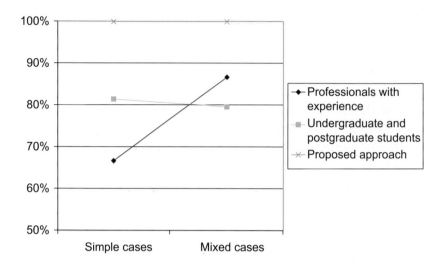

Fig. 10. Results of the validation.

This would appear to prove, then, that the fitness measure proposed here can assess which is the best CM for a given problem. This provides some confidence in the soundness of the value provided by the fitness measure, as, given two CMs (CM_1 and CM_2), where CM_1 provides a better representation capability than CM_2, the fitness measure provides a value $v(CM_1) > v(CM_2)$. That is, the fitness measure at least establishes a relationship of order $\geq$ with respect to the representation capability of CMs for problems in concrete domains. Furthermore, the effectiveness of the fitness measure is greater than the measure achieved by the subjects participating in the validation using subjective criteria (that is, knowledge of and experience in conceptual modelling).

Additionally, Fig. 10 brings to light two other points, which, although not related to the main theme of this chapter, should not be overlooked. The first refers to the fact that the undergraduate and postgraduate students are, on average, more effective at identifying the best suited CM than the experienced professionals. The second is that the experienced professionals are less effective in simple cases, contrary to what would be expected, due to their clear bias.

Both points are due to the fact that, as can be inferred from the non-clustered data shown in Annex C, the experienced professionals tend to always use the same CM, irrespective of the test case with which they are presented, whereas the students are more flexible in this respect. The effect of always using the same CM means that, in the simple cases, the chances of success are 1 in 3, whereas, in the mixed cases, they are 2 in 3. The students achieve a similar result (around 80%) in both the simple and mixed cases, whereas the experienced professionals come suspiciously close to the minimums implied in the design of the validation. We might ask, therefore, whether experience is a factor that raises the power of judgement, at least as far as CM fitness for problem domains is concerned, or whether, on the other hand, the repeated use of a CM or a methodology eventually leads to experienced analysts viewing all problems similarly.

5. Conclusions

In this chapter, we have proposed a new CM completeness measure, called fitness. This new measure emerges as a result of the deficiencies perceived in the completeness measures proposed by quality frameworks and metrics and for the purpose of more faithfully representing the match between CMs and problems defined in concrete domains. Fitness has been defined as the number of interesting or relevant propositions that a CM can represent about a problem in a given domain dived by the total number of interesting propositions existing in the domain.

To determine what interesting propositions there are in a domain, we have proposed a generic CM, called concept map. As it hardly categorises the elements of the problem domain, the concept map has a very wide representation capability, allowing recording of any domain aspect, irrespective of whether it is static, dynamic or logical. Consequently, as opposed to the traditional CMs, like class diagram or data flow diagram, the concepts map does not previously filter the problem domain, therefore providing a complete model of this domain.

The number of problem domain propositions that can be expressed in a CM is also calculated on the basis of the concept map. For this purpose, the concept map and the constructs of the different traditional CMs are compared in what has been termed interpretation. As a result of the interpretation, the contents of the concept map can be directly related to the different forms of expression of the traditional CMs, taking into account only the semantic characteristics of the CM constructs and the syntactic constraints that govern the possibilities of combination of the above-mentioned constructs.

Having identified all the important aspects of the domain (by modelling the domain using the concepts map) and established the match between the concepts map and the traditional CM constructs, fitness can be directly determined and involves a simple division.

The fitness measure, as well as all the steps taken to arrive at this measure, have been validated in practice. The validation affirms the soundness of the proposed approach.

Acknowledgements

This research is part of the MCP-IS&IC project, supported by "Ministerio de Educación y Ciencia" (Spain) (PB-0721) and the MUML project financed by "University of Castilla-La Mancha" (011.100623).

References

Batini, C., Ceri, S. and Navathe, S. (1992). *Conceptual Database Design. An Entity Relationship Approach*, Benjamin. Cummings Publishing Company.

Boman, M., Bubenko, J., Johannesson, P. and Wangler, B. (1997). *Conceptual Modelling*. Prentice Hall.

Bonfatti, F. and Monari, P.D. (1994). Towards a General-Purpose Approach to Object-Oriented Analysis. *Proceedings of the International Symposium of Object Oriented Methodologies and Systems*, Palermo, Italy, pp. 108–122.

Borgida, A. (1991). Knowledge Representation, Semantic Modeling: Similarities and Differences. Ed. H. Kangasalo, *Entity-Relationship Approach: The Core of Conceptual Modeling*. Elsevier Science Publishers, pp. 1–24.

Ceri, S. (Ed.) (1983). *Methodology and Tools for Database Design*. North Holland.

Curtis, B., Krasner, H. and Iscoe, N. (1988). A Field Study of the Software Design Process for Large Systems. *Communications of the ACM*, Vol. 31, No. 11, pp. 1268–1287.

Beringer, D. (1994). Limits of Seamless in Object Oriented Software Development. *Proceedings of the 13th International Conference on Technology of Object Oriented Languages and Systems*, Versailles, France, pp. 161–171.

Davis, A.M., Jordan, K. and Nakajima, T. (1997). Elements Underlying the Specification of Requirements. *Annals of Software Engineering*, Vol. 3, pp. 63–100.

Dieste, O. (2003). *POAM: Un Método de Análisis Orientado a la Necesidad.* Unpublished doctoral dissertation. Departamento de Informática, Universidad de Castilla-La Mancha.

Dieste, O., Juristo, N., Moreno, A.M., Pazos, J. and Sierra, A. (2000). Conceptual Modelling in Software Engineering and Knowledge Engineering: Concepts, Techniques And Trends. Ed. K. Chang, *Handbook of Software and Knowledge Engineering*, Vol. 1. World Scientific Publishing, pp. 763–766.

Høydalsvik, G.M. and Sindre, G. (1993). On the Purpose of Object Oriented Analysis. *Proceedings of the Conference on Object Oriented Programming, Systems, Languages and Applications*, New York, USA, pp. 240–255.

Kesh, S. (1995). Evaluating the Quality of Entity Relationship Models. *Information and Software Technology*, Vol. 37, No. 12, pp. 681–689.

Krogstie, J., Lindland, O. and Sindre, G. (1995). Towards a Deeper Understanding of Quality in Requirements Engineering. Eds. J. Iivari, K. Lyytinen and M. Rossi. *Proceedings of the CAiSE '95, Lecture Notes in Computer Science 932*. Springer Verlag, pp. 82–95.

Lindland, O., Sindre, G. and Solvberg, A. (1994). Understanding Quality in Conceptual Modelling. *IEEE Software*, Vol. 11, No. 2, pp. 42–49.

Loucopoulos, P. and Karakostas, V. (1995). *Systems Requirements Engineering.* McGraw-Hill.

Maier, R. (1996). Benefits and Quality of Data Modeling — Results of an Empirical Analysis. Ed. B. Thalheim. *Proceedings of the ER '96, Lecture Notes in Computer Science 1157*. Springer Verlag, pp. 245–260.

Mayr, H.C. and Kop, C. (1998). Conceptual Predesign — Bridging the Gap Between Requirements and Conceptual Design. *Proceedings of the International Conference on Requirements Engineering*. IEEE Computer Society Press, pp. 90–98.

McGregor, J.D. and Korson, T. (1990). Understanding object-oriented: A Unifying Paradigm. *Communications of the ACM*, Vol. 33, No. 9, pp. 40–60.

Moody, D., Shanks, G. and Darke, P. (1998). Improving the Quality of Entity Relationship Models — Experience in Research and Practice. Eds. T. Wang Ling, S. Ram and M.-L. Lee. *Proceedings of the ER '98, Lecture Notes in Computer Science 1507.* Springer Verlag, pp. 255–276.

Motschnig-Pitrik, R. (1993). The Semantics of Parts versus Aggregates in Data/Knowledge Modelling. Eds. C. Rolland, F. Bodart and C. Cauvet. *Proceedings of the CAiSE '93, Lecture Notes in Computer Science 685.* Springer Verlag, pp. 352–373.

Novak, D. and Gowin, D.B. (1984). *Learning to Learn.* Cambridge University Press.

Piattini, M., Genero, M., Calero, C., Polo, M. and Ruiz, F. (2000). Database Quality. Eds. O. Diaz and M. Piattini. *Advanced Database Technology and Design.* Artech House.

Reingruber, M. and Gregory, W. (1994). *The Data Modelling Handbook. A Best-Practice Approach to Building Quality Data Models.* John Wiley and Sons.

Schuette, R. and Rotthowe, T. (1998). The Guidelines of Modeling — An Approach to Enhance the Quality in Information Models. Eds. T. Wang Ling, S. Ram and M.-L. Lee. *Proceedings of the ER '98, Lecture Notes in Computer Science 1507.* Springer Verlag, pp. 240–254.

van Griethuysen, J.J. (1982). *ISO — Concepts and Terminology for the Conceptual Schema and the Information Base.* N695. ISO/TC9/SC5/WG3.

Annex A: Identification Tables

Table 8. Permitted combinations in the canonical mode between elements, links and propositions (part 1/2).

Element 1	Link	Element 2	entity [repl]	entity [notrepl]	process	predicate	transition	message	constraint	value	statespace
entity [repl]	-sends-	message			activate	activate	receives	stimulus			
transition	response	transition						stimulus			
transition	stimulus	transition						stimulus			
predicate	stimulus	transition						stimulus			
process	response	transition						stimulus			
process	stimulus	transition						stimulus			
predicate	operand	predicate								operand	
process	activate	predicate							Stimulus/ response		-operando	
entity [notrepl]	operand	predicate								operand	
Entity [repl]	operand	predicate								operand	
process	activate	process			Activate/ activate		activate activate	Stimulus/ response		-operando	
process	pof	process									
process	spec	process									
process	-activate-	process					-activate	Stimulus/ response		-operando	
process	receives	process					-activate	Stimulus/ response			
process	sends	process					operand activate	Stimulus/ response			
process	pof	process									
process	-activate-	process					-activate	Stimulus/ response		-operando	
process	receives	process					-activate	Stimulus/ response			
process	sends	process					operand activate	Stimulus/ response			
process	pof	process									
entity [notrepl]	activate	entity [notrepl]						Stimulus/ response		-operando	
entity [notrepl]	rel	entity [notrepl]	Pof rel	Pof rel							pof
entity [notrepl]	pof	entity [notrepl]									pof
entity [notrepl]	sqns	entity [notrepl]									
entity [notrepl]	spec	entity [notrepl]									
entity [repl]	activate	entity [notrepl]						Stimulus/ response		-operando	
entity [repl]	rel	entity [notrepl]	Pof Rel	Pof rel							pof
entity [repl]	pof	entity [notrepl]									pof
entity [repl]	sqns	entity [notrepl]									
entity [repl]	spec	entity [notrepl]									
entity [repl]	activate	entity [repl]						Stimulus/ response		-operando	pof
entity [repl]	rel	entity [repl]	Pof rel	Pof rel	receives sends						pof
entity [repl]	pof	entity [repl]			receives sends						
entity [repl]	sqns	entity [repl]									
entity [repl]	spec	entity [repl]									

Table 9. Permitted combinations in the canonical mode between elements, links and propositions (part 2/2).

Element 1	Link	Element 2	entity [repl]	entity [notrepl]	process	predicate	transition	message	constraint	value	statespace
statespace	pof	statespace	-pof	-pof			operand				
statespace	spec	statespace	-pof	-pof							
value	hval	statespace						response			
constraint	-operand	statespace									
message	-operand	statespace									
transition	-response	statespace					stimulus				
transition	-stimulus	statespace					stimulus				
predicate	-operand	statespace					operand				
process	pof	statespace					operand				
process	-receives	statespace					stimulus				
process	-sends	statespace					operand	stimulus			
entity [notrepl]	pof	statespace					operand				
entity [repl]	pof	statespace					operand				
value	pof	value			Sends receives		operand				
constraint	-operand	value									
message	-operand	value									
transition	-response	value					stimulus				
transition	-stimulus	value					stimulus				
predicate	-operand	value					operand				
process	pof	value					operand				
process	-receives	value			sends			Stimulus response			
process	-sends	value			receives		operand	Stimulus response			
constraint	operand	constraint							operand		
message	operand	Constraint							operand		
transition	operand	constraint							operand		
predicate	operand	constraint							operand		
process	pof	constraint									
entity [notrepl]	operand	constraint							operand		
entity [repl]	operand	constraint							operand		
message	pof	message	sends	sends	Sends receives sends						
transition	-response	message	sends	sends			stimulus				
transition	-stimulus	message	sends	sends			stimulus				
predicate	-operand	message	sends	sends			stimulus				
process	-receives	message	sends	sends			stimulus				
process	-sends	message	active	active	receives		stimulus				
entity [notrepl]	-receives	message	receives	receives			stimulus				
entity [notrepl]	-sends	message	sends	sends	receives		stimulus				
entity [repl]	-receives	message	sends	sends			stimulus				

Annex B: Identification Tables

Table 10. Identification table for the link sends (part 1/3).

	entity [repl]	entity [notrepl]	process	predicate	transition	message	constraint	value	statespace
entity [repl]									
entity [notrepl]									
process									
predicate									
transition									
message	—	—	DFDRT						
constraint			—						
value	DFD DFDRT	DFD DFDRT	DFD DFDRT						
statespace	DFD DFDRT	DFD DFDRT	DFD DFDRT						

Table 11. Identification table for the link sends (part 2/3).

			entity [repl]	entity [notrepl]	process	predicate	transition	message	constraint	value	statespace
message	-sends	entity [repl]									
transition	response	transition									
transition	stimulus	transition									
transition	stimulus	predicate									
transition	response	process									
transition	stimulus	process									
predicate	operand	predicate									
predicate	activate	process									
predicate	operand	entity [notrepl]									
predicate	operand	Entity [repl]									
process	activate	process									
process	pof	process									
process	spec	process									
process	-activate	entity [notrepl]									
process	receives	entity [notrepl]									
process	sends	entity [notrepl]									
process	pof	entity [notrepl]									
process	-activate	entity [repl]									
process	receives	entity [repl]									
process	sends	entity [repl]									
process	pof	entity [repl]									
entity [notrepl]	activate	entity [notrepl]									
entity [notrepl]	rel	entity [notrepl]									
entity [notrepl]	pof	entity [notrepl]									
entity [notrepl]	sqns	entity [notrepl]									
entity [notrepl]	spec	entity [notrepl]									
entity [notrepl]	activate	entity [repl]									
entity [notrepl]	rel	entity [repl]									
entity [notrepl]	pof	entity [repl]									
entity [notrepl]	sqns	entity [repl]									
entity [notrepl]	spec	entity [repl]									
entity [repl]	activate	entity [repl]									
entity [repl]	rel	entity [repl]				DFD DFDRT					
entity [repl]	pof	entity [repl]				DFD DFDRT					
entity [repl]	sqns	entity [repl]									
entity [repl]	spec	entity [repl]									

Table 12. Identification table for the link sends (part 3/3).

			entity [repl]	entity [notrepl]	process	predicate	transition	message	constraint	value	statespace
statespace	pof	statespace									
statespace	spec	statespace									
value	hval	statespace									
constraint	-operand	statespace									
message	-operand	statespace									
transition	-response	statespace									
transition	-stimulus	statespace									
predicate	-operand	statespace									
process	pof	statespace									
process	-receives	statespace									
process	-sends	statespace									
entity [notrepl]	pof	statespace									
entity [repl]	pof	statespace									
value	pof	value			DFD DFDRT						
constraint	-operand	value									
message	-operand	value									
transition	-response	value									
transition	-stimulus	value									
predicate	-operand	value									
process	pof	value									
process	-receives	value			DFD DFDRT						
process	-sends	value									
constraint	operand	constraint									
message	operand	Constraint									
transition	operand	constraint									
predicate	operand	constraint									
process	pof	constraint									
entity [notrepl]	operand	constraint									
entity [repl]	operand	constraint									
message	pof	message	DFDRT DFD	DFDRT DFD	DFDRT						
transition	-response	message	DFDRT DFD	DFDRT DFD	DFDRT						
transition	-stimulus	message	DFDRT DFD	DFDRT DFD	DFDRT						
predicate	-operand	message	DFDRT DFD	DFDRT DFD	DFDRT						
process	-receives	message	DFDRT DFD								
process	-sends	message									
entity [notrepl]	-receives	message									
entity [notrepl]	-sends	message	DFDRT DFD								
entity [repl]	-receives	message	DFDRT DFD								

Table 13. Identification table for the receives (part 1/3).

	entity [repl]	entity [notrepl]	process	predicate	transition	message	constraint	value	statespace
entity [repl]									
entity [notrepl]									
process									
predicate									
transition									
message	—	—	DFDRT						
constraint	—	—	—						
value	DFD DFDRT	DFD DFDRT	DFD DFDRT						
statespace	DFD DFDRT	DFD DFDRT	DFD DFDRT						

Table 14. Identification table for the link receives (part 2/3).

			entity [repl]	entity [notrepl]	process	predicate	transition	message	constraint	value	statespace
entity [repl]	spec	entity [repl]									
entity [repl]	subs	entity [repl]									
entity [repl]	pof	entity [repl]	DFD DFDRT								
entity [repl]	rel	entity [repl]	DFD DFDRT								
entity [repl]	activate	entity [repl]									
entity [repl]	spec	entity [notrepl]									
entity [repl]	subs	entity [notrepl]									
entity [repl]	pof	entity [notrepl]									
entity [repl]	rel	entity [notrepl]									
entity [repl]	activate	entity [notrepl]									
entity [notrepl]	spec	entity [notrepl]									
entity [notrepl]	subs	entity [notrepl]									
entity [notrepl]	pof	entity [notrepl]									
entity [notrepl]	rel	entity [notrepl]									
entity [notrepl]	activate	entity [notrepl]									
entity [repl]	pof	process									
entity [repl]	sends	process									
entity [repl]	receives	process									
entity [repl]	-activate	process									
entity [notrepl]	pof	process									
entity [notrepl]	sends	process									
entity [notrepl]	receives	process									
entity [notrepl]	-activate	process									
process	spec	process									
process	pof	process									
process	activate	process									
Entity [repl]	operand	predicate									
entity [notrepl]	operand	predicate									
process	activate	predicate									
predicate	operand	predicate									
process	stimulus	transition									
process	response	transition									
predicate	stimulus	transition									
transition	stimulus	transition									
transition	response	transition									
message	-sends	entity [repl]	DFDRT								

Table 15. Identification table for the link receives (part 3/3).

			entity [repl]	entity [notrepl]	process	predicate	transition	message	constraint	value	statespace
message	-receives	entity [repl]									
message	-sends	entity [notrepl]		DFDRT							
message	-receives	entity [notrepl]	DFDRT	DFDRT							
message	-sends	process	DFDRT								
message	-receives	process									
message	-operand	predicate									
message	-stimulus	transition									
message	-response	transition									
message	pot	message	DFDRT								
constraint	operand	entity [repl]									
constraint	operand	entity [notrepl]									
constraint	pot	process									
constraint	operand	predicate									
constraint	operand	transition									
constraint	operand	message									
constraint	operand	constraint									
value	-sends	process	DFD DFDRT	DFDRT							
value	-receives	process									
value	pot	process									
value	-operand	predicate									
value	-stimulus	transition									
value	-response	transition									
value	-operand	message									
value	-operand	constraint									
value	pot	value	DFD DFDRT	DFDRT							
statespace	pot	entity [repl]									
statespace	pot	entity [notrepl]									
statespace	-sends	process									
statespace	-receives	process									
statespace	pot	process									
statespace	-operand	predicate									
statespace	-stimulus	transition									
statespace	-response	transition									
statespace	-operand	message									
statespace	-operand	constraint									
statespace	hval	value									
statespace	spec	statespace									
statespace	pot	statespace									

Annex C: Validation Data

		CP 1	CP 2	CP 3	CP 4	CP 5	CP 6
	Fittest CM*	F	O	E	FO	FE	OE
Experienced professionals	Specialist 1	O	O	O	O	O	O
	Specialist 2	O	O	O	F	O	O
	Specialist 3	F	O	E	O	F	E
	Specialist 4	F	O	E	F	F	O
	Specialist 5	F	O	F	F	F	O
	Success rate	60%	100%	40%	100%	60%	100%
Undergrad & postgrad students	Student 1	F	O	E	F	E	E
	Student 2	F	O	E	O	E	E
	Student 3	F	O	O	O	O	O
	Student 4	E	O	E	O	E	E
	Student 5	O	O	O	O	E	O
	Student 6	F	O	E	F	E	F
	Student 7	F	O	E	O	E	F
	Student 8	F	O	E	O	E	E
	Student 9	O	O	F	O	F	E
	Student 10	F	O	E	O	O	O
	Student 11	F	O	E	–	O	O
	Student 12	F	O	E	F	O	E
	Student 13	O	F	O	O	O	E
	Student 14	F	O	E	O	E	E
	Student 15	F	O	E	F	E	F
	Student 16	F	F	E	F	O	E
	Student 17	F	O	E	F	E	E
	Student 18	F	O	E	O	E	E
	Success rate	78%	89%	78%	94%	61%	83%
Proposed approach	Students**	F	O	E	O	F	O
	Success rate	100%	100%	100%	100%	100%	100%

* F = DFD; O = CD/ER; E = STD/SCT
** The results were similar for the 3 students participating in the validation

Chapter 3

METRICS FOR USE CASES: A SURVEY
OF CURRENT PROPOSALS

BEATRIZ BERNÁRDEZ[*,a], AMADOR DURÁN[*,b] and MARCELA
GENERO[†]

Department of Computer Languages and Systems
University of Seville
Avda. Reina Mercedes, s/n. 41012 Sevilla, Spain
[a]*beat@lsi.us.es*
[b]*amador@lsi.us.es*

[†]*ALARCOS Research Group, Department of Computer Science*
University of Castilla-La Mancha
Paseo de la Universidad, 4 – 13071 – Ciudad Real, Spain
Marcela.Genero@uclm.es

1. Introduction

In this chapter, the current state-of-the-art of use cases metrics is presented. Before describing the different proposals, the concept of *use case*
itself is discussed. This discussion is necessary because of the different
use case approaches that have been proposed since the original work by
Jacobson et al. (1992) was published. These approaches vary from use cases
expressed as informal, plain prose to extremely detailed message sequence
diagrams, causing confusion about the concept and role of use cases in
software development. This confusion has been increased by the ambiguity of the use-case specification in the UML standards (OMG, 2003),

especially by the so-called *use case relationships*. Obviously, the concrete form in which use cases are used and expressed dramatically affects their measuring, as noted in Henderson-Sellers et al. (2002). Therefore, use cases metrics must always be understood in the context of a specific use case format and purpose.

After introducing the reader to the concept of use case in the next section, several proposals for use cases metrics are discussed. The proposals are grouped depending on their measurement goal. In Sec. 3, use cases metrics for project estimation are presented, including proposals by Karner (Schneider and Winters, 1998), Marchesi et al. (1998) and Smith (1999). In Sec. 4, use case metrics for improving the requirements engineering process are discussed, including proposals by Saeki (2003) and Bernárdez et al. (2004). Finally, in Sec. 5, the conclusions and a summary of the main proposals are presented.

The reader must always have in mind that the metrics proposals discussed in this chapter are still in a very early stage. Most of them are only initial proposals that have not been neither theoretically not empirically validated yet, as commented in the conclusions section.

2. The Concept of Use Case

Use cases are a scenario-based technique initially proposed by Jacobson et al. (1992) that can be used for different purposes in software development, especially during requirements engineering. As a scenario-based technique, use cases tell *stories* describing interactions between some so-called *actors*, i.e. people or other systems with some goal to be achieved, and a *system under discussion* (SuD) providing some services needed to achieve actors' goals. The SuD does not necessarily have to be a software system. It may be a computer-based information system encompassing hardware, software and people (see section on *Dimensions of use cases* for details on *use case scoping*).

2.1. *Roles of use cases in requirements engineering*

As commented in Cockburn (2001), one of the best books on use cases, they can play different roles in the requirements engineering process, the following being the most usual:

- As a mean of understanding and describing current business processes, where they are called *business use cases* by some authors like Cockburn (2001) or Leffingwell and Widrig (2000), or simply *scenarios* as in Leite et al. (2000).
- As a mean of focusing discussion about the requirements of the system to be built, but not to be the requirements description, i.e. as a requirements elicitation technique but not as a requirement documentation or specification technique. In this case, use cases are eventually transformed into lists of *typical* functional requirements.
- As part of the functional requirements of the system to be built, which is probably the role they play more often. This is the main purpose of use cases as described in the latest UML specification (OMG, 2003) and in other publications (Cockburn, 2001; Leffingwell and Widrig, 2000; Schneider and Winters, 1998).

Notice that, as stated by Cockburn (2001), *"they really are requirements but they are not all of the requirements"*. Other kinds of requirements like information requirements, business rules or non-functional requirements cannot be expressed as use cases but must be part of any complete requirements specification.

At the moment of writing, use cases are the most popular requirements elicitation technique in software industry[1] and they are becoming an actual alternative to typical specifications of functional requirements composed of hundreds of sentences starting with *"the system shall"*. As discussed in Cockburn (2001), use cases can be considered as *contracts for behaviour*, thus rising Meyer's *contract* concept from programming to requirements.

All of the analysed proposals for use case metrics assume that the measured use cases are part of a system or software requirements specification. We will also make the same assumption in the rest of this chapter for the sake of simplicity.

---

[1]The interested reader can see the article by Weidenhaupt et al. (1998) for an excellent survey on how use cases are applied in European software industry.

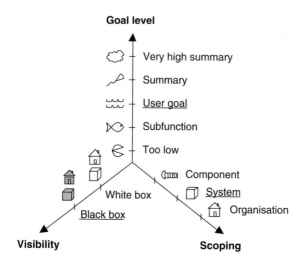

Fig. 1. Cockburn's dimensions of use cases.

2.2. Dimensions of use cases

Other criteria for classifying use cases apart from their purpose are their *scoping*, *goal level* and *visibility*, as proposed in Cockburn (2001) and graphically depicted in Fig. 1 as three orthogonal dimensions.

2.2.1. Scoping

The scoping of a use case can be at an *organisational level* if it describes *stories* between actors and organisations, which is the usual scope of the previously mentioned *business use cases*. The scoping is at a *system level* or *component level* if actors interact with a computer-based system or with a subsystem or a component of a computer-based system. The two latter scoping levels are the usual when writing system or software requirements specifications.

2.2.2. Goal level

The goal level of a use case indicates its level of abstraction with respect to user goals. For expressing the goal level, Cockburn proposes a metaphor in which height relative to sea level resembles goal level. The sea level corresponds to the *user goal* level, which is the level at which most use cases are usually described. Those higher-level use cases in which interactions are themselves user goals are said to be at a *summary* or *very high summary* level, depending on their level of abstraction. Since these use cases are *above the sea level*, they are represented by a kite (*summary*) or by a cloud (*very high summary*).[2] User-goal-level use cases are usually performed in no more than a few minutes (what Cockburn calls a *single-sitting*), whereas summary use cases requires the completion of several user goals to be performed and can take longer to complete.

2.2.3. *Visibility*

The visibility of a use case indicates whether it describes the internal structure of the SuD or only its external, observable behaviour. In the former case, the use case is said to have a white box visibility, whereas in the latter case it is said to have a black box visibility. Needless to say, the latter is the usual visibility when using use cases as specifications of functional requirements, following Davis recommendations (Davis et al., 1993).

Most of the metrics proposed for use cases focus on use cases with the underlined characteristics in Fig. 1, i.e. use cases at system scope, at user goal level and with a black box visibility. Because of that, these will be considered as the default values of Cockburn's dimensions for the rest of this chapter.

2.3. *Specification of use cases*

Jacobson et al. (1992) made use cases very popular, but they did not provide much guidance on how to specify them. As a result, a plethora of use case templates, notations and writing guidelines have bloomed in the last years. Use cases, as a scenario-based technique, are fundamentally text-based. Others formats like UML activity and sequence diagrams or Petri nets can be used for specifying use cases but, as recognised by Cockburn (2001), Kulak and Guiney (2000) and other practitioners, stakeholders without a software engineering background usually understand written *stories* using

---

[2]A similar classification is described in Regnell et al. (1996), where *environment*, *structure* and *event* are proposed as levels of use case detail.

the vocabulary of the problem domain better than any other software-oriented diagrammatic notation.

Assuming that use cases are basically text, there are still many possible ways of specifying them, from plain prose to structured English. Regardless of the writing style, one commonly agreed point is that any use case specification must describe a sequence of interactions between actors and the SuD, usually numbering the *steps* performed during the interactions in order to achieve some actor's goals.

A thorough discussion of all the proposed templates for use case specification is out of the scope of this chapter, but a summary of some of them is essential in order to understand some of the metrics proposals. Notice that, as actual requirements templates, use cases templates usually include *requirements attributes*[3] like a unique identifier, version, status, stakeholders, writers, dependencies on other requirements, associated non-functional requirements, etc. As commented in the following sections, use-case metrics based on some of these attributes like the number of stakeholders with a stake on the use case, the number of dependencies of the use case or the number and type of associated non-functional requirements should be taken into consideration when using use cases for effort estimation.

2.3.1. *Cockburn's template*

One of the first, most widely used templates for use case specification was initially proposed in (Cockburn, 1997) and later reviewed by its author in (2001). Its most relevant elements are the following:

- **Name, scope, level and visibility:** the name of the use case is the primary actor's goal in a short, active verb phrase. The primary actor is the actor requesting services from the system, usually triggering the use case. In Cockburn's template, the use case name is decorated with the corresponding scope, level and visibility icons (see Fig. 1).
- **Preconditions:** the preconditions of a use case are assertions about the state of the SuD and its environment — the *state of the world* in

---

[3]The interested reader can see Davis (1993) or Sommerville and Sawyer (1997) for more details on requirements attributes and requirements management.

Cockburn's words — that will be checked before letting the use case start and that will not be checked again during the use case execution.

- **Minimal and success guarantees:** Cockburn considers two different groups of postconditions depending on whether the use case ends successfully or not, i.e. whether the primary actor's goal is achieved or abandoned. Minimal guarantees must hold regardless of the success or failure of primary actor's goal. Success guarantees must hold only when the use case concludes successfully.

- **Trigger:** a trigger is an event that fires the execution of a use case. Depending on the writing style, it can be considered as the first step of the use case or specified outside the main success scenario.

- **Main success scenario:** the main success scenario is a numbered sequence of steps performed during the execution of a use case that leads to a situation in which the primary actor's goal is achieved. Apart from including another use case, Cockburn considers three possible kinds of action to be performed in a step: an interaction between two actors (considering the SuD as a special kind of actor), a validation step, and a internal change of the SuD (even if the visibility of the use case is black box). The number of actions to be included in a single step depends on the writing style,[4] although one or two actions are the usual number. Cockburn also recommends not using conditional steps in the main success scenario but considering them as extensions.

- **Extensions:** extensions are branches of the main success scenario depending on a particular condition — the extension condition — in a given step. Some of these branches can lead to success while other can lead to failure of the use case. Cockburn recommends using extensions for handling both situations, while other authors like Leite et al. (2000) or Durán et al. (2002) use conditional steps for successful, usual branches and exceptions for branches triggered by exceptional conditions usually leading to use case failure.

- **Technology and data variations:** Cockburn considers different ways of performing a step as variations, like using different payment methods, different data during an identification of a user, etc. They are not

---

[4]See Cockburn (2001), pages 93–95, for details about including a reasonable set of actions in a single step.

considered to be alternative branches, i.e. they have neither condition nor steps.

2.3.2. *RUP template*

The *Rational Unified Process* (RUP) (Kruchten, 2000) is a software engineering methodology developed by the Rational company (now a company of IBM) after the *Unified Process* (UP) (Jacobson et al., 1999). One of its defined artefacts is the *RUP use case template*, including the following elements:

- **Name:** like in Cockburn's template, the name of the use case in the RUP template is a short description of the primary actor's goal, although it is augmented with a brief description in which a short summary of the use case is provided.
- **Pre- and postconditions:** in the RUP template, a precondition is defined as the state of the system that must be present before the use case starts. Postconditions are defined as a list of the possible states the system can be in after a use case has finished. Kruchten (2000) does not specify if postconditions must always hold or if they must only hold on successful ending of the use case, which seems to be the usual semantics. Notice that unlike in Cockburn's template, pre- and postconditions in the RUP template do not take the SuD environment into consideration.
- **Basic flow:** the basic flow is a numbered sequence of steps describing what actors do and what the system does in response. In the RUP template, conditional branches are allowed provided they are composed of only a few steps. In the case of complex alternative branches, using an *alternative flow* is preferred. As in Cockburn's template, the action of a step can be an *inclusion* of another use case (or an *extension* if the step is conditional).
- **Alternative flows:** alternative flows describe alternative behaviour usually due to exceptions that occur in specific steps in the main flow. When an alternative flow ends, the main flow is resumed unless otherwise stated. If needed, alternative flows can be divided into alternative subflows at arbitrary depth, although that use is discouraged.
- **Extension points:** in the UML 1.5 specification (OMG, 2003), an *extension point* is defined as a reference to one or a collection of

locations in a use case where the use case may be *extended*. An *extend relationship* defines that a use case may be — i.e. depending on a *extension condition* — augmented with some additional behaviour defined in another use case.

From our point of view, one of the problems of this vague description of, a probably unnecessary, concept is that extensions points are not related to any step in neither the basic flow nor the alternative flow. In other words, they seem to be unattached labels for the starting points of alternative flows expressed as separate use cases.

2.3.3. *Leite's template*

Leite et al. (2000) proposes not only a scenario template but also a whole process for scenario construction. An important difference in this approach is that Leite's scenarios are tightly coupled with a *lexicon* containing concepts from the problem domain. In this way, Leite ensures that scenarios are written using the vocabulary of customers and users, thus enforcing their communicability. The most relevant elements of this template are the following:

- **Title and goal:** Leite's template includes both a name and a goal. Usually, the former is a short form of the latter.
- **Context and resources:** in Leite's template, preconditions are part of the context of the scenario, which describes a geographical location, a temporal location and preconditions. Leite also includes information about relevant resources, i.e. physical elements or information, which must be available during the scenario performance. Postconditions are not considered in this template.
- **Episodes:** the episodes of Leite's scenario template are basically the same as the numbered sequences steps of previously discussed templates. In this template, episodes can include other scenario or describe a simple interaction. Conditions can be included in the episode sequence, but they affect only one episode. For conditional branches composed of more than one episode, scenario inclusion must be used. Leite also considers *optional episodes*, i.e. steps that may or may not be performed depending on conditions that cannot be explicitly detailed. Notice that groups of

non-sequential episodes can also be defined in a Leite's template, thus allowing a parallel or indistinct sequential order.

- **Exceptions:** this section of Leite et al.'s template contains the specifications of exceptional situations due to the lack or malfunction of some of the previously mentioned resources. The main differences with other templates are that exceptions are not associated to specific steps, and that only one action can be specified as the exception treatment, although that action can be a scenario inclusion.

2.3.4. *Durán's template*

Durán's template for use cases, formerly published in Durán et al. (1999), is one of the results of the PhD thesis of one of the authors of this chapter (Durán, 2000). The most relevant characteristic of this template is that for a number of its elements some *linguistic patterns* are provided, thus easing use case writing.[5] Another interesting aspect of this template is that it is fully supported by the free requirements management tool *REM* (Durán, 2003), as shown in Fig. 2. Its basic elements are the following:

- **Name:** the name of the use case is, as in Cockburn's template, a short verb phrase stating the goal of the use case from the primary actor's point of view.
- **Description:** the description is based on a linguistic pattern including the triggering event of the use case. The simplified structure of this linguistic pattern is *"the system shall behave as described in the following use case when <triggering event>"*. Notice that Durán considers the triggering event at the business level, whereas the first step of the *ordinary sequence* is usually a request of service from an actor to the system (see Fig. 3 for an example).
- **Preconditions:** preconditions include assertions that must be true in order to reach the goal of the use case. Like in Cockburn's and Leite's

---

[5]A description of linguistic patterns is out of the scope of this chapter. The interested reader can see Durán et al. (1999) for details. A more extensive work on the use of linguistic patterns for use cases can be found in Ben Achour et al. (1999), one of the results of the CREWS project.

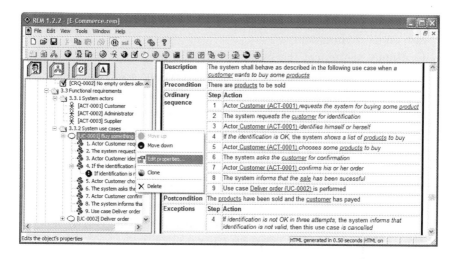

Fig. 2. Support for use cases in REM.

UC–0015	Register Book Loan	
Dependencies	• OBJ–0001 *To manage book loans (objective)* • OBJ–0005 *To know library users' preferences (objective)* • CRQ–0003 *Maximum number of simultaneous loans (business rule)* • CRQ–0014 *Return date for a loan (business rule)*	
Description	The system shall behave as described in the following use case when *a library user requests a loan of one or more books.*	
Precondition	*The library user has been identified by means of his or her identity card and has picked up the books to loan from the shelves.*	
Ordinary sequence	**Step**	**Action**
	1	The librarian *requests the system for starting the book loan registering process.*
	2	The system *requests for the identification of the library user requesting a loan.*
	3	The librarian *provides identification data of the library user to the system.*
	4	The system *requests for the identification of the books to be loaned.*
	5	The librarian *provides identification data of the books to be loan to the system.*
	6	The system *displays the return date for each of the books to be loan and requests loan confirmation for each of them.*
	7	The librarian *tells the user library the return dates displayed by the system and ask him/her if he or she still wants to loan each book.*
	8	The library user *confirms the librarian which books he or she wants to loan after knowing return dates.*
	9	If *some of the confirmed books have an associated multimedia item*, then use case "*Add item multimedia to loan*" is performed.
	10	The librarian *re–confirms the book loans confirmed by the library user to the system.*
	11	The system *informs that the book loans have been successfully registered.*
Postcondition	*The library user can take the loaned books away and the system has registered the book loans*	
Exceptions	**Step**	**Action**
	3	If *the library user has already reached the maximum number of simultaneous loans or has a penalty*, the system *informs of the situation, then this use case cancelled.*
Comments	*The maximum number of simultaneous book loans and the loan period depend on the library policy and can change in the future. See business rules CRQ–0003 y CRQ–0014.*	

Fig. 3. Use case example using a simplified version of Durán's template.

templates, preconditions are expressed not only on the system state but also on its environment.

- **Ordinary sequence:** the ordinary sequence describes the steps performed to achieve the use case goal when everything goes right, including single conditional steps like in Leite's template. The actions performed in any step can be actor actions (*actor-to-actor* or *actor-to-system* actions), system actions (usually only externally observable actions) or the performance of another use case (an UML *inclusion* or *extension*, depending on whether the step is conditional or not).
- **Postcondition:** postconditions include assertions about the system and its environment that must hold provided the use case ends successfully.
- **Exceptions:** exceptions have the same structure than in Leite's template plus additional information specifying if the use case is resumed or canceled after exception treatment.

2.4. *Use case diagrams*

Apart from their textual specification, use cases, their actors and their relationships can be depicted in the so-called *use cases diagrams*. Use case diagrams were part of the initial proposal by Jacobson et al. (1992) and, with minor changes, they are also present in the current UML specification (OMG, 2003).

As commented by some authors like Cockburn (2001) or Kulak and Guiney (2000), use case diagrams must be understood only as a *table of contents* of use cases, not as an alternative of their textual specification. In use case diagrams, only the name of the use cases, the participating actors and some use case relationships are shown. The *essence* of use cases, i.e. their sequence of actor-system interactions, cannot be in anyway derived from use case diagrams. An example of a use case diagram can be seen in Fig. 4, where the system boundary is represented as a box containing some use cases. Actors are represented as stick men and their participations in use cases are depicted as association lines.

2.5. *Use cases in the UML specification*

As commented in the introduction of this chapter, the UML specification has caused confusion about some concepts related to use cases. Apart

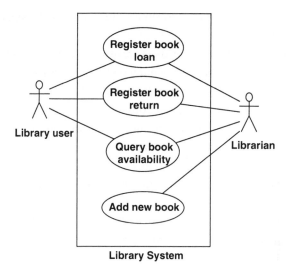

Fig. 4. Use case diagram example.

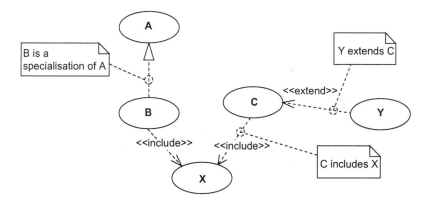

Fig. 5. UML notation for use case relationships.

from focusing only in the diagrammatic notation, the introduction of three different kinds of *use case relationships*, i.e. *inclusion*, *extension* and *generalisation* (see Fig. 5 for their graphical notation), has led many developers to build extremely complex use case models impossible to understand for their customers and users because of an excessive use of these relationships.

We agree with Cockburn and other authors about the meaning of the so-called *include* and *extend* relationships. They must be considered as a means of avoiding redundancy in use cases specifications, but always taking into account communicability and understandability as the primary goals of use cases. In other words, a certain degree of redundancy is acceptable if it makes communication easier. Their counterparts in textual specification are those steps invoking or calling other use cases. Unconditional invocations are considered as *inclusions* and conditional invocations, i.e. conditional steps or exceptions, are considered as *extensions*.

Without a doubt, the most confusing use case relationship in UML is *use case generalisation*. There are no clear semantics about the relationships of the sequence of steps of two use cases when one is a generalisation of the other. In the UML specification, the semantics of use-case generalisation are described in this way:

> *Generalisation between use cases means that the child is a more specific form of the parent. The child inherits all features and associations of the parent, and may add new features and associations (pages 2–132).*
> *[...]*
> *A generalisation relationship between use cases implies that the child use case contains all the attributes, sequences of behaviour, and extension points defined in the parent use case, and participates in all relationships of the parent use case. The child use case may also define new behaviour sequences, as well as add additional behaviour into and specialise existing behaviour of the inherited ones. One use case may have several parent use cases and one use case may be a parent to several other use cases (pages 2–138).*

As the reader can see in the previous definition of use-case generalisation, its semantics are extremely ambiguous. On one hand, *child use cases* must contain the whole sequence of the *parent use case*. On the other hand, *child use cases* may define *new sequences, add new behaviour and specialise exisiting behaviour.* It is not clear at all how a child use case can redefine the sequence of steps of its parent use case — not to mention if the child use case has more than one parent!

Ambler (2001) interprets use case generalisation in a different way:

Inheritance between use cases should be applied whenever a single condition would result in the definition of several alternate courses.
[...]
The inheriting use case is much simpler than the use case from which it inherits. It should have a name, description, and identifier, and it should also indicate from which use case it inherits in the "Inherits From" section. This includes any section that is replaced, particularly the pre-conditions and post-conditions as well as any courses of action. If something is not replaced, then leave that section blank, assuming it is inherited from the parent use case (you might want to put text, such as "see parent use case," in the section).

Ambler's definition of use-case generalisation is more concrete than the official one. It seems that use-case generalisation should be use when a single condition is responsible for several alternate courses. In other words, if you find several — more than three, perhaps? — non-contiguous, conditional steps, all of them sharing the same condition, you should consider extracting all affected steps and create a child use case.

An obvious alternative to Ambler's proposal is using conditional steps — action steps or inclusion steps, i.e. extensions — instead of introducing a new kind of use-case relationship.

Cokburn (2001) recognises the problems of use-case generalisation and proposes a completely different use:

In general, the problem with the generalises relation is that the professional community has not yet reached an understanding of what it means to subtype and specialize behaviour, that is, what properties and options are implied. Since use cases are descriptions of behaviour, there can be no standard understanding of what it means to specialise them.
If you use the generalises relation, my suggestion is to make the generalised use case empty [...]. Then the specialising use case will supply all the behaviour [...].

What Cockburn does not say is the reason for keeping the empty generalised use case, which seems to be useless.

As the reader can see, there is no consensus about what use-case gener-alisation means. This situation is reflected in the fact that, as far as we know, no use-case metrics proposal takes use-case generalisation into account.

2.6. *Conclusions on the concept of use case*

After analysing the concept of use case, their roles in software development, and some templates for their specification,[6] we have reached the following conclusions:

- Although other uses are possible, use cases are mainly used as textual specifications of functional requirements. Hence, they can be considered as partial specifications of the system to be built for estimation purposes.
- Use case templates usually include the use-case goal, preconditions, trigger, main successful scenario, postconditions, successful alternative branches and failure alternative branches. Some of them distinguish between usual and abnormal, i.e. exceptional, conditions of alterna-tive branches. Some of them include information about the environment whereas other focus only on the software system.
- The usual number of actions specified in each step is usually one or two. Step actions are usually one of the three possible classes — actor action, system action and use case inclusion/extension.
- Use case relationships must be used carefully, keeping use case specifi-cations clear and easy to understand. Inclusion and extension should be used only as means of avoiding redundancy. Generalisation should be used only when non-ambiguous semantics were commonly agreed.

Taking these considerations into account, the different proposals for use-case metrics are analysed in the following sections.

3. Metrics for Project Estimation

As Smith (1999) commented, *"Intuitively, it seems as though it should be possible to form estimates of size and effort that development will require*

---

[6]The interested reader can see other use case templates proposals — (Schneider and Winters, 1998), (Kulak and Guiney, 2000), and (Coleman, 1998).

based on characteristics of the use case model. After all, the use case model captures the functional requirements ..."

In this section, the main proposals to estimate size, effort and complexity of the system based on use cases will be presented.

3.1. *Size and complexity estimation*

3.1.1. *Fectcke's et al. proposal*

The *function points* (Albrecht, 1979) is one of the method that allows measuring the functional size of software systems. One of the main reasons for its use is because *function points* measures the functionality of software from the user viewpoint independently of technology used for implementation. With OO methods implantation it is advisable to adapt the *functions points* for the OO conceptual models.

In order to allow this goal, in Fetcke et al. (1997) a method to calculate *function points* based on conceptual models is shown. These conceptual models are use cases model, domain model and analysis objects model.

In order to calculate *function points*, previously it was necessary to know *unadjusted function points* that are calculated by adding the number of internal files and external files of the application, together with the inputs, outputs and inquiries from and to the user.

In particular, for the use cases model, Feckte et al. (1997) assume that some use cases will be mapped to direct interaction user-system and others will not because of the different possible detail levels of the use cases.

In order to correctly select use cases, the method proposed by these authors explains that first we have to apply the mapping actors rules that lie in choosing those actors (human or not) that are not part of the system under consideration, i.e. the system users and the others systems. Afterward, the use cases that are related with some of the selected actors will be chosen. Furthermore, we have to add the use cases that are related with a particular one by means of an *extend* relationship.

Those use cases will be counted as systems interactions and will be added to the rest of elements selected in the analysis model or domain model in order to obtain *unadjusted function points*.

Fetcke et al. (1997) state how the method is applied to three development projects getting system size in *unadjusted functions points*. The main advantage is that the method is based on system requirements, collected at the very beginning of the system development process. The disadvantage is that it is only applicable when you use OOSE (Object Oriented Software Engineering) (Jacobson et al., 1992).

3.1.2. Marchesi et al.'s proposal

Also based on the use case model, metrics are defined to estimate system complexity. One of these proposal, explained in (Marchesi, 1998), which is based on possible mapping between use case and *function points* assures that the number of use cases (N_{CU}), the number of actors (N_a) and the number of *include* and *extend* relationships are good indicators of system complexity.

To estimate system complexity based on the metrics mentioned above, Marchesi proposes the metric $UC4$ of which the equation is as follows:

$$UC4 = K_1 UC1^2 + UC3 + K_2[smm([C]) - smm([E])]$$

where:

- The coefficients K_1 and K_2 are constants (less than one) and must be calculated empirically.
- $UC1$ represents the number of use cases in the requirements specification. According to Henderson-Sellers et al. (2002), it is unknown why $UC1$ appears squared. The author argues reasons of homogeneity because the other parts of the equation are proportional to $N_a \times N_{CU}$ and $UC1$ is only N_{CU}.
- $UC3$ is the total amount of communications among use cases and actors without redundancies introduced by *extend* and *include* relationships, taking into account the fact that the complexity of a use case increases more than linearly with the number its communications.
- $[C]$ is a matrix (with dimension $N_a \times N_{CU}$) and the element c_{ik} of $[C]$ has value 1 if the actor i has a relationship with use case k, and value 0 otherwise.
- $[E]$ is a matrix ($N_a \times N_{CU}$) representing the relationships between use cases after eliminating the redundancies due to *include* and *extend* relationships. Assuming a matrix $[M]$, then $smm([M])$ is defined as the sum of all elements of matrix $[M]$, taking into account that the difference

$smm([C]) - smm([E])$ is a measurement of the communications inherited by all use cases *extending* or *using* other use cases.

In our point of view, once the metric $UC4$ is defined, it is advisable to try to empirically validate it in order to establish a correlation between this metric and system complexity, for example, doing a *correlational study* according to (Briand and Wüst, 2002). In the results of this study, it would be possible to establish the coefficients values (K_1 and K_2). On the other hand, it is difficult to fix the measure unit of $UC4$ and how the value bears upon the project schedule.

3.1.3. *Feldt's proposal*

Feldt (2000) studies how the complexity and size of use cases influence system complexity and size.

In order to specify use cases, this author proposes to use UML sequence diagrams (OMG, 2003). For this reason, the metrics proposed in this section are suitable when it works with low-level use cases. The only participants in the sequence diagrams used by Feldt are *actor* and *system*. They interchange messages as "calls to procedures" which can have parameters. Furthermore, repetition sequences and alternatives can appear as well as other elements usually seen in these types of diagrams (stimulus and interruptions).

In our opinion, it is preferable to specify functional requirements with some of the textual use case proposals (summarised in Sec. 2.3. Specification of use cases) to make the communication between software developers and clients and users possible. Nevertheless, this proposal is interesting to see the aspects of use cases considered necessary to estimate size and system complexity.

In order to characterise the size and complexity of use cases, Feldt proposes the following metrics:

- Number of stimulus (external events that have influences in the use case performance).
- Number of alternative branches.
- Number of interruptions.
- Number of system responses (calls to procedures).
- Number of system actions (relationships with other use cases).

- Number of exceptions.
- Number of actors.

It is convenient to take into account that Feldt (2000) considers size and complexity as attributes that can be measured as a whole. Furthermore, it is interesting to study how he approximates the system complexity through the time invested in writing the sequence diagram.

3.2. *Estimation of system effort*

It is difficult to determine *a priori* the effort required to implement a use case. This is because use cases are used in different ways depending on engineer's requirements or on the active rules in the organisation. Consequently, use cases can have different abstraction levels.

In order to solve this problem, there are some alternatives. Some of them suggest to classify use cases according to their detail level and then estimate the effort to implement them according to their assigned level. Other proposals count the number of analysis classes, which correspond to each use case, and based on this, they can estimate the extend of its implementation.

3.2.1. *Karner's proposal*

The proposal done by Karner (Rational Software) and collected in Schneider and Winters (1998) defines the concept *use case points*, analogue to the *function points* concept. *Use case points* is useful to estimate the effort (in man-hours) of development project.

The metric *use case points* (*UCP*) is defined as:

$$UCP = UUCP \cdot TCF \cdot EF$$

where

- *UUCP* is the metric called *unadjusted use case points*. This metric is calculated as the weighted sum in number of actors and number of use cases in the requirements specification. Each actor and use case can have a different complexity. This provokes the weighing in the calculation of *UUCP*. The weights of the actors figure are in Table 1. The complexity of use cases depends on one of two factors: the number of steps, and the

Table 1. Actor weighting factors.

Actor type	Description	Factor
Simple	Program interface	1
Average	Interactive, or protocol-driven interface	2
Complex	Graphical interface	3

Table 2. Transaction-based weights factors.

Use case type	Description	Factor
Simple	3 or fewer transactions	5
Average	4 to 7 transtractions	10
Complex	More than 7 transctions	15

Table 3. Analysis class-based weighting factors.

Use case type	Description	Factor
Simple	Fewer than 5 analysis classes	5
Average	5 to 10 analysis classes	10
Complex	More than 10 analysis classes	15

number of analysis classes corresponding to the use case. Tables 2 and 3 show the possible weights of the use case.

- *TCF* represents a technical complexity factor. This factor increases if there are complex non-functional requirements, for example, if the system is distributed, the code must be reusable or easy to change, etc. In Table 4, you can see which factors have influence in *TCF*. Those factors have a weight between 0.5 and 2. According to the importance of this factor in the system, this weight will be multiplied by a number between 0 and 5 (0 means that the factor is not present in the system).

- *EF* represents the level of experience of the technical personnel that work in the project. The stability of the project also has influence on the value of *EF*.

Once the value of *UCP* is calculated, and to estimate system effort, Karner suggests applying a factor of 20 man-hours per *UCP*. However, data obtained from its application in real projects advises that it is convenient to adjust this quantity.

One of these revisions is shown in Schneider and Winters (1998) which comments that it would be beneficial to adjust this quantity depending on

Table 4. Technical factors for system and weights.

Factor number	Factor description	Weight
T1	Distributed system	2
T2	Response or throughput performance objectives	1
T3	End-user efficiency (online)	1
T4	Complex internal processing	1
T5	Code must be reusable	1
T6	Easy to install	0.5
T7	Easy to use	0.5
T8	Portable	2
T9	Easy to change	1
T10	Concurrent	1
T11	Includes special security features	1
T12	Provides direct access for third parties	1
T13	Special user training	Facilities are required

the *EF* value. If the *EF* is highly affected by change in staff, this will provoke more effort in training team members or provoke the convenience of solving instability problems. In this case, Schneider advises to use 28 man-hours per *UCP*.

In Banerjee (2001), it also provided another possibility: to increase the number of man-hours to 36 per *UCP*. The reason for this approach is that negative numbers mean extra effort spent on training team members or problems due to instability. However, using this method of calculation means that even small adjustments of an environmental factor, for instance, by half a point, can make a great difference in the estimate.

Furthermore, the *use case points* method has been applied to different types of projects. Thus, in Arnold and Pedross (1998), usage in large-scale software systems is explained. Experiences, based on empirical data of a productivity benchmark of 23 measured projects, have revealed the usefulness of the method in order to measure the size of a software system.

The method has also been applied in building Web Application Systems (Stoica, 2000) coming to the conclusion that this technique can be used by adding front-ends to the best existing cost models.

Furthermore, some CASE tools solve the calculation of *UCP*. One of them is Enterprise Architect (Systems, 2003), a modelling UML tool.

In our opinion, the most relevant thing of this approach is to consider technical factors *TCF* and *EF*. More or less, this shows that it is insufficient about the information collected in requirements specification to estimate effort because there are other factors whose influence is essential to take into account.

3.2.2. Smith's proposal

The approach described in this section presents a fundamental difference with the one described in the previous section; which is the detail level of the use cases object of the estimation. In the Karner's proposal, it is necessary that use cases have sufficient detail level, in order to know how many analysis classes correspond to each use case.

In brief, Smith (1999) defines four possible types of use cases according to detail level: Subsystem ($L1$), Group of subsystem ($L2$), System ($L3$) and System of subsystem ($L4$). A concrete use case can belong to a sole level, or to several of them in a concrete percentage.

The concept of subsystem coincides with the concept proposed by UML (OMG, 2003). The concept of subsystem group coincides with CSCI[7] (Computer Software Configuration Item) (DoD, 1993).

The basic idea is that a use case of level $L(i)$ needs less effort than a level $L(i+1)$ to be implemented in C++ language. This is because a use case of level $L(i+1)$ comprises several use cases of level $L(i)$. On the other hand, the type of system also has influence in the effort of implementation of the use case. Thus, three types of systems are considered — simple business system, scientific system and complex command and control system.

Table 5 shows the level size in SLOCS (Source Lines of Code). In order to build Table 5, the following sentences are assumed, whose justification are in Smith (1999):

- A subsystem ($L1$) implements 8 classes.
- To implement a class in C++ approximately 850 SLOCS are necessary.
- The level $L(i+1)$ is composed by 8 components of the level $L(i)$.

---

[7]A configuration item for computer software, where a *Configuration Item* is an aggregation of hardware or software that satisfies an end use function and is designed by the acquirer for separate configuration management.

Table 5. Size of sytem (in SLOCS).

Level	Size (SLOCS)
L1	7,000
L2	56,000
L3	448,000
L4	3,584,000

Table 6. Effort of use case depending on detail level and system type.

Level	Effort h/UC simple business system	Effort h/UC scientific system	Effort h/UC complex command and control system
L1	55 (range 40–75)	120 (range 90–160)	260 (range 190–350)
L2	820 (range 710–950)	1,700 (range 1,500–2,000)	3,300 (range 2,900–3,900)
L3	12,000	21,000	38,000
L4	148,000	252,000	432,000

Once the level size is known, it is necessary to take into account the following statements:

- To describe the functionality of 8 classes, 300 scenarios are necessary.
- 10 use cases of level $L1$ can describe 300 scenarios.

Now, if models like COCOMO and SLIM are applied, the results obtained in Table 6 show the effort in hours/use case (h/UC) necessary to implement a use case of level and type of a system in particular.

In order to apply this estimation technique, we would have to take the set of use cases of the requirements specification and fit each of them in the suitable level $L(i)$ or partially in several of them. Furthermore, it is convenient to take into account the number of pages that fill each use case. Subjectively, Smith exposed that a use case of a simple business system must occupy an average length of 5 pages, a use case of a scientific system, 9 pages, and a complex command or control system, 12 pages.

One example in Smith (1999) assumes a scientific system where the actual use cases count was 5, and one of them split at $L4$ and 4 at $L3$, further, the $L4$ use case is 12 pages and the $L3$ use cases average 10 pages, then the effort is: $1 \times 250 \times 12/9 + 4 \times 21000 \times 10/9 = \approx 2800$ staff months. The quotients 12/9 and 10/9 are used to account for the apparent complexity due to the 9 pages represented as the average length use case because the system is a scientific type.

3.2.3. *Henderson-Sellers's proposal*

Henderson-Sellers et al. (2002) provide some metrics for size and complexity of use cases. According to the authors they could be useful for estimating external attributes (Fenton and Pfleeger, 1997), such as system effort and maintainability.

In order to measure the size of a use case, the following metrics are suggested:

- Number of atomic actions in the main flow.
- Number of atomic actions in each alternative flow.
- The longest path between the first atomic action of the use case to the final atomic action of the use case.
- Number of alternative flows (alternative flows are measured from the start of the use case to its termination).

On the other hand, the following *environment factors* contribute to the use cases complexity independently of size metrics shown above:

- Number of stakeholders.
- Number of actors.
- Total number of goals.

The author argues that these metrics measure complexity in the presence of two use case models with similar values in defined size metrics, but different values in environment metrics, probably the one with greater values requires more effort in doing any change. This is because there are more elements that must be reviewed to solve possible conflicts.

Other indirect metrics can be derived from the above metrics and include:

- Total number of atomic actions in the alternative flows.
- Total number of atomic actions in all flows.
- Number of atomic actions per actor.
- Number of atomic actions per goal.
- Number of goals per stakeholder.

After showing different proposed metrics to measure use cases size and complexity, most of the authors coincide that the main factor that has influence in the use cases complexity is the increase of the resources required to do a change in the use case. The greater the effort required to do a change the greater will be the complexity of the specification.

In these circumstances, also dependencies between requirements increase complexity. These dependencies appear in *traceability matrix* and in our point of view must be included as a factor to measure use cases complexity.

4. Metrics for Requirements Engineering

Leaving aside the project estimation and focussing on requirements engineering process, there are reasons to think that it would be beneficial to define metrics. Nevertheless, because the requirements engineering is a recent discipline, there are not too many proposals. The reasons mentioned are as follows:

- In Kamstiems and Rombach (1997), the importance of early detection of requirements problems is recognised to improve the quality in the software development process. This is because the cost of repairing defects increases as the project moved forward (Boehm, 1975).
- In order to increase the control and monitoring during the development of this task, it is necessary to know in detail the requirements engineering process. The fact of control in the process allows knowing early needs for change. This has advantages because one of the main problems in the development process is changing requirements and specifications, as TSG (1995) shows. These changes affect technology, schedule, budget and staff organisation as commented in Costello and Liu (1995) quoting the paper of Glaseman and Davis (1980).

4.1. *Quality in requirements specification*

At the moment, there are not too many proposals, which specify how to predict quality requirements based on use cases. In spite of that, there are some proposals to evaluate quality of natural requirements. Generally, some of them can be applied to evaluate use cases quality. In this area, the following approaches exist:

- Manual verification of requirements: these approaches study aspects as stability, ambiguity or traceability of requirements. Some of them can be consulted in Davis et al. (1993), Costello and Liu (1995) or Hyatt and Rosemberg (1996).
- Automated verification of requirements: these proposals generally are based on NLP (Natural Language Processing). According to Fabbrini et al. (1998), the goal of NLP applied to requirements engineering is to know the vocabulary used, writing style, ambiguity (degree of syntactic and semantic uncertainty of the sentence), information conveyed by requirements, discovering underspecifications, missing information and unconnected statements.

One of these proposals applied to use cases was collected in Fantechi et al. (2002). The idea of this proposal is to automatically identify defects in requirements specification. In order to achieve this goal, a tool CASE automatically identifies words in the text of use cases that denote lack of expressiveness (due to ambiguity or incompressibility), lack of consistency or incompleteness.

On the other hand, some proposals to evaluate the design quality of use cases models have been done. For example, these metrics have been proposed:

- NumAss: The number of associations the use case participates in.
- ExtPts: The number of extension points of the use case.
- Including: The number of use cases which this one includes.
- Included: The number of use cases which include this one.
- Extended: The number of use cases which extend this one.
- Extending: The number of use cases which this one extends.

Some of these metrics were automated by the tool SDMetrics (SDMetrics, 2003).

4.1.1. *Saeki's proposal*

The modifiability is one of the desirable properties of the requirements specification. IEEE (1993) defines a modifiable requirements specification as one whose structure and style is so that any change can be performed in an easy, complete and consistent way maintaining its structure and style.

In Saeki (2003), a set of metrics for use cases diagrams are defined. Based on these, the rate of modifiability can be calculated. The basic idea of the defined metrics is that if a use case needs a change, probably other use cases will also need a change: those that have a relationship with the originally changed use case. In short, *include* and *extend* relationships and the control[8] and data[9] dependency relationships are considered. The intuition suggests that the more existing relationships in the model, the more difficult it will be to make any change.

Another factor that has influence in the modifiability of use cases is the type of use case. Simplifying the idea, if a use case has several goals (*types* to Saeki), it is more susceptible of changing than if it only has one goal.

In order to approximate the modifiability, the defined metrics are *NOD* (Number Of Dependencies) and *NUCT* (Number of Use Case Types).

The next equation is the pattern that stands for *NO_extends*, *NO_uses*, *NO_CD* and *NO_DD* metrics. These metrics express the modifiability index due to *extend*, *include*, control dependency and control data relationships, respectively.

$$NOD = \frac{AllDependencies - \#Dependency}{AllDependencies}$$

where $\#S$ stands for the number of the elements of the set S, *UseCase* stands for the set of all use cases in the diagram, $AllDependencies = (\#UseCase \times (\#UseCase - 1))/2$ is the set of all the possible dependencies that exist. In our opinion, term *AllDependencies* is a theoretical term since semantically it would not make sense that all use cases are connected between them in the model.

On the other hand, the equation shown below expresses the modifiability index due to the fact that a use case covers more than one goal (*types*).

$$NUCT = \frac{1}{\underset{u \in UseCase}{AVE} \{\#\{ut \in UseCaseType \mid aggregates(u, ut)\}\}}$$

---

[8]Control dependency expresses the order of execution of use cases.
[9]Data dependency expresses that one use case gives data to another.

where $u \in UseCase$ represents one of the use cases in the diagram, *aggregates*(u, ut) means that a use case u has a type ut, $AVE_{p(x)}\{s(x)\}$ means the average value of a set of numbers $s(x)$ constructed from x such that $p(x)$. *NUCT* is the reciprocal number of an average of attached use case *types* for each use case.

Based on these metrics the rate of modifiability (*MODIFIABILITY*) of the use cases diagram is computed as:

$$MODIFIABILITY = w_1 \times NO\_extends + w_2 \times NO\_uses + w_3$$
$$\times NO\_CD + w_4 \times NO\_DD + w_5 \times NUCT$$

where each w_i represents the weighting factor of the corresponding metric and the sum $w_1 + w_2 + w_3 + w_4 + w_5$ may be equal to 1 and $0 \leq w_i \leq 1$ ($i = 1, \ldots, 5$). One possible solution is proposed by Saeki: $w_i = 0, 2 \forall i$.

This manner of defining the metrics is not obvious but it is justifiable in our point of view. The goal achieved by the author was to find an indicator rate ($0 \leq MODIFIABILITY \leq 1$) that would reveal the modifiability degree of a use cases model.

This proposal is interesting because of its capability to measure one of the desirable properties in requirements specifications, the modifiability. The traces existing between use cases should also be included in the calculation of modifiability because the traced requirements can change with the original requirements. In general, the coupling between use cases is caused by *include* and *extend* relationships and by the use cases connected in a *traceability matrix* which should be considered in the modifiability calculation. The control and data dependencies reveal that use cases technique has been used in an inferior specification level, close to the sequence diagram.

4.1.2. *Bernárdez and Durán's proposal*

Bernárdez et al. (2004) have empirically revised a set of heuristics to identify use cases that potentially can have defects.

These heuristics, presented in Durán et al. (2002), are based on a set of use case metrics defined for the use cases model of REM (Durán, 2003). In this use cases model, a use case is seen as a sequence of steps that can be action-step, system-step or realise another use case as commented in

Sec. 2.3.4: Durán's template. An example of a use case of this model can be seen in Fig. 3.

The heuristics, based on the metrics shown in Table 7, rely on a basic concept: there is a normal range of values for each metric $m[m_1, m_2]$, out of which the probability of a use case c presenting defects ($P_{def}[c]$) increases.

$$m(c) \notin [m_1, m_2] \Rightarrow P_{def}[c] \gg 1 - P_{def}[c].$$

In Table 8, we will apply the outlined metrics to the use case example shown in Fig. 3.

The normal range of values (see Table 9) was set using data from 414 non-verified (i.e. containing defects) use cases from students of computer science at the University of Seville.

In order to consolidate the intuition of these heuristics, Bernárdez et al. (2004) have verified 8 requirements specifications from their students, containing 127 use cases. Some of the results achieved reveal that use cases outside the normal range are fault-prone requirements. This fact is confirmed in Fig. 6, which shows the percentage of use cases that have defects in and out of the normal range.

The main source of defects in use cases, which are revealed by the empirical data, are incompressibility, incompleteness (both defined by

Table 7. Use case metrics which Durán's heuristics are based.

Metric	Description
NOS	Number of steps of the use case (NOS = NOAS + NOSS + NOUS)
NOAS	Number of actor action steps of the use case
NOSS	Number of system action steps of the use case
NOUS	Number of use case action steps of the use case (inclusion or extension)
NOCS	Number of conditional steps of the use case
NOE	Number of exceptions of the use case
NIE	Number of times the use case is included or extends other use cases
NOAS/NOS	Rate of actor action steps of the use case
NOSS/NOS	Rate of system action steps of the use case
NOUS/NOS	Rate of use case action steps of the use case
CC	Cyclomatic complexity of use case (NOCS + NOE + 1)

Table 8. Use case metric values for the use case of Fig. 3.

Metrics	Value	Explanation
NOS	11	There are 11 steps in use case "Ordinary sequence"
NOAS	6	There are 6 actor (*librarian* and *library user*) steps
NOSS	4	There are 4 system steps
NOUS	1	There is one *include* in step 9
NOCS	1	There is only a conditional step (step 9)
NOE	1	There is only an exception associated to step 3
NIE	0	This use case is not performed during another use case execution (The "Description" of the use case not include other use cases)
NOAS/NOS	0.54	6 divided by 11
NOSS/NOS	0.37	4 divided by 11
NOUS/NOS	0.09	1 divided by 11
CC	3	NOCS + NOE + 1 (= 1 + 1 + 1)

Table 9. Use case metrics normal range.

Metrics	Normal range
NOS	[3, 9]
NOAS/NOS	[30%, 70%]
NOSS/NOS	[40%, 80%]
NOUS/NOS	[0%, 25%]
CC	[1, 4]

Davis et al. (1993) and the incorrect use of the use cases technique (according to Lilly (1999)). If the findings shown in Fig. 6 were confirmed by a family of controlled experiments, we could conclude that these metrics really allow the prediction of potential defects in requirements.

4.2. *Progress of requirements engineering process*

Some authors like (Costello and Liu, 1995) advise the calculation of some metrics as indicators of the requirements engineering process. As commented above, this would be beneficial because it would permit project managers and requirements engineers to monitor and better control the requirements engineering process.

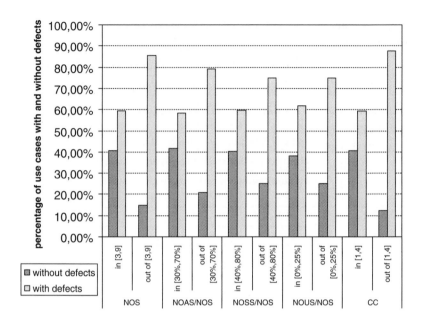

Fig. 6. Empirical results on heuristics reviews.

4.2.1. *Kim and Boldyreff's proposal*

Kim and Boldyreff (2002) propose the following metrics:

- NAU (Number of Actors associated with a Use case): The goal of this metric is to measure the importance of the requirement. If there are many actors interested in performing the use case, it must be very important to the system.
- NMU (Number of Messages associated with a Use case): This metric is calculated from a UML interaction diagram (OMG, 2003). NMU is useful to trace requirements to design elements.
- NSCU (Number of System Classes associated with a Use case): This metric measures the number of classes of which objects take part in a use case scenario. This metric goal is to know the impact of the change in a use case.

4.2.2. *Alexander's proposal*

Alexander (2001) proposes some metrics to learn the status and progress of requirements engineering and some metrics to reveal possible problems in requirements. Those metrics (that are shown below) can be calculated using the Scenario Plus Use Case Toolkit (Plus, 2003).

The first group of metrics points out the status and progress of the requirements engineering process:

- The number of use cases.
- The number of actors.
- The number of alternative steps of the use case.
- The number of exceptions.
- The number of constraints.

The second group reveals problems in requirements:

- The number of use cases without exceptions.
- The number of use cases without steps.
- The number of use cases isolated.
- The number of relationships between use cases.

5. Conclusions

In this chapter, the basic main ideas to learn the use cases technique have been presented. Also, the main proposals to estimate software project attributes (in brief, size, complexity and effort) based on use cases metrics has been collected. Furthermore, the main proposals to improve the requirements engineering process based on use cases metrics have been presented.

Tables 10 and 11 summarise the most relevant proposals analysed in this chapter. The first column contains the author of the proposal. The second column contains the use cases metrics defined in the proposal. The third column lists the external attributes to be estimated. The fourth column indicates whether the proposal provides a prediction equation or not. The fifth column indicates whether computation of the proposed metrics and estimated attributes is supported by any CASE tool or not.

Looking at Table 10, we can see that the more estimated attribute is development effort. In order to estimate this attribute, authors usually measure attributes like size and complexity of use cases. Nevertheless, most

Table 10. Summary of use case metrics proposals for project management.

Author	What is measured?	What is estimated?	Prediction equation?	CASE tool support?
Marchesi (1998)	Number of use cases, number of actors, number of *include* and *extend* relationships	System complexity	No	No
Schneider et al. (1998)	*Use case points*	Development effort	Yes	Yes (Sparx System)
Smith (1999)	Number of use cases in each detail level, number of pages of the use case	Development effort	Yes	No
Feldt (2000)	Use cases complexity and size	System complexity and size	No	No
Software Solutions on Time (2001)	Number and type of use cases	Development time	Yes	Yes (Metric Data)
Henderson-Sellers et al. (2002)	Use cases complexity and size	Development effort or maintainability	No	No
In et al. (2003)	Number of actors and number of use cases	Development effort	Yes	Yes (OSMAT)

of the proposals do not provide a prediction equation and they are not supported by CASE tools.

Table 11 reveals that the relationships in use case models and use cases themselves can be used to predict attributes like modifiability and the existence of potential problems and defects in requirements. There is not any prediction equation, but there are some CASE tools available to calculate the proposed metrics.

Table 11. Summary of use case metrics proposals for improving the requirements engineering process.

Author	What is measured?	What is estimated?	Prediction equation?	CASE tool support?
Alexander (2001)	Number of use cases, number of actors, number of use cases without exceptions, etc.	Status of requirements and potential problems	No	Yes (DOORS)
Kim et al. (2002)	Number of actors, number of messages in the interaction diagram associated with the use case, number of system classes associated with the use case	Importance of the requirement, impact caused by change a requirement	No	No
Saeki (2003)	Number of relationships and dependencies between use cases	Modifiability	No	No
Bernárdez et al. (2004)	Number of steps of use case steps, rate of each type of step and ciclomatic complexity	Fault-proneness	No	Yes (REM)

At the moment, there are no proposals to deal with the theoretical validation of these metrics. Concerning empirical validation, there are no thorough studies that guarantee the causal relationship between the use cases metrics and the external attributes, such as development time, development effort, system complexity, etc., i.e. *internal validity* according to Wholin et al. (2000). However some of the estimation methods explained in this chapter have been applied to real projects.

In order to empirically validate the metrics to estimate effort, it is suitable to perform experiments in a real environment because the experiment will cover several phases of the life cycle. But in real environments, it is difficult to do controlled experiments and moreover too many resources are needed.

We have reached the conclusions that there is a general intuition among several authors who think that some metrics regarding use cases are useful to project estimation or to improve the requirements engineering process, thus increasing quality in requirements specifications. On the other hand, the different metrics explained here are based on different use cases models and this makes the possibility of adapting the proposal to other situations difficult.

Furthermore, there are other proposals which have not been deeply investigated in this chapter, that define use cases metrics to estimate project cost or development time instead of effort. For example, the proposal presented in In et al. (2003), which presents a CASE tools called OSMAT (Ontology Software Metrics Analysis Tool). This tool is useful to estimate project cost based on UML models. In particular, the proposed metrics to use cases are: Number Of Actors (NOA) and Number of Use Cases (NOUC). On the other hand, there are some development CASE tools companies that propose techniques of project estimation based on use cases. For example, Software Solutions on Time (2001) estimates the time that will be invested in each use case along with each phase of the development process.

Acknowledgements

This research is part of the AgilWeb project (TIC2003-02737-C02-01) financed by "Subdirección General de Proyectos de Investigación, — Ministerio de Ciencia y Tecnología" (Spain), the TAMANSI project (PCB-02-001) financed by "Consejería de Ciencia y Tecnología de la Junta de Comunidades de Castilla-La Mancha" and the MUML project (011.100623) financed by the University of Castilla-La Mancha.

References

Albrecht, A. J. (1979). Measuring Application Development Productivity. *Proceedings of the IBM Application Development Symposiu*m. Monterey, CA, pp. 83–92.

Alexander, I. (2001). Visualising Requirements in UML. *Telelogic Newsbyte*. Available in http://easyweb.easynet.co.uk/˜iany/consultancy/reqts_in_uml/ reqts_in_uml.htm.

Ambler, S. W. (2001). *The Object Primer*. Cambridge University Press. 2nd edition.

Arnold, M. and Pedross, P. (1998). Software Size Measurement and Productivity Rating in Large-Scale Software Development Department. *Proceedings of the*

1998 International Conference on Software Engineering. Los Alamitos, CA, USA, pp. 490–493.

Barnejee, G. (2001). Use Case Points. *White paper*, Isavix.

Ben Achour, C., Rolland, C., Maiden, N. A. M. and Souveyet, C. (1999). Guiding Use Case Authoring: Results of an Empirical Study. *Proceedings of the Fourth IEEE International Symposium on Requirements Engineering.* Limerick, pp. 36–43.

Bernárdez, B., Durán, A. and Genero, M. (2004). An Empirical Review of Use Cases Metrics for Requirements Verification. *Proceedings of the SOFT-WARE MEASUREMENT EUROPEAN FORUM (SMEF'04)*. Rome. Accepted for publication.

Boehm, B. W. (1975). Some Experience with Automated Aids to the Design of Large-Scale Reliable Software. *IEEE Transactions on Software Engineering*, Vol. 1, No. 1, March, pp. 125–133.

Briand, L. C. and Wüst, J. (2002). Empirical Studies of Quality Models in Object-Oriented Systems. *Advances in Computers*, Academics Press, Vol. 59, pp. 97–166.

Cockburn, A. (1997). Structuring Use Cases with Goals. *Journal of Object-Oriented Programming*, Sep–Oct, 1997.

Cockburn, A. (2001). *Writing Effective Use Cases*. Addison-Wesley.

Coleman, D. (1998). A use case template: Draft for discussion. Available in http://www.bredemeyer.com/pdf_files/use_case.pdf.

Costello, R. J. and Liu, D. (1995). Metrics for Requirements Engineering. *Journal Systems Software*, Vol. 29, pp. 39–63.

Davis, A., Overmyer, S., Jordan, K., Caruso, J., Dandashi, F., A. Dinh, Kincaid, G., Ledeboer, G., Reynols, P., Sitaran, P., Ta, A. and Theofanos, M. (1993). Identifying and Measuring Quality in Software Requirements Specification. *Proceedings of the 1st International Software Metrics Symposium*. Los Alamitos, California, IEEE Computer Society Press, pp. 164–175.

Davis, A. M. (1993). *Software Requirements: Objects, Functions and States.* Prentice-Hall. 2nd edition.

DoD (1993). *DoD-STD-2167, Defense System Software Development*. Department of Defense, United States of America.

Durán, A. (2000). A Methodological Framework for Requirements Engineering of Information Systems (in Spanish). Doctoral dissertation, University of Seville.

Durán, A. (2003). REM web site. http://klendathu.lsi.us.es/REM.

Durán, A., Bernárdez, B., Ruiz, A. and Toro, M. (1999). A Requirements Elicitation Approach Based in Templates and Patterns. *Proceedings of the 2nd Workshop on Requirements (WER'99)*. Buenos Aires, pp. 17–29.

Durán, A., Ruiz-Cortés, A., Corchuelo, R. and Toro, M. (2002). Supporting Requirements Verification Using XSLT. *Proceedings of the IEEE Joint International Requirements Engineering Conference (RE'02)*. Essen, pp. 165–172.

Fabbrini, F., Fusani, M., Gervasi, V., Gnesi, S. and Ruggieri, S. (1998). Achieving Quality in Natural Language Requirements. *Proceedings of the 11th International Software Quality Week*. San Francisco.

Fantechi, A., Gnesi, S., Lami, G. and Macari, A. (2002). Application of Linguistic Techniques for Use Case Analysis. *Proceedings of the IEEE Joint International Requirements Engineering Conference (RE'02)*, Essen, Germany, pp. 157–164.

Feldt, P. (2000). Requirements Metrics Based on Use Cases. Master's thesis, Department of Communication Systems, Lund Institute of Technology, Lund University, Box 118, S-221 00 Lund, Sweden.

Fenton, N. and Pfleeger, S. (1997). *Software Metrics: A Rigorous and Practical Approach*. PWS Publisher.

Fetcke, T. A., Abran, A. and Nguyen, T. (1997). Mapping the OO-Jacobson Approach into Function Point Analysis. *Proceedings of the 23rd Technology of Object-Oriented Languages and Systems (TOOLS-23)*. Santa Barbara, California, pp. 1–11.

Glaseman, S. and Davis, M. (1980). *Software Requirements for Embedded Computers: A Preliminary Report*. Document R-2567-AF. U. S. Air Force.

Henderson-Sellers, B., Zowghi, D., Klemola, T. and Parasuram, S. (2002). Sizing use cases: How to create a standard metrical approach. *Proceedings of the 8th Object-Oriented Information Systems 2002*, Montpellier, France, Springer-Verlag, pp. 409–421.

Hyatt, L. and Rosenberg, L. (1996). A Software Quality Model and Metrics for Identifiying Project Risk and Assessing Software Quality. *Proceedings of the 8th Software Technology Conference*. Available in http://satc.gsfc.nasa.gov/support/STC_APR96/quality/sct_qual.html.

IEEE (1993). *IEEE Recommended Practice for Software Requirements Specifications* (IEEE/ANSI Standard 830–1993). Institute of Electrical and Electronics Engineers.

In, P., Kim, S. and Barry, M. (2003). Uml-Based Object-Oriented Metrics for Architecture Complexity Analysis. *Proceedings of Ground System Architectures Workshop*. El Segundo, CA. Available in http://sunset.usc.edu/gsaw/gsaw2003/s8e/in.pdf.

Jacobson, I., Booch, G. and Rumbaugh, J. (1999). *The Unified Software Development Process*. Addison-Wesley.

Jacobson, I., Christerson, M., Jonsson, P. and Övergaard, G. (1992). *Object-Oriented Software Engineering: A Use Case Driven Approach*. Addison-Wesley.

Kamsties, E. and Rombach, H. D. (1997). A Framework for Evaluating System and Software Requirements Specification Approaches. *Proceedings of Requirements Targeting Software and Systems Engineering*. Bernried, Germany, pp. 203–222.

Kim, H. and Boldyreff, C. (2002). Developing Software Metrics Applicable to UML Models. *Proceedings of the 6th International Workshop on Quantitative Approaches in Object-Oriented Software Engineering*. Málaga, Spain, pp. 67–76.

Kruchten, P. (2000). *The Rational Unified Process: An Introduction*. Addison-Wesley. 2nd edition.

Kulak, D. and Guiney, E. (2000). *Use Cases: Requirements in Context*. Addison-Wesley.

Leffingwell, D. and Widrig, D. (2000). *Managing Software Requirements: A Unified Approach*. Addison-Wesley.

Leite, J. C. S. P., Hadad, H., Doorn, J. and Kaplan, G. (2000). A Scenario Construction Process. *Requirements Engineering Journal*, Vol. 5, No. 1, pp. 38–61.

Lilly, S. (1999). *Use Case-Based Requirements: Review Checklist* (Technical Report). SRA International, Inc.

Marchesi, M. (1998). OOA Metrics for the Unified Modeling Language. *Proceedings of the 2nd EUROMICRO Conference on Software Manteinance and Reengineering*, pp. 67–73.

Meyer, B. (1997). *Object-Oriented Software Construction*. Prentice-Hall. 2nd edition.

OMG (2003). OMG Unified Modeling Language Specification, v1.5.

Regnell, B., Anderson, M. and Bergstrand, J. (1996). A Hierarchical Use Case Model with Graphical Representation. *Proceedings of the IEEE International*

Symposium and Workshop on Engineering of Computer-Based Systems. Friedrichshafen, pp. 65–84.

Plus, S. (2003). Use Case Toolkit for DOORS. Available in http://www.scenarioplus.org.uk.

Saeki, M. (2003). Embedding Metrics into Information System Development Methods: An Application of Method Engineering Technique. *Lecture Notes in Computer Science 2681*, pp. 374–389.

Schneider, G. and Winters, J. P. (1998). *Applying Use Cases: A Practical Guide.* Addison-Wesley.

SDMetrics (2003). SDMetrics: The Software Design Metrics Tool for the UML. Available in http://www.sdmetrics.com/.

Smith, J. (1999). *The Estimation of Effort Based on Use Cases* (Rational Software white paper). Rational Software. Available in http://www.rational.com/media/whitepapers/finalTP171.PDF.

Software Solutions on Time (2001). A Fresh and Innovative Approach to Systems Development and Software Project Management. Available in http://www.tassc-solutions.com/omx/pages/metric_data.htm#usecase-metrics.

Sommerville, I. and Sawyer, P. (1997). *Requirements Engineering: A Good Practice Guide.* Wiley.

Stoica, A. (2000). Aspect of Building Web Application Systems Using the MBASE Approach. *Proceedings of the 15th International Forum on SCM/Focused Workshop.* USC-CSE.

Systems, S. (2003). Enterprise Architect: UML Modeling and Design Tool. Available in http://www.sparxsystems.com.au.

TSG (1995). *The CHAOS Report.* The Standish Group. Available in http://www.standishgroup.com/chaos.html.

Weidenhaupt, K., Pohl, K., Jarke, M. and Haumer, P. (1998). Scenarios in System Development: Current Practice. *IEEE Software*, Vol. 15, No. 2, pp. 34–45.

Wholin, C., Runeson, P., Höst, M., Ohlsson, M. C., Regnell, B. and Wesslén, A. (2000). *Experimentation in Software Engineering: An Introduction.* Kluwer Academic Publishers.

Chapter 4

DEFINING AND VALIDATING METRICS
FOR UML CLASS DIAGRAMS

MARCELA GENERO*,a, GEERT POELS†, ESPERANZA MANSO‡
and MARIO PIATTINI*,b

*Alarcos Research Group, Department of Computer Science
University of Castilla-La Mancha
Paseo de la Universidad, 4 – 13071 – Ciudad Real, Spain
a Marcela.Genero@uclm.es
b Mario.Piattini@uclm.es

†Department of Management Information, Operations Management
and Technology Policy, Faculty of Economics
and Business Administration Ghent University
Hoveniersberg, 24 – 9000 – Gent, Belgium
geert.poels@ugent.be

‡GIRO Research Group, Department of Computer Science
University of Valladolid
Campus Miguel Delibes, E.T.I.C. – 47011 – Valladolid, Spain
manso@infor.uva.es

1. Introduction

In the development of object-oriented (OO) software the class diagram is the key outcome of the conceptual modelling phase. Indeed, class diagram lays the foundation of all later design and implementation work. Hence, class diagram quality is a crucial issue that must be evaluated (and improved if necessary) in order to obtain quality OO software, which is the main concern of present day software development organisations.

The early focus on class diagram quality may help OO software designers build better software, without unnecessary reworking at later stages of the development when changes are more expensive and more difficult to perform. It is in this arena where software measurement plays an important role, because metrics contribute to class diagram quality evaluation in an objective way avoiding bias in the quality evaluation process.

We focus this chapter on class diagrams developed using the Unified Modelling Language (UML) (OMG, 2001), because it has become the standard language of OO modelling.

Measuring UML class diagram quality at conceptual level allows OO software designers:

- A quantitative comparison of design alternatives, and therefore an objective selection among several class diagram alternatives with equivalent semantic content.
- A prediction of external quality characteristics, like maintainability in the initial phases of the OO software life cycle and a better resource allocation based on these predictions.

The goal of this chapter is two-fold:

(1) To give a brief overview of the existing proposals of metrics that can be applied to UML class diagrams at conceptual level.
(2) To define and validate a new set of metrics to measure UML class diagrams structural properties.

2. Overview of the Existing Proposals of Metrics

The main idea of this section is to show a summary of the most relevant existing proposals of metrics that can be applied to UML class diagrams at conceptual level, looking at their strengths and weaknesses. Most of the metric proposals we will consider and list below were not originally defined to measure UML class diagrams. Nevertheless, they can be tailored for this purpose:

- Chidamber and Kemerer's metrics (1991, 1994): These metrics were defined at class level and their purpose is to measure design complexity in relation to their impact on external quality attributes such as maintainability, reusability, etc.
- Li and Henry's metrics (1993): These metrics measure different internal attributes such as coupling, complexity and size, and were successfully used to predict maintenance effort. They were defined at class level.
- Brito e Abreu and Carapuça's metrics (1994): They were defined to measure the use of OO design mechanisms such as inheritance, information hiding, coupling and polymorphism and the consequent relation with software quality and development productivity. They can be applied at class diagram level.
- Lorenz and Kidd's metrics (1994): They were defined at class level to measure the static characteristics of software design, such as the usage of inheritance, the amount of responsibilities in a class, etc.
- Briand et al.'s metrics (1997): These metrics are defined at class level, and are counts of interactions between classes. Their aim is the measurement of the coupling between classes.
- Marchesi's metrics (1998): The aim of these metrics is the measurement of system complexity, of balancing responsibilities among packages and classes, and of cohesion and coupling between system entities.
- Harrison et al.'s metrics (1998): They have proposed the metric Number of Associations per class metric as an inter-class coupling metric.
- Bansiya et al.'s metrics (1999, 2002): These metrics were defined at class level for assessing design properties such as encapsulation, coupling, cohesion, composition and inheritance.

Table 1 reflects the published studies related to the theoretical and the empirical validation of the proposals of metrics previously mentioned. Regarding theoretical validation, we considered two approaches:

- Property-based approaches (Weyuker, 1998; Briand et al., 1996): They aim to formalise the properties that a generic attribute of a software system (e.g. complexity, size, etc.) must satisfy in order to be used in the

Table 1. Summary of proposals of metrics for UML class diagrams.

Source	Validation			
	Empirical		Theoretical	
	Experiments	Case studies	Property-based approaches	Measurement theory-based approaches
Chidamber and Kemerer (1991, 1994)	Chidamber and Kemerer (1994), Basili et al. (1996), Daly et al. (1996), Cartwright (1998), Unger and Prechelt (1998), Harrison et al. (2000), Poels and Dedene (2001), Briand et al. (2001), Bandi et al. (2003) Subramanyan and Krishnan (2003)	Li and Henry (1993), Chidamber et al. (1998), Tang et al. (1999), Briand et al. (1998, 2000b)	Briand et al. (1996), Chidamber and Kemerer (1994)	Zuse (1998), Poels and Dedene (1999)
Li and Henry (1993)		Li and Henry (1993)		
Brito e Abreu and Carapuça (1994)		Brito e Abreu et al. (1995), Brito e Abreu and Melo (1996), Brito e Abreu et al. (1996b), Harrison et al. (1999)		Harrison et al. (1998)
Lorenz and Kidd (1994)		Lorenz and Kidd (1994)		
Briand et al. (1997)		Briand et al. (1998, 2000b), El-Emam et al. (1999), Galsberg et al. (2000)	Briand et al. (1999)	
Marchesi (1998)		Marchesi (1998)		
Harrison et al. (1998)		Harrison et al. (1998)		
Bansiya et al. (1999, 2002)		Bansiya et al. (1999, 2002)		

analysis of any measurement proposed for those attributes. They provide properties that are necessary but not sufficient, so they can be used as a filter to reject proposed measures (Kitchenham and Stell, 1997), but they are not sufficient to prove the validity of the measure.

- Measurement theory-based approaches (Zuse, 1998; Poels and Dedene, 1999, 2000a): They check for specific measure if the empirical relations between the elements of the real world established by the attribute being measured, are respected when measuring the attributes. Also measurement-theory based approaches are useful for knowing the scale of a measure, which is a must when analysing data obtained in empirical studies.

Related to empirical validation, we considered two empirical strategies:

- Experiments. Experiments are formal, rigorous and controlled investigations. They are launched when we want control over the situation and want to manipulate behaviour directly, precisely and systematically. Hence, the objective is to manipulate one or more variables and control all other variables at fixed levels. An experiment can be carried out in an off-line situation, for example in a laboratory under controlled conditions, where the events are organised to simulate their appearance in the real world. Experiments may alternatively be carried out on-line, which means that the investigation is executed in the field under normal conditions. Experiments in the context of empirical software engineering research are further discussed in Wohlin et al. (2000) and in Juristo and Moreno (2001).
- Case studies. A case study is an observational study, i.e. it is carried out by observation of an on-going project or activity. The case study is normally aimed at tracking a specific attribute or establishing relationships between different attributes. The level of control is lower in a case study than in an experiment. Case study research is further discussed in Robson (1993), Stake (1995), Pfleeger (1994, 1995) and Yin (1994).

From Table 1, we can observe that work relating to the theoretical validation of metrics is scarce. Although more emphasis has been placed on the empirical validation of metrics in order to find conclusive results of their usefulness in practice, claiming the validity of the current metrics proposals requires replication of the experiments. Above all, external replications are needed as most metrics suites have only been 'validated' by their own authors. Further, empirical validation using data taken from "real projects" is required.

Moreover, on further analysis, taking the scope of the metrics (class or class diagram) and the UML construct they are related to into account, we found that most of the presented metric proposals lack metrics referring to associations, aggregations and dependencies. Analysing Tables 2 and 3 can deduce this fact. It is also evident that generalisation has been the area most widely addressed in the field of OO metrics.

Table 2. Comparison of class-scope metrics.

Scope → Proposals ↓	Classes					
			Relationships			
	Attributes	Methods	Gen.	Agg.	Assoc.	Dep.
Li and Henry (1993)						
Lorenz and Kidd (1994)	X	X	X			
Chidamber and Kemerer (1994)		X	X			
Briand et al. (1997)	X	X				
Harrison et al. (1998)					X	
Bansiya et al. (1999, 2002)	X	X				

Table 3. Comparison of class diagrams-scope metrics.

Scope → Proposals ↓	Class diagrams					
			Relationships			
	Attributes	Methods	Gen.	Agg.	Assoc.	Dep.
Brito e Abreu and Carapuça (1994)	X	X	X			
Marchesi (1998)[*]	X		X		X	

[*] Marchesi (1998) considered all relationships (except generalisations) as dependencies, without distinguishing between them.

The lack of metrics for the structural complexity of class diagrams due to the usage of UML relationships revealed in Tables 2 and 3, leaded us to define a set of metrics, which will be presented in the next section.

3. Proposal of Metrics for UML Class Diagrams

In order to guarantee, to some extent, the success of metrics, it is essential that the process of obtaining them should be carried out in a disciplined manner, following a method, which guarantees their validity. In this respect we have defined a method for the definition of metrics, which consists of three main steps: metric definition, theoretical validation and empirical validation (Calero et al., 2001). In the rest of the chapter, we will show how we carried out each of these three activities.

We considered that the structural complexity of UML class diagram is determined by the different elements of which it is composed, such as classes, attributes, relationships, etc. Fenton has formally proven that a single measure of complexity cannot capture all possible aspects or viewpoints on complexity (Fenton, 1994). Hence, it is not advisable to define a single measure for class diagram structural complexity. The approach taken here is to propose several objective and direct measures applied at diagram level, each one focussing on a different class diagram modelling construct. Therefore, in the next sub-section we will first enumerate the UML modelling constructs that we consider a UML class diagram has at conceptual level. Next, in a second sub-section, our suite of structural complexity metrics is presented, where the metric definitions are stated informally, in natural language. Formal definitions, using set theoretic constructs, will be provided in Sec. 4, where the formal validation of the metrics is presented. The empirical validation of the metrics are in Secs. 5 and 6.

3.1. *UML modelling constructs*

For our purpose, we consider that at a high-level design stage, a UML class diagram has the following elements:

- Packages.
- Classes.

- Each class has attributes and methods.
- Attributes have their name, type, visibility and scope.
- Methods have their name, list of parameters, return type and also their visibility and scope.
- Relationships, considering four kinds of relationships:

  - Association. This is a connection between classes, which means that it is also a connection between objects of those classes. In UML, an association is defined as a semantic connection among a tuple of objects.
  - Aggregation. This is a special case of association. The aggregate indicates that the relationship between the classes is some sort of "whole-part". UML considers two special kinds of aggregation: common aggregation and composition.
  - Generalisation. This is a relationship between a more general and more specific element. An instance (an object is an instance of a class) of more specific element may be used wherever the more general element is allowed.
  - Dependency. This is a relationship between elements, one independent and one dependent. A change in the independent element will affect the dependent element.

3.2. *Metric definition*

Using the GQM (Basili and Rombach, 1988; Basili and Weiss, 1984; Van Solingen and Berghout, 1999) template for goal definition, the goal pursued with the definition of the metrics for UML class diagrams is:

Analyse	*UML class diagrams*
For the purpose of	*measuring*
With respect to their	*structural complexity*
From the point of view of	*the researcher*
In the context of	*software quality studies*

The metrics we propose are shown in Table 4. These metrics were defined to measure UML class diagram structural complexity, due to the use of different kinds of relationships, such as associations, generalisations,

Table 4. Metrics for the structural complexity of UML class diagrams.

Metric name	Metric definition
Number of Associations (NAssoc)	The total number of associations
Number of Aggregations (NAgg)	The total number of aggregation relationships within a class diagram (each whole-part pair in an aggregation relationship)
Number of Dependencies (NDep)	The total number of dependency relationships
Number of Generalisations (NGen)	The total number of generalisation relationships within a class diagram (each parent-child pair in a generalisation relationship)
Number of Aggregation Hierarchies (NAggH)	The total number of aggregation hierarchies (whole-part structures) within a class diagram
Number of Generalisation Hierarchies (NGenH)	The total number of generalisation hierarchies within a class diagram
Maximum DIT (MaxDIT)	It is the maximum of the DIT (Depth of Inheritance Tree) values obtained for each class of the class diagram. The DIT value for a class within a generalisation hierarchy is the longest path from the class to the root of the hierarchy
Maximum HAgg (MaxHAgg)	It is the maximum of the HAgg values obtained for each class of the class diagram. The HAgg value for a class within an aggregation hierarchy is the longest path from the class to the leaves

aggregations and dependencies. Further details on them may be found in Genero et al. (2000) and Genero (2002), where the authors proposed them.

These metrics accomplish the ISO 9126 (ISO, 2001) required properties for measures used for comparison, because:

- They are objective, i.e. there is an agreed procedure for assigning values to the metrics.
- They are empirical, i.e. the data is obtained by observation.

- They are repeatable, i.e. the procedures for measurement result in the same measures being obtained by different persons making the same measurement of the same ER diagram on different occasions.

The ISO 9126 also proposes that the metrics shall be characterised in an interval or higher scale, and should also have predictive validity. These last two properties will be evaluated by the theoretical (see Sec. 4) and the empirical validation (see Secs. 5 and 6), respectively.

Another relevant property is that the proposed metrics are simple, which is as Fenton and Neil (2000) remark in a work related to the future of software metrics, is a desirable property for software metrics in general.

3.3. *An example*

Now, we will apply the outlined metrics to the example shown in Fig. 1, taken from Fowler and Scott (1999) and modified to illustrate the calculation of the metrics proposed.

Table 5 shows the value of the metrics extracted from the example shown above.

4. Theoretical Validation of the Proposed Metrics

We have chosen to carry out the theoretical validation of the proposed metrics using a measurement-based approach called the DISTANCE framework (Poels, 1999; Poels and Dedene, 2000a). Firstly, in this section, we will present the main concepts of the DISTANCE framework, and later we will show how we used this framework for defining and theoretically validating the metrics we presented in Table 4.

4.1. *The DISTANCE framework for software measure construction*

The DISTANCE framework provides constructive procedures to model software attributes and define their measures (Poels, 1999; Poels and Dedene, 2000a). The different procedure steps are inserted into a process model for software measurement that (i) details the required inputs for

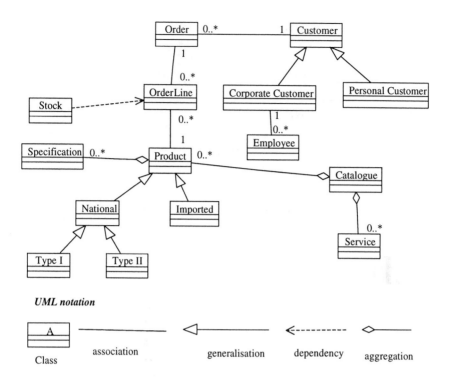

Fig. 1. Example of an UML class diagram (Fowler and Scott, 1999).

each task, underlying assumptions and expected results, (ii) prescribes the order of execution, providing for iterative feedback cycles, and (iii) embeds the measurement procedures into a typical goal-oriented measurement approach such as, for instance, GQM (Basili and Weiss, 1984; Basili and Rombach, 1988; Van Solingen and Berghout, 1999). In this section, we summarise the procedures for attribute definition and measure construction for ease of reference.

The framework is called DISTANCE as it builds upon the concepts of distance and dissimilarity (i.e. a non-physical or conceptual distance). Software attributes are modelled as conceptual distances between the software entities they characterise and other software entities that serve as reference points or norms for measurement. These distances are then measured by functions that are called 'metrics' in mathematics. These 'metrics' are functions that satisfy the metric axioms, i.e. a set of axioms that are

Table 5. UML class diagrams metric values for the class diagram of Fig. 1.

Metrics	Value	Explanation
NAssoc	4	**Associations** = (Order-Customer), (Order-Order Line), (Order Line-Product), (Corporate Customer, Employee)
NAgg	3	**Aggregations** = (Catalogue, Product), (Catalogue, Service), (Product, Specification)
NDep	1	**Dependencies** = (Stock, Order Line)
NGen	6	**Generalisations** = (Customer, Corporate Customer), (Customer, Personal Customer), (Product, National), (Product, Imported), (National, Type I), (National, Type II)
NAggH	1	There is only one aggregation hierarchy with a whole Catalogue.
NGenH	2	There are two generalisation hierarchies, the first has as root class the class Customer, and the other the class Product.
MaxHAgg	2	HAgg (Specification) = 0, HAgg (Product) = 1, HAgg (Catalogue) = 2, HAgg (Service) = 0; The Maximum value of HAgg is 2.
MaxDIT	2	DIT (Type II) = 2, DIT (Type I) = 2, DIT (National) = 1, DIT (Product) = 0, DIT (Imported) = 1, DIT (Corporate Customer) = 1, DIT (Personal Customer) = 1, DIT (Customer) = 0; The maximum value of DIT is 2.

necessary and sufficient to define measures of distance (Poels and Dedene, 2000a).

The measurement theoretic interpretation of the concept of dissimilarity is built into the framework. This ensures that the theoretical validity of the measures obtained with DISTANCE can be formally proven within the framework of measurement theory (Krantz et al., 1971; Roberts, 1979). A key feature of DISTANCE is that the constructive attribute modelling and measure definition procedures as presented in the process model, hide the complexity of the underlying measurement theoretic constructs from the user. Poels and Dedene (2000a) take full advantage of the intuitiveness and flexibility of the distance concept to arrive at a measure construction framework that is transparent with respect to measurement theory and that is generic, i.e. not limited to the measurement of a specific software attribute.

The distance-based measure construction process consists of five steps. The process is triggered by a request to find or build a measurement instrument for a software attribute *attr* that characterises the software entities in a set P. There might for instance be a request that expresses the need for a measure of some structural complexity aspect of a UML class diagram.

Find a measurement abstraction. A measurement abstraction for the software entities must be found. The software entities of interest must be modelled so that the attribute of interest is emphasised. This means that the model should allow us to observe to what extent a software entity is characterised by the attribute. The result of this step is a set of software entities M that can be used as measurement abstractions or models of the software entities in P for the attribute of interest *attr*. Also a function $abs: P \rightarrow M$ is defined that formally describes the rules of the mapping.

Model distances between measurement abstractions. Distances between the elements of M are modelled as sequences of elementary transformations. Such a sequence represents a series of atomic changes applied to an element of M to arrive at another element of M. The number of atomic changes that are required to transform one element into the other determines the distance between these elements. The formal outcome of this step is a set T_e of elementary transformation types on M that must be used to build the sequences.

Quantify distances between measurement abstractions. A metric $\delta: M \times M \rightarrow \mathfrak{R}$ is defined to quantify the distances between the elements of M. Formally, this step results in the definition of a metric space (M, δ).

Find a reference abstraction. We need to determine what the model of a software entity in P must look like in case that entity is characterised by the theoretical lowest value of *attr*. This hypothetical 'null' model or reference model can then be used as a reference point or norm for measurement. The result of this step is thus the definition of a function *ref*: $P \rightarrow M$ that returns for each software entity in P a reference abstraction for *attr* in M.

Define the software measure. The software attribute *attr* is defined and measured as a specific distance within M. The extent to which *attr* characterises a software entity $p \in P$ is defined by the distance between the actual model of p for *attr* (i.e. $abs(p)$) and the reference model for *attr* (i.e. $ref(p)$). The larger this distance, the more the actual measurement abstraction differs from the norm that has been set and thus the greater the extent to which *attr* characterises p. Hence, the value of *attr* for p

is the value returned by the metric δ for the pair $(abs(p), ref(p))$. The formal outcome of this step is the measure $\mu: P \rightarrow \mathfrak{R}$ defined such that $\forall p \in P: \mu(p) = \delta(abs(p), ref(p))$.

From a measurement theory point of view, the distance-based software measure construction process results in the definition of an attribute as a segmentally additive proximity structure and in the definition of a measure as a metric with additive segments (Suppes et al., 1989). According to the uniqueness theorem associated with the representation theorem for segmentally additive proximity structures the resulting measures are characterised by the ratio scale type. For further details on the measurement theoretical principles underlying the approach you can refer to Poels (1999) and Poels and Dedene (2000a).

Before proceeding to the distance-based definition of the UML class diagram structural complexity measures in the next section, we wish to clarify why we emphasise the theoretical validation of the proposed measures. In our opinion, the validity of the measurement instruments used for the variables of an empirical study is a key factor in the overall study validity. On the one hand, the theoretical validity of the structural complexity measures is used to claim their construct validity when used as measures of structural complexity, which is the independent variable in the empirical studies described in Sec. 4. On the other hand, knowledge of the scale type of the measures helps to choose the appropriate statistical technique(s) to analyse the data obtained in an experiment.

4.2. Definition of metrics using the DISTANCE framework

Next, we will follow each of the steps for measure construction proposed in the DISTANCE framework for the metric NAssoc. In order to exemplify the process, we will use the UML class diagrams shown in Fig. 2.

Step 1: Find a measurement abstraction. In our case the set of software entities is the Universe of class diagrams (UCD) that are relevant to the Universe of Discourse (UoD). The attribute of interest is the number of associations, i.e. a particular aspect of class diagram structural complexity. Let UAssoc be the Universe of Associations relevant to UoD. All the sets of associations within the class diagrams of UCD are elements of the power

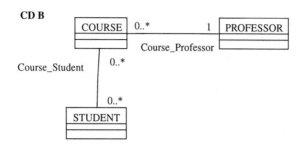

Fig. 2. Two examples of class diagrams.

set of UAssoc, denoted by $\wp$(UAssoc). We can therefore equate the set of measurement abstractions to $\wp$(UAssoc) and define the abstraction function as:

abs_{NAssoc}: UCD $\rightarrow$ $\wp$(UAssoc): $CD \rightarrow$ SAssoc(CD),

where SAssoc is a function that projects a class diagram upon its set of associations.

Example:

$abs_{\text{NAssoc}}(CD\ A) = $ SAssoc($CD\ A$) $= \{$Course_Professor$\}$

$abs_{\text{NAssoc}}(CD\ B) = $ SAssoc($CD\ B$) $= \{$Course_Student,

Course_Professor$\}$.

Step 2: Model distances between measurement abstractions. The next step is to model distances between the elements of $\wp$(UAssoc). We need to find a set of elementary transformation types for the set of measurement abstractions such that any set of associations can be transformed into any other set of associations by means of a finite sequence of elementary transformations. Finding such a set in the case of a power set is a trivial task. Since the elements of $\wp$(UAssoc) are sets of associations, T_e must only contain two types of elementary transformations: one for adding an association to a set and one for removing an association from a set. Given two sets of associations $s_1 \in \wp(\text{UAssoc})$ and $s_2 \in \wp(\text{UAssoc})$, s_1 can always be transformed into s_2 by removing first all associations from s_1 that are not in s_2, and then adding all associations to s_1 that are in s_2, but not in the original s_1. In the "worst case scenario", s_1 must be transformed into s_2 via an empty set of associations. Formally, $T_e = \{t_{0\text{-NAssoc}}, t_{1\text{-NAssoc}}\}$, where $t_{0\text{-NAssoc}}$ and $t_{1\text{-NAssoc}}$ are defined as:

$$t_{0\text{-NAssoc}}: \wp(\text{UAssoc}) \to \wp(\text{UAssoc}): s \to s \cup \{a\}, \quad \text{with } a \in \text{UAssoc}$$

$$t_{1\text{-NAssoc}}: \wp(\text{UAssoc}) \to \wp(\text{UAssoc}): s \to s - \{a\}, \quad \text{with } a \in \text{UAssoc}.$$

In our example, the distance between $abs_{\text{NAssoc}}(CD\ A)$ and $abs_{\text{NAssoc}}(CD\ B)$ can be modelled by a sequence of elementary transformations, as shown below.

$$\text{SAssoc}(CD\ A) = \{\text{Course\_Professor}\}$$
$$\text{SAssoc}(CD\ B) = \{\text{Course\_Professor, Course\_Student}\}$$
$$= t_{0\text{-NAssoc}}(\text{SAssoc}(CD\ A)).$$

This sequence of one elementary transformation is sufficient to transform SAssoc($CD\ A$) into SAssoc($CD\ B$). All "shortest" sequences of elementary transformations qualify as models of distance.

Step 3: Quantify distances between measurement abstractions. In this step, the distances in $\wp(\text{UAssoc})$ that can be modelled by applying sequences of elementary transformations of the types contained in T_e are quantified. A function δ_{NAssoc} of these distances is a metric (in a mathematical sense) that is defined by the symmetric difference model, i.e. a particular instance of the contrast model of Tversky (Suppes et al., 1989). It has been proven in Poels (1999) that the symmetric difference model can always be used to define a metric when the set of measurement abstractions is a power set:

$$\delta_{\text{NAssoc}}: \wp(\text{UAssoc}) \times \wp(\text{UAssoc}) \to \Re: (s, s') \to (|s - s'| + |s' - s|).$$

This definition is equivalent to stating that the distance between two sets of associations, as modelled by a shortest sequence of elementary transformations between these sets, is measured by the count of elementary transformations in the sequence. Note that for any element in s but not in

s' and for any element in s' but not in s, an elementary transformation is needed.

The symmetric difference model results in a value of 1 for the distance between the set of associations of *CD A* and *CD B*.

$$\delta_{\text{NAssoc}}(abs(CD\ A), abs_{\text{NAssoc}}(CD\ B))$$
$$= |\{\text{Course\_Professor}\} - \{\text{Course\_Professor, Course\_Student}\}|$$
$$+ |\{\text{Course\_Professor, Course\_Student}\} - \{\text{Course\_Professor}\}|$$
$$= |\emptyset| + |\{\text{Course\_Student}\}| = 1.$$

Step 4: Find a reference abstraction. In our example the obvious reference point for measurement is the empty set of associations. It is desirable that a class diagram without associations should have the lowest possible value for the NAssoc measure. Therefore, we define the following function:

$$ref_{\text{NAssoc}}: \text{UCD} \rightarrow \wp\,(\text{UAssoc}): CD \rightarrow \emptyset.$$

Step 5: Define the software measure. In our example, the number of associations of a class diagram *CD* can be defined as the distance between its set of associations SAssoc(*CD*) and the empty set of associations $\emptyset$. Hence, the NAssoc measure can be defined as a function that returns the value of the metric δ_{NAssoc} for the pair of sets SAssoc(c) and $\emptyset$ for any class diagram:

$$\forall\, CD \in \text{UCD}: \text{NAssoc}\,(CD) = \delta_{\text{NAssoc}}(\text{SAssoc}(CD), \emptyset)$$
$$= |\text{SAssoc}(CD) - \emptyset| + |\emptyset - \text{SAssoc}(CD)|$$
$$= |\text{SAssoc}(CD)|.$$

Consequently, a measure that returns the count of associations within a class diagram qualifies as a measure of the number of associations.

The rest of the proposed class diagram metrics can be modelled by means of a set abstraction (see Table 6) and as a consequence all the measures take the form of a simple count, so their process construction is analogous followed by the metric NAssoc.

Table 6. Abstract functions for the rest of UML class diagram metrics.

Metric	Abstraction function
NAgg	abs_{HAgg}: UCD $\rightarrow$ $\wp(\text{UR}^1)$: $CD \rightarrow$ SAgg(CD) where UR is the Universe of Relationships relevant to an UoD, SAgg(CD) $\subseteq$ UR is the set of aggregation relationships within an CD. An aggregation relationship is each whole-part pair within an aggregation hierarchy that to belongs to a CD.
NDep	abs_{Ndep}: UCD $\rightarrow$ $\wp(\text{UR})$: $CD \rightarrow$ SDep(CD) where UR is the Universe of Relationships relevant to an UoD, SDep(CD) $\subseteq$ UR is the set of dependencies within a CD.
NGen	abs_{NGen}: UCD $\rightarrow$ $\wp(\text{UR})$: $CD \rightarrow$ SGen(CD) where UR is the Universe of Relationships relevant to an UoD, SGen(CD) $\subseteq$ UR is the set of generalisation relationships within a CD. A generalisation relationship is each a child-parent pair within a generalisation hierarchy that belongs to a CD.
NGenH	abs_{NgenH}: UCD $\rightarrow$ $\wp(\text{UGenH})$: $CD \rightarrow$ SGenH(CD) where UGenH is the Universe of Generalisation Hierarchies relevant to an UoD, SGenH(CD) $\subseteq$ UGenH is the set of generalisation hierarchies within a CD.
NAggH	abs_{NaggH}: UCD $\rightarrow$ $\wp(\text{UAggH})$: $CD \rightarrow$ SAggH(CD) where UAggH is the Universe of Aggregation Hierarchies relevant to the UoD, SAggH(CD) $\subseteq$ UAggH is the set of aggregation hierarchies within a CD.
MaxDIT	The DIT metric is defined at class level as: abs_{DIT}: UC $\rightarrow$ $\wp(\text{UC})$: C $\rightarrow$ SAncestorsLongest(D) where UC is the Universe of classes relevant to an UoD, SAncestorsLongest(C) $\subseteq$ UC is the set of ancestors. In the case of multiple inheritance it considers the classes in the longest path between the class and the root of the generalisation hierarchy. The Max DIT metric is the maximum value of DIT calculated for all the classes of a CD.
MaxHAgg	The HAgg metric is defined at class level as: abs_{HAgg}: UC $\rightarrow$ $\wp(\text{UC})$: C $\rightarrow$ SPartsLongest(CD) where UC is the Universe of Classes relevant to an UoD, SPartsLongest(CD) $\subseteq$ UC is the set of part classes that are in the longest path between the class and the leaves of the aggregation hierarchy. The Max HAgg metric is the maximum value of HAgg calculated for all the classes of a CD.

---

[1] In the Universe of Relationships (UR) we consider all possible relationships (associations, aggregations, generalisations and dependencies) relevant to a UoD.

5. Empirical Validation of the Proposed Metrics

Empirical validation is crucial for the success of any software measurement project (Basili et al., 1999; Fenton and Pfleeger, 1997; Kitchenham et al., 1995; Schneidewind, 1992). A proposal of metrics has no value if its practical use is not demonstrated empirically, either by means of case studies taken from real projects or by controlled experiments. Therefore, our main motivation is to investigate, through experimentation, whether the metrics we proposed for UML class diagram structural complexity (see Table 5) are useful and reliable indicators of UML class diagram maintainability.

We focus on class diagram maintainability because it is one of the main software product quality characteristics (ISO, 2001). Concerns with software development organisations are mostly related to this characteristic; in fact, maintenance is still the major resource consumer of the whole software life cycle (Pigoski, 1997).

But as Miller (2000) and Basili et al. (1999), among others, suggested, simple studies rarely provide definite answers. Therefore, we have carried out a family of three experiments[2] (Genero, 2002) for empirically validating the proposed metrics (see Table 5). Each of them will be described in this section. We are aware that only after performing a family of experiments can we build an adequate body of knowledge to extract useful measurement conclusions regarding the use of metrics to be applied in real measurement projects (Basili et al., 1999; Briand et al., 1998).

In order to carry out the experiments we have followed some suggestions provided in the literature by some experts in the field of empirical software engineering such as Briand et al. (2000a), Perry et al. (2000), Wohlin et al. (2000), Juristo and Moreno (2001) and Kitchenham et al. (2002).

---

[2]We considered a family of experiments in the sense that the three experiments we carried out do not vary the hypothesis, i.e. they try to ascertain if there exists correlation between the structural complexity and size of UML class diagrams and their maintainability subcharacteristics. This family of experiments are not considered as replication of experiments as Shull et al. (2003) commented.

Table 7. Metrics for the size of UML class diagrams.

Metric name	Metric definition
Number of Classes (NC)	The total number of classes.
Number of Attributes (NA)	The total number of attributes.
Number of Methods (NM)	The total number of methods.

We considered in this study the set of 8 measures for UML class diagram structural complexity we proposed (see Table 5), and also three traditional size metrics, which are shown in Table 7.

5.1. *Experimental goals*

On the basis of the main objective, which is *"To investigate, through experimentation, whether the metrics we proposed for UML class diagram structural complexity and traditional size metrics are useful and reliable indicators of UML class diagram maintainability"*, two partial goals have arisen:

- First goal: To perform an *exploratory study of the UML class diagrams* to *detect redundancy* with respect to *a set of structural complexity and size metrics*, from the point of view of *the researchers*, in the context of *undergraduate students and professors in the Department of Computer Science at the University of Castilla-La Mancha, in Spain.*
- Second goal: To analyse *the structural complexity and the size of the UML class diagrams*, to *evaluate them* with respect to *their correlation with class diagram maintainability*, from the point of view of *the researchers*, in the context of *students and professors in the Department of Computer Science at the University of Castilla-La Mancha, in Spain.*

The first goal will be achieved through Principal Component Analysis (PCA) (Johnson, 1998; Kleinbaum, 1987). PCA allows us to analyse if the information that the metrics provide is redundant or not. When a group of metrics in a data set are strongly correlated, these variables are likely to measure the same underlying dimensions (i.e. class internal quality attribute) of the object to be measured. PCA can identify the underlying, orthogonal (and so not correlated) dimensions that explain relations between the metrics in the data set.

In the experimental research in software engineering PCA has been used in different kind of studies — Briand et al. (2002) used the PCA to assess a fault-proneness model, Westland (2002) to model the costs of errors in software development, Manso et al. (2002) and Hanebutte et al. (2003) to characterise a set of a class diagrams taken from real projects.

The second goal will be achieved through correlation analysis. A correlation coefficient measures the strength and direction of the relationship between two numerical variables. The correlation coefficient can have any value between -1 and $+1$. If the correlation coefficient is -1, this means that the two variables are perfectly negatively correlated. If the correlation coefficient is $+1$, this means that the two variables are perfectly positively correlated. If the correlation coefficient is 0, this means that the two variables are not correlated at all.

Two measures of correlation are commonly used when analysing software measurement data. Spearman's rank correlation coefficient must be used when the data is ordinal, or when data is far from normally distributed. Pearson's correlation coefficient can be used when data is of an interval or ratio type. Pearson's correlation coefficient is based on two assumptions: (1) the data is normally distributed, and (2) the relationship is linear (Maxwell, 2002). The theoretical foundations can be found in statistical elementary books such as Siegel and Castellan (1988) and Snedecor and Cochran (1989).

5.2. *Experiment process*

We have used the experiment process proposed by Wohlin et al. (2000) — with only minor changes — which consists of the following six steps:

- Definition: In this step, the foundation of the experiment is determined. The purpose of the definition phase is to define the goals of an experiment, formulated from the problem to be solved. This step determines why the experiment is conducted.
- Planning: This step prepares how the experiment is to be conducted.
- Operation: In this step, the experiment is carried out in order to collect the data that should be analysed.
- Analysis and interpretation: In this step the data collected must be analysed in an appropriate way.

- Validation: The degree of credibility of any experiment depends on the validity of how conclusions are drawn. Therefore, in this step those issues that could threaten the conclusion validity, construct validity, internal validity and external validity must be evaluated.
- Presentation and package: When an experiment has been carried out, the intention is often to present the findings. This could for example be done in a paper for a conference, a report for decision-making, a lab package for replication of the experiment or as educational material.

5.3. *First experiment*

We begin this section by describing the first experiment we carried out, following the experimental process mentioned above.

5.3.1. *Definition*

Using the GQM template for goal definition, the goal of the experiment is defined as follows:

Analyse	*UML class diagram structural complexity and size metrics*
For the purpose of	*Evaluating*
With respect to	*the capability to be used as class diagram maintainability indicators*
From the point of view of	*the researchers*
In the context of	*Undergraduate Computer Science students and professors of the Software Engineering area at the Department of Computer Science at the University of Castilla-La Mancha*

5.3.2. *Planning*

The planning phase can be divided into six steps — context selection, hypothesis formulation, variables selection, selection of subjects, experiment design and instrumentation.

- Context selection. The context of the experiment is a group of undergraduate students and professors of the software engineering area, and hence the experiment is run off-line (not in an industrial software development environment). The subjects were seven professors and ten students enrolled in the final-year of computer science in the Department of Computer Science at the University of Castilla-La Mancha in Spain. All of the professors belong to the software engineering area. The experiment is specific since it is focused on UML class diagram structural complexity metrics. The ability to generalise from this specific context is further elaborated below when discussing threats to the experiment. The experiment addresses a real problem, i.e. what indicators can be used for the maintainability of class diagrams? With this end in view, it investigates the correlation between class diagram structural complexity and size metrics and maintainability sub-characteristics.

- Selection of subjects. The subjects are chosen for convenience, i.e. the subjects are undergraduate students and professors who have experience in the design and development of OO systems using UML.
- Variable selection. The independent variable is the class diagram structural complexity and size. The dependent variables are three maintainability sub-characteristics

  – Understandability: The capability of the software product to be understood by it users (software designers, developers).
  – Analysability: The capability of the software product to be diagnosed for deficiencies or causes of failures in the software, or for the parts to be modified need to be identified.
  – Modifiability: The capability of the software product to enable the implementation of a specified modification. The implementation includes the changes in design, code and documentation.

- Instrumentation. The objects were 28 UML class diagrams. The independent variables was measured through the metrics we proposed. The dependent variables were measured according to subject ratings of the maintainability sub-characteristics using an ordinal scale with linguistic labels (see Table 9).
- Hypothesis formulation. We wish to test the following hypotheses:

  – Null hypothesis, H_0: There is no significant correlation between the size (NC, NA, NM) and the structural complexity metrics (NAssoc, NAgg, NDep, NGen, NAggH, NGenH, MaxHAgg, MaxDIT) and the

subject ratings of three maintainability sub-characteristics, such as understandability, analysability and modifiability.
- Alternative hypothesis, H_1: There is a significant correlation between the size (NC, NA, NM) and the structural complexity metrics (NAssoc, NAgg, NDep, NGen, NAggH, NGenH, MaxHAgg, MaxDIT) and the subject ratings of three maintainability sub-characteristics, such as understandability, analysability and modifiability.

• Experiment design. We selected a within-subject design experiment, i.e. all the tests (experimental tasks) had to be solved by each of the subjects. The tests were put in a different order for each subject.

5.3.3. Operation

The operational phase is divided into three steps — preparation, execution and data validation.

• Preparation. By the time the experiment was done all the students had taken two courses in software engineering, in which they learnt how to design OO software using UML. All the selected professors had more than four years of experience in the design and development of OO software using UML. Moreover, subjects were given an intensive training session before the experiment took place. However, the subjects were not aware of what aspects we intended to study. Neither were they aware of the actual hypothesis stated. We prepared the material we handed to the subjects, consisting of 28 UML class diagrams of the same universe of discourse, related to Bank Information Systems. The structural complexity and size of each diagram is different, because as Table 8 shows, the values of the metrics are different for each diagram.

Each diagram had a test enclosed, which includes the description of three maintainability sub-characteristics — understandability, analysability and modifiability. Each subject had to rate each sub-characteristic using a scale consisting of seven linguistic labels. For example for understandability, we proposed the following linguistic labels shown in Table 9.

We chose seven linguistic labels because we considered they are enough to cover all the possible categories of our variable, the understandability.

Table 8. Metric values for each class diagram.

Diagram	NC	NA	NM	NAssoc	NAgg	NDep	NGen	NAggH	NGenH	MaxHAgg	MaxDIT
D0	2	4	8	1	0	0	0	0	0	0	0
D1	3	6	12	1	1	0	0	1	0	1	0
D3	4	9	15	1	2	0	0	1	0	2	0
D4	5	14	21	1	3	0	0	2	0	2	0
D5	3	6	12	2	0	0	0	0	0	0	0
D6	4	8	12	3	0	1	0	0	0	0	0
D7	6	10	14	2	2	0	2	1	1	2	1
D8	3	9	12	1	0	1	0	0	0	0	0
D9	7	14	20	2	3	0	2	1	1	2	1
D10	9	18	26	2	3	0	4	1	2	3	1
D11	7	18	37	3	3	0	2	1	1	3	1
D12	8	22	35	3	2	1	2	1	1	3	1
D13	5	9	26	0	0	0	4	0	1	0	2
D14	8	12	30	0	0	0	10	0	1	0	3
D15	11	17	38	0	0	0	18	0	1	0	4
D16	20	42	76	10	6	2	10	2	3	2	2
D17	23	41	88	10	6	2	16	2	3	4	3
D18	21	45	94	6	6	1	20	2	2	4	4
D19	29	56	98	12	7	3	24	3	4	4	4
D20	9	28	47	1	5	0	2	2	1	4	1
D21	18	30	65	3	5	0	19	1	2	3	4
D22	26	44	79	11	6	0	21	2	5	4	3
D23	17	32	69	1	5	0	19	1	1	2	5
D24	23	50	73	9	7	2	11	3	4	4	1
D25	22	42	84	14	4	4	16	2	3	2	3
D26	14	34	77	4	9	0	7	2	2	3	4
D27	17	34	47	6	6	0	11	3	2	2	2

Table 9. Linguistic labels for understandability.

Extremely difficult to understand	Very difficult to understand	A bit difficult to understand	Neither difficult nor easy to understand	Quite easy to understand	Very easy to understand	Extremely easy to understand

The selection of an odd number of labels has been carried out based on some suggestions provided in Godo et al. (1989) and Bonissone (1982) where they justify that odd numbers contribute to the achievement of better results because they are balanced.

We also prepared a debriefing questionnaire. This questionnaire included (i) personal details and experience, (ii) opinions on the influence of different components of UML class diagrams, such as classes, attributes, associations, generalisations, etc, on their maintainability.

- Execution. The subjects were given all the materials described in the previous paragraph. We explained to them how to carry out the tests. We allowed one week to do the experiment, i.e. each subject had to carry out the test alone, and could use unlimited time to solve it. We collected all the data, including subjects' rating obtained from the responses of the experiment and the metric values automatically calculated by means of a metric tool we had designed.
- Data validation. We collected all the tests, checking if they were complete. As all of them were complete and the subjects had at least medium experience in building class diagrams (this fact was corroborated analysing the responses of the debriefing questionnaire) we consider their subjective evaluation reliable.

5.3.4. *Analysis and interpretation*

After collecting the experimental data in the operation phase, we want to be able to draw conclusions based on this data.

First we will do a PCA to achieve the first goal of this study — the reduction of Redundant metrics. Later, we will carry out a correlational analysis to find out if there exists correlation between the PCs found in the previous PCA and the maintainability sub-characteristics, which is the second goal of this study.

For these purposes, we summarised the data collected. We had the metric values calculated for each class diagram (see Table 8), and we calculated the median of the subjects' rating for each maintainability sub-characteristic (see Table 10). So this is the data we want to analyse to test the hypotheses stated above.

Table 10. Median of the subjects' ratings.

Diagram	Understandability median	Analysability median	Modifiability median
D0	1	1	1
D1	2	2	2
D2	2	2	2
D3	2	2	2
D4	2	2	2
D5	1	2	2
D6	3	3	3
D7	3	3	4
D8	2	2	2
D9	3	3	3
D10	3	3	3
D11	3	2	3
D12	3	3	3
D13	1	2	2
D14	2	2	3
D15	4	4	4
D16	6	6	6
D17	6	6	6
D18	6	6	6
D19	7	7	7
D20	2	3	3
D21	5	5	5
D22	6	6	6
D23	4	5	5
D24	5	5	5
D25	5	5	6
D26	4	5	5
D27	4	4	4

5.3.4.1. Principal component analysis
Using PCA three rotated PCs were obtained (see Table 11), with the constraint that the eigenvalue is larger than 1.0. With these PCs, 93.76% (see Table 12) of the total variability is explained.

As you can observe in Table 11:

- The PC1 picks out information of the structural complexity relative to the aggregation.
- The PC2 picks out information of the structural complexity given by the generalisation.
- The PC3 refers to the structural complexity given by the relations of association and dependencies among classes.

The metrics NA, NGenH, NM and NC seem not to be relevant in the PCA. Because the correlation with the metrics that do appear in the PCA is

Table 11. Rotated components.

Metrics	PCs		
	PC1	PC2	PC3
MaxHAgg	**0.911**	0.231	0.126
NAggH	**0.879**	0.141	0.349
NAgg	**0.873**	0.382	0.185
NA	0.669	0.539	0.492
NGenH	0.586	0.494	0.513
MaxDIT	0.187	**0.962**	0.408
NGen	0.263	**0.893**	0.300
NM	0.567	0.675	0.429
NC	0.560	0.648	0.501
NDep	0.123	0.136	**0.943**
NAssoc	0.450	0.265	**0.817**

Table 12. Total variation explained by the PCs.

PCs	Eigenvalue	Percentage	Accumulated percentage
PC1	4.112	37.383	37.383
PC2	3.441	31.278	68.661
PC3	2.761	25.101	**93.763**

high (see Table 13), we can assume that the information that they contain has already been transmitted through the metrics that are relevant in the PCA.

5.3.4.2. Correlational analysis

We have tested the Null Hypothesis (there is correlation of the new components with dependent variables, understandability, analysability and modifiability) using the Spearman correlation coefficient (see Table 14). The three components of each class diagram in the new space were previously calculated with the Anderson–Rubin method (Anderson and Rubin, 1956).

The observed results were the following:

- Understandability is highly correlated with PC2 (generalisations) (0.679, $p = 0.000$) and less with PC1 (aggregations) (0.520, $p = 0.005$).
- Analisability is highly correlated with PC2 (generalisations) (0.702, $p = 0.000$) and less with PC1 (aggregations) (0.544, $p = 0.003$).
- Modifiability is highly correlated with PC2 (generalisations) (0.747, $p = 0.000$) and less with PC1 (aggregations) (0.502, $p = 0.006$).

In conclusion, it seems that PC3, that refers to dependencies and associations, is not correlated with any of the studied dependent variables. This fact might have been produced because, after analysing the class diagrams

Table 13. Correlation between metrics.

	NAssoc	NAgg	NAggH	NDep	NGen	MaxHAgg	MaxDIT
NC	0.843	0.817	0.761	0.607	0.893	0.717	0.728
NA	0.830	0.884	0.841	0.627	0.802	0.784	0.659
NM	0.776	0.851	0.728	0.591	0.856	0.732	0.786
NGenH	0.849	0.759	0.723	0.548	0.753	0.712	0.568

Table 14. Spearman's correlation coefficient.

	PC1 (Generalisation)	PC2 (Aggregation)	PC3 (Association and dependencies)
Understandability	0.520 ($p = 0.005$)	0.679 ($p = 0.000$)	0.312 ($p = 0.106$)
Analisability	0.544 ($p = 0.003$)	0.702 ($p = 0.000$)	0.265 ($p = 0.174$)
Modifiability	0.502 ($p = 0.006$)	0.747 ($p = 0.000$)	0.268 ($p = 0.168$)

that were used in the experiment, it was observed that on the whole they had few associations and even less dependencies. From that comes the necessity of making another experiment in which more emphasis is put on this type of relation. Definitively, after analysing the data obtained in the first experiment, we can say that apparently the metrics that have to do with the aggregation and the generalisation, influence the maintainability of class diagrams. Although these results are partial, they are similar to the ones found in different empirical researches made to evaluate the effect of the relation of generalisation about the OO software maintainability (Daly et al., 1996; Briand et al., 1998; Cartwright, 1998; Harrison et al., 2000; Poels et al., 2001). Otherwise, as Deligiannis et al. (2002) affirm, the relations of aggregation have been less studied from an empirical point of view. That is why they insist on the necessity to look into this subject in more depth. There exists the suspicion that the usage of the aggregation might complement the design of more extensive and reusable products.

5.3.5. *Validity evaluation*

Next, we will discuss the empirical study's various threats to validity and the way we attempted to alleviate them:

- Threats to conclusion validity. The conclusion validity defines the extent to which conclusions are statistically valid. The only issue that could affect the statistical validity of this study is the size of the sample data (476 values, 28 diagrams and 17 subjects), which is perhaps not enough for both parametric and non-parametric statistic tests (Briand et al., 1995). We are aware of this, so we will consider the results of the experiment only as preliminary findings.
- Threats to construct validity. The construct validity is the degree to which the independent and the dependent variables are accurately measured by the measurement instruments used in the study. The dependent variables are three maintainability sub-characteristics — understandability, analysability and modifiability. We proposed subjective metrics for them (using linguistic variables), based on the judgement of the subjects. As the subjects involved in this experiment have medium experience in OOIS design using UML, we think their ratings could be considered significant. The construct validity of the metrics used for the independent

variables is guaranteed by Poels and Dedene's framework used to define and validate them (see Sec. 4).

- Threats to Internal Validity. The internal validity is the degree to which conclusions can be drawn about cause-effect of independent variables on the dependent variables. The following issues have been dealt with:

  - Differences among subjects. Using a within-subjects design, error variance due to differences among subjects is reduced. As Briand et al. (2001) remark when dealing with small samples in software engineering experiments, variations in participant skills are a major concern that is difficult to fully address by randomisation or blocking. In this experiment, professors and students had approximately the same degree of experience in modelling with UML.

  - Knowledge of the universe of discourse among class diagrams. Class diagrams were from the same universe of discourse, the only variant being the number of attributes, classes or associations, i.e. their constituent parts. Consequently, knowledge of the domain does not affect the internal validity.

  - Accuracy of subject responses. Subjects assumed the responsibility for rating each maintainability sub-characteristic. As they have medium experience in OO software design and implementation, we think their responses could be considered valid. However, we are aware that not all of them have exactly the same degree of experience, and if the subjects have more experience minor inaccuracies could be introduced by subjects.

  - Learning effects. The subjects were given the test in a different order, to cancel out learning effects. Subjects were required to answer in the order in which the tests appeared.

  - Fatigue effects. On average the experiment lasted for less than one hour (this fact was corroborated summing the total time for each subject), so fatigue was not very relevant. Also, the different order in the tests helped to cancel out these effects.

  - Persistence effects. In order to avoid persistence effects, the experiment was run with subjects who had never done a similar experiment.

  - Subject motivation. All the professors who were involved in this experiment have participated voluntarily, in order to help us in our research. We motivated students to participate in the experiment, explaining to them that similar tasks to the experimental ones could be done in exams or practice.

- Other factors. Plagiarism and influence among students could not really be controlled. Students were told that talking with each other was forbidden, but they did the experiment alone without any supervision, so we had to trust them as far as that was concerned. We are conscious that this aspect at some extent could threat the validity of the experiment, but at that moment it was impossible to join all the subjects together.

- Threats to external validity. The external validity is the degree to which the results of the research can be generalised to the population under study and other research settings. The greater the external validity, the more the results of an empirical study can be generalised to actual software engineering practice. Two threats of validity have been identified which limit the possibility of applying any such generalisation:

  - Materials and tasks used. In the experiment we tried to use class diagrams, which can be representative of real cases. Related to the tasks, the judgement of the subjects is to some extent subjective, and does not represent a real task.
  - Subjects. To solve the difficulty of obtaining professional subjects, we used professors and advanced students from software engineering courses. We are aware that more experiments with practitioners and professionals must be carried out in order to be able to generalise these results. However, in this case, the tasks to be performed do not require high levels of industrial experience, so, experiments with students could be appropriate (Basili et al., 1999). Moreover, students are the next generation of professionals, so they are close to the population under study (Kitchenham et al., 2002).

5.3.6. Presentation and package

As the diffusion of the experimental data is important to external replication (Brooks et al., 1996) of the experiments we have published this experiment in detail in Genero et al. (2001a), and we have also put all the material of this experiment on our web site http://alarcos.inf-cr.uclm.es.

5.4. *Second experiment*

As our preliminary (but limited) findings obtained in the first experiment were encouraging, we decided to carry out another experiment trying to improve the design of the previous one. We were looking particularly for more objective tasks to be solved by the subjects, because we realise that the obtained ratings of maintainability sub-characteristics are subjective and could have been influenced by the specific experience that the subjects of the first experiment had with UML class diagrams.

As the majority of the steps of the second experiment process are identical to those of the first experiment, we will focus on those issues in our discussion, which are different:

- The subjects were ten professors and 20 students enrolled in the final-year of computer science in the Department of Computer Science at the University of Castilla-La Mancha in Spain. All the professors belong to the software engineering area.
- The dependent variable was measured by the time the subjects spent carrying out the tasks required in the experiment. We called this time "maintenance time". Maintenance time comprises the time to comprehend the class diagram, to analyse the required changes and to implement them. Our assumption here is that for the same modification task, the faster a class diagram can be modified, the easier it is to maintain.
- The hypotheses we wanted to test are the following:
  - Null hypothesis, H_0: There is no significant correlation between the size (NC, NA, NM) and the structural complexity metrics (NAssoc, NAgg, NDep, NGen, NAggH, NGenH, MaxHAgg, MaxDIT) and the maintenance time.
  - Alternative hypothesis, H_1: There is a significant correlation between the size (NC, NA, NM) and the structural complexity metrics (NAssoc, NAgg, NDep, NGen, NAggH, NGenH, MaxHAgg, MaxDIT) and the maintenance time.
- The material we gave to the subjects consisted of a guide explaining UML notation and nine UML class diagrams of different application domains that were easy enough to be understood by each of the subjects. The diagrams have different structural complexity, covering a broad range of metric values (see Table 15).

Table 15. Metric values for each class diagram.

Diagram	NC	NA	NM	NAssoc	NAgg	NDep
D1	7	11	22	1	0	0
D2	8	12	31	1	6	0
D3	3	17	24	2	0	0
D4	10	12	21	15	3	0
D5	9	19	29	3	3	0
D6	7	16	7	6	0	0
D7	23	33	66	4	5	2
D8	20	30	65	6	5	0
D9	23	65	80	20	3	2
Diagram	NGen	NAggH	NGenH	MaxDIT	MaxHAgg	
D1	5	0	1	2	0	
D2	1	1	1	1	2	
D3	0	0	0	0	0	
D4	0	2	0	0	1	
D5	3	3	1	2	1	
D6	0	0	0	0	0	
D7	16	2	3	3	3	
D8	14	4	3	3	2	
D9	3	3	1	2	3	

Each diagram had an enclosed test that included a brief description of what the diagram represented and two new requirements for the class diagram. Each subject had to modify the class diagrams according to the new requirements and to specify the start and end time. The difference between the two is what we call maintenance time (expressed in minutes and seconds). The modifications to each class diagram were similar, including adding attributes, methods, classes, etc.

- We collected all the data including the modified class diagrams with the maintenance time obtained from the responses of the tests and the metrics values automatically calculated by means of a metric tool we designed.

    Once the data was collected, we checked that the tests were complete and if the modifications had been done correctly. We discarded

Table 16. Mean of the maintenance.

Diagram	Mean of the maintenance time (seconds)
1	269.38
2	353.00
3	410.00
4	174.66
5	244.00
6	305.94
7	523.00
8	305.17
9	234.39

the tests of seven subjects, which included a required modification that was done incorrectly. Therefore, we took into account the responses of 23 subjects.

We had the metric values calculated for each class diagram (see Table 15), and we calculated the mean of the maintenance time (see Table 16). So this is the data we want to analyse to test the hypotheses stated above.

5.4.1. *Principal component analysis*

The solution obtained in the PCA after the rotation of the components, with an eigenvalue larger than 1 (see Table 17), explains 79.151% of the total variability (see Table 18).

In this case, the conclusions that can be extracted are the following:

- The PC1 is determined because of the complexity given by generalisations and aggregations.
- The PC2 otherwise, picks out the complexity of the associations and the number of attributes.

In this research, the metrics that allows elimination because of having redundant information, are NC, NM, NAgg, NDep and NAggH. The information they contain will be picked out through the metrics with the correlated ones (see Table 19) that intervene in the PCs.

Table 17. Rotated components.

Metrics	PCs	
	PC1	PC2
NC	0.796	0.561
NA	0.359	**0.862**
NM	0.683	0.686
NAssoc	−0.08817	**0.911**
NAgg	0.729	0.239
NDep	0.728	−0.248
NGen	**0.927**	0.009
NAggH	0.632	0.348
NGenH	**0.870**	0.399
MaxHAgg	**0.872**	0.269
MaxDIT	**0.832**	0.330

Table 18. Total variation explained by the PCs.

PCs	Eigenvalue	Percentage	Accumulated percentage
PC1	5.768	52.440	52.440
PC2	2.938	26.711	**79.151**

Table 19. Correlation between metrics.

	NA	NGen	NGenH	MaxHAgg	MaxDIT
NC	**0.775**	**0.794**	**0.886**	**0.833**	**0.822**
NM	**0.900**	**0.651**	**0.887**	**0.760**	**0.827**
NAggH	0.341	0.570	**0.710**	**0.634**	**0.607**
NAgg	0.338	0.501	**0.651**	**0.928**	0.536
NDep	0.148	**0.684**	0.438	**0.610**	0.406

5.4.2. Correlational analysis

The correlation of the new PCs with the maintenance time has been studied using the Pearson's correlation coefficient (see Table 20). Therefore, the coefficients for the factorial punctuations were previously calculated with the Anderson–Rubi method. These are the two components of the class diagrams in the new space of two dimensions.

Table 20. Pearson's correlation coefficient.

	PC1 Generalisation	PC2 Associations & attributes
Maintenance time	0.485 ($p = 0.185$)	**0.853 ($p = 0.003$)**

As Table 20 reveals the correlation between maintenance time and the PCs is only significant for the PC2 that corresponds to associations and attributes.

5.5. Third experiment

This experiment is different from the second one in the sense that we added tasks in order to ascertain whether the subjects understood the class diagrams or not, which we called "understandability tasks".

The subjects were 24 undergraduate students enrolled on the third-year of Computer Science at the Department of Computer Science at the University of Castilla-La Mancha in Spain.

The material we gave to the subjects consisted of nine UML class diagrams of different application domains. The diagrams have different structural complexity, covering a broad range of metric values (see Table 21).

Each diagram had an enclosed test that included a brief description of what the diagram represented, and the two types of tasks:

- Understandability tasks: where the subjects had to answer a questionnaire (four questions) that reflected whether or not they had understood each diagram, and they also had to note how long it took to answer the questions. The Understandability Time, expressed in minutes and seconds, was obtained from that.
- Modifiability tasks: Where the subjects had to modify the class diagrams according to four new requirements, and specify the start and end time. The difference between the two times is what we call Modifiability Time (expressed in minutes and seconds). The modifications to each class diagram were similar, including adding attributes, methods, classes, etc.

The subjects were given all the materials described in the previous paragraph and we explained to them how to carry out the tests. We allowed them one week to undertake the experiment, i.e. each subject had to carry out the test alone, and had an unlimited amount of time to solve it.

Table 21. Metric values of the UML class diagram used in the third experiment.

Diagram	NC	NA	NM	NAssoc	NAgg	NDep
1	13	30	47	11	5	3
2	22	43	56	11	6	4
3	9	24	25	6	1	1
4	7	17	26	1	4	0
5	9	2	40	2	3	1
6	11	26	36	5	0	2
7	52	76	35	15	23	8
8	22	62	39	7	12	0
9	7	23	31	3	1	1
Diagram	**NGen**	**NAggH**	**NGenH**	**MaxHAgg**	**MaxDIT**	
1	3	2	1	2	1	
2	15	1	7	4	3	
3	5	1	2	1	2	
4	3	2	1	1	1	
5	5	1	2	1	1	
6	7	0	4	0	3	
7	17	3	6	7	4	
8	2	4	1	1	1	
9	2	1	1	1	1	

The independent variables are the same as the second experiment. The dependent variables are the two maintainability subcharacteristics modifiability and understandability, measured as is usual in empirical studies (Briand et al., 2001; Poels and Dedene, 2001):

- Understandability Time is time spent by the subjects on answering the understandability questions.
- Modifiability Time is the time spent by the subjects doing the modifications tasks.

The metric values for each class diagram are in Table 21, and we calculated the mean of the maintenance time (see Table 22). So this is the data we want to analyse to test the hypotheses stated above.

Table 22. Mean of the Understandability and Modifiability times of the third experiment.

Diagram	Mean of the understandability time	Mean of the modifiability time
1	111.00	332.00
2	135.00	243.00
3	91.00	309.00
4	65.00	174.00
5	78.00	370.00
6	101.00	310.00
7	165.00	435.00
8	167.00	263.00
9	157.00	208.00

Table 23. Rotated components.

Metrics	PCs	
	PC1	PC2
NC	0.643	0.753
NA	0.423	**0.859**
NAssoc	0.667	0.579
NAgg	0.397	**0.901**
NDep	**0.855**	0.414
NGen	**0.956**	0.221
NAggH	−0.247	**0.955**
NGenH	**0.961**	0.044
HAggMax	0.741	0.591
MaxDIT	**0.941**	0.111

5.5.1. *Principal component analysis*

While studying the table of correlations between the metrics, it was observed that NM was not correlated with any of the others. That is why the PCA was made without including it, because it constitutes a dimension.

After the rotation, the PCA presented the results of Table 23, with the same restriction as in the previous cases (autovalues that are bigger than one), and explained 92.075% of the total variability (Table 24).

Table 24. Total variation explained by the PCs.

PCs	Eigenvalue	Percentage	Accumulated percentage
PC1	5.260	52.596	52.596
PC2	3.948	34.480	**92.075**

Table 25. Correlation between metrics.

	NC	NAssoc	NA	NAgg	NDep	NGen	MaxHAgg	MaxDIT
NC	1.000	0.819	0.928	0.953	0.863	0.778	0.909	0.714
NM	0.214	0.509	0.281	0.133	0.342	0.394	0.314	0.176
NAssoc	0.819	1.000	0.763	0.714	0.862	0.714	0.828	0.654
HAggMax	0.909	0.828	0.748	0.834	0.926	0.858	1.000	0.688

From the PCs shown in Table 23, the following can be concluded:

- The PC1 picks out the information related to dependencies and generalisations.
- The PC2 picks out the information related to aggregations and attributes.

In this research, the metrics that allow elimination because of having redundant information are NC, NAssoc and MaxHAgg. As seen in Table 25, they are very correlated among themselves, besides others being part of the selected PCs. In this way, NC is very correlated with metrics that determine PC2, meanwhile, NAssoc and MaxHAgg are very correlated with metrics of PC1.

5.5.2. *Correlational analysis*

We have studied the correlation of new PCs (PC1 and PC2) and NM with the dependent variables (the understandability and modifiability time) using Pearson's correlation coefficient (see Table 26). For this reason, the coefficients for factorial punctuations were previously calculated with the Anderson–Rubin method, which are the two components of the class diagrams in the new space of two dimensions.

Analysing the obtained results in Table 26, it can be observed that:

- The understandability time is highly correlated with PC2, which is related with aggregations and attributes. The maintenance time is not correlated with the PCs.

Table 26. Pearson's correlation coefficients.

	PC1 Dependencies and generalisations	PC2 Aggregations and attributes	NM
Understandability time	0.355 ($p = 0.348$)	**0.769** ($p = 0.016$)	0.401 ($p = 0.285$)
Maintenance time	0.472 ($p = 0.199$)	0.365 ($p = 0.376$)	0.146 ($p = 0.709$)

Table 27. Pearson's correlation coefficients.

	PC1 Dependencies and generalisations	PC2 Aggregations and attributes	NM
Total maintenance time	0.472 ($p = 0.199$)	**0.669** ($p = 0.049$)	0.146 ($p = 0.709$)

- Besides, the third dimension that NM represents is not related to any of the two dependent variables.
- Given that in the previous experiment the maintenance time has been evaluated without making the difference between understandability and modifiability time, a new dependent variable has been introduced in this case, Total Maintenance Time, that measures the maintenance time as the sum of both of them. In this way, the results of both experiments can be better compared (Table 27).

As we can see in Table 27, only the component PC2, which picks out the information of the aggregations and the number of attributes, is positively correlated with the maintenance time. As expected, the sum of the two times reduces the correlation grade, from 0.769 to 0.669, and the level of signification gets worse, from 0.016 to 0.049, although the result keeps being significant at the level 0.05.

5.6. *Comparison of the experiments and conclusions*

It is well known that software product metrics are very useful in the evaluation of the different characteristics that affect the quality of OO software, for example the maintainability (Fenton and Pflegeer, 1997). With this idea in mind, we have carried out three controlled experiments to test whether the metrics we had defined for class diagram structural complexity, and other traditional metrics related to class diagram size, could really be used as class diagram maintainability indicators in the early phases of the OO software life-cycle. With the aim of discovering which of the metrics used might not be redundant in these empirical studies, we have used PCA in this work. After performing the PCA we managed to observe in the three samples of data, that the PCs containing non-redundant information present well-known characteristics of the OO design, which are related to the usage of UML relationships.

The results of the first experiment deserve a separate comment, because the dependent variables are subjective measures. No size metric appears to be relevant in the PCA. The PC1 and PC2, that pick out the information of the aggregation and the generalisation, are the ones being significantly correlated with dependent variables, so the results are in favour of the hypothesis about a relation between a subset of considered metrics and maintainability.

It seems that PC3 (dependencies and associations) is not correlated with the dependent variables, maybe because the class diagrams had few associations and even less dependencies (Table 11). That is the reason why for the rest of the experiments class diagrams have more associations and dependencies.

About the second and third experiment, the metrics related to the size do not seem to be relevant, like NC and NM, but NA is. Although it is reasonable to think that the more classes there are in a diagram, the more dependencies and associations could exist, and experimental results show that it is better to measure the use of these relationships directly than to rely on size metrics.

If we examine the correlation between the maintainability and/or the understandibility and the PCs in the two experiments where they are measured objectively, using the maintenance time (see Table 28), it is clear that it is correlated in the first experiment with the PC that picks out the structural complexity of class diagrams due to the number of associations together with the number of attributes. In the second experiment, it is correlated with the PC that picks out the number of aggregations and the number of attributes.

In conclusion, although the PC's obtained depend on the sample of the study, what is already known (Briand et al., 1998; Briand and Wüst, 2002) the results are in favour of there being dependency between some of the

Table 28. Summary of the controlled experiments.

Empirical studies	Dependent Variables (D.V.)	PCs and metrics that emerge through	Correlation between PCs and D.V.
Experiment 1	Understandability (U) Analysability (A) Modifiability (M) (subjective ratings)	PC1 → Aggregations PC2 → Generalisation PC3 → Associations and Dependencies	U → PC2, PC1 A → PC2, PC1 M → PC2, PC1
Experiment 2	Maintenance Time (MT)	PC1 → Generalisation PC2 → Associations and NA	MT → PC2
Experiment 3	Understandability Time (UT) Modifiability Time (ModT)	PC1 → Dependencies and Generalisation PC2 → Aggregations and NA	UT → PC2 (MT = UT + ModT) → PC2

considered metric ones and maintainability sub-characteristics. When separating the maintenance time considering the modifiability and the understandability time, the degree of dependence and the signification improve, so it would seem correct to make this difference.

6. Building a Prediction Model for Class Diagrams Maintainability

In the previous sections, we have found, by analysing the empirical data, that to some extent the metrics we presented for the structural complexity of UML class diagrams seem to be correlated with the class diagram maintainability sub-characteristics. This fact led us to think about building a prediction model for class diagram maintainability based on metric values. We have used all the metrics to build the prediction models because we considered it to be too premature to discard some metrics. Seeing the encouraging results obtained by the application of the Fuzzy Deformable Prototypes for building prediction models applied to different domains (Olivas et al., 2000; Olivas et al., 2002), we decided to use it for our purpose. For the sake of brevity we will not explain in depth all the steps of the prediction process. Further details can be found in Olivas (2000). The main goals of the prediction process, in our case, are:

(1) The automatic search and extraction of fuzzy prototypes to characterise the class diagrams across its maintainability expressed as the time of

maintenance. This step is called Fuzzy Prototypical Knowledge Discovery (FPKD) process.

(2) The obtaining of a prediction model of the maintenance time of the class diagrams accomplishing the deformation of the previously discovered fuzzy prototypes.

To build the prediction model, we used the data obtained in the third experiment. Firstly, it was necessary to transform the data in order for it to be useful for the FPKD process. On the one hand, we obtained the table with the metric values of the class diagrams (see Table 21). On the other hand, we obtained the maintenance time for each diagram for each subject. From these times, the minimum, average and maximum times for each diagram are obtained, filtering that data, which does not accomplish a certain level of correctness and completeness. ($\geqslant 0.9$) (see Table 29).

In this way, we obtained one table with 9 rows and 4 columns, which is joined with the table of the metrics values for each diagram (see Table 21) by means of the column, which represents each diagram.

In order to build the prediction model we followed the next step:

- Obtaining the prototypes using clustering techniques.
- Parametric definition of the prototypes.
- Fuzzy representation of the prototypes.
- Deforming the fuzzy prototypes to predict class diagram maintainability.
- Validation of the prediction model.

Next, we will explain how we carried out each of the steps.

Table 29. Maintenance times obtained in the transformation process.

Diagram	Average of the maintenance time (seconds)	Minimum of the maintenance time (seconds)	Maximum of the maintenance time (seconds)
1	269.38	50	580
2	353	353	353
3	410	390	430
4	174.615	36	305
5	244	215	273
6	305.9375	120	535
7	523	261	785
8	305.166	165	567
9	234.391	80	498

6.1. *Obtaining the prototypes using clustering techniques*

With the aim of detecting the relationships between the class diagrams to be able to later ascertain whether they have a low, medium or high maintenance time, we will carry out a hierarchical clustering process in the way of Repertory Grids's technique (Bell, 1990).

A similarity matrix was constructed of 9×9 elements whose values on the diagonal represent the degrees of similarity among the diagrams. By converting these values into percentages and unleashing the algorithm of hierarchical clustering, we obtained the results illustrated trough the dendrogram of Fig. 4.

Having obtained the results of the clustering, and with the heuristic previous knowledge of having three prototypes, a cut is carried out to a similarity lower than 55%. The diagrams are grouped in three prototypes according to the values of the metrics that reflect their structural complexity and size, as Table 30 shows.

6.2. *Parametric definition of the prototypes*

Considering the data prototypes found in the previous section and their values of the maintenance time shown in Table 29, we obtained the parametric definition of the prototype, as Table 31 shows. The prototypes were defined

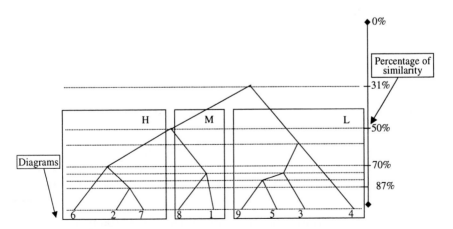

Fig. 4. Clustering Results (H = High value of maintenance time, M = Medium value of maintenance time, L = Low value of maintenance time).

Table 30. Diagrams grouped taking into account the prototypes.

Prototypes	Diagrams
Low value of maintenance time	3, 5, 9, 4
Medium value of maintenance time	1, 8
High value of maintenance time	2, 7, 6

Table 31. Parametric definition of the prototypes.

	Time
High value of maintenance time	
Average	6 min. 30 sec.
Maximum	10 min. 45 sec.
Minimum	1 min. 50 sec.
Medium value of maintenance time	
Average	4 min. 50 sec.
Maximum	9 min. 30 sec.
Minimum	1 min. 20 sec.
Low value of maintenance time	
Average	4 min. 20 sec.
Maximum	8 min. 45 sec.
Minimum	1 min. 10 sec.

by means of the average, the maximum and minimum of the values of their maintenance time.

6.3. *Fuzzy representation of the prototypes*

The obtained prototypes were represented as "fuzzy numbers", which will allow us to obtain a degree of membership (between 0 and 1) of a new class diagram with each of the prototypes (see Fig. 5). To use triangular fuzzy numbers, it is only necessary to know their center (named center in Table 32) and the size of the base of the triangle (named (a) and (b) in Table 32).

In the FPKD process, the formal definition of the prototypes as fuzzy numbers is obtained by means of a normalisation process, carried out in the following way $x'_n = \frac{x_n - x_{min}}{x_{max} - x_{min}}$, and the aggregation by means of the

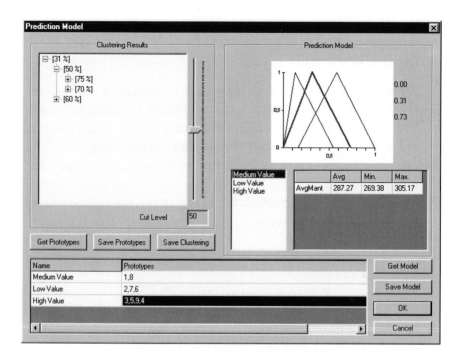

Fig. 5. Fuzzy representation of the prototypes.

Table 32. Fuzzy definition of the prototypes.

Prototypes	Diagrams	a	centre	b
L: Low time of Maintenance	3, 5, 9, 4	0.00	0.12	0.54
M: Medium time of Maintenance	1, 8	0.00	0.31	0.73
H: High time of Maintenance	2, 7, 6	0.16	0.58	1

average of the data corresponding to the metrics values (see Table 21). These prototypes are called Fuzzy Deformable Prototypes (Olivas, 2000).

6.4. *Deforming the fuzzy prototypes to predict UML class diagram maintainability*

In this section, we will show how to predict the maintenance time for a new class diagram. Given the values of the metrics of a new class diagram, the parametric definition of the prototype, which has the greatest degree of membership, is adapted or deformed in order to predict the maintenance time of this new class diagram.

The process is as follows:

(1) Normalisation of the values measured by means of the indexes of normalisation associated with the obtained prediction model. The same formula is used as in the definition of the fuzzy numbers and with the same coefficients of minimum and maximum.

(2) Calculate the average of the previously normalised values (this value is called X).

(3) Obtain the degrees of membership to the prototypes represented by means of the fuzzy numbers.

$$X > centre_{pi} \Rightarrow \mu_{pi} = \frac{X - a_{pi}}{centre_{pi} - a_{pi}}$$

$$X \leq centre_{pi} \Rightarrow \mu_{pi} = \frac{c_{pi} - X}{c_{pi} - centre_{pi}}.$$

(4) To obtain the predicted value of the maintenance time for the new class diagram, the fuzzy prototype which has the greatest degree of membership, is "deformed". Applying the concept of Fuzzy Deformable Prototypes, defined in Olivas (2000), the characterisation of the proposed new class diagram can be described by the following linear combination:

$$C_{real}(w_1, \ldots, w_n) = \left| \sum \mu_p(v_1, \ldots, v_n) \right|$$

where

C_{real} Real case proposed.

$(w_1, \ldots, w_n)$ Parameters that describe the real case proposed.

μ_p Degree of membership with the Fuzzy Deformable Prototypes which has the greatest degree of membership.

$(v_1, \ldots, v_n)$ Parameters of these Fuzzy Deformable Prototypes.

Now, we will apply the steps mentioned above to a new class diagram whose metrics values are shown in Table 33.

(1) First, we normalised the metrics values, obtaining the values shown in Table 34.

Table 33. An example of the metrics value of a new class diagram.

NC	NA	NM	NAssoc	NAgg	NDep
21	30	50	10	6	3
NGen	NAggH	NGenH	HAggMax	MaxDIT	
16	2	3	4	2	

Table 34. Normalised values of the metrics.

NC	NA	NM	NAssoc	NAgg	NDep
0.4	0.39	0.89	0.67	0.26	0.38
NGen	NAggH	NGenH	HAggMax	MaxDIT	
0.94	0.5	0.43	0.57	0.5	

Table 35. Degree of membership of the new class with the prototypes.

Prototypes		Affinities
L: Low time of maintenance	$0.54 - 0.54/0.54$	0
M: Medium time of maintenance	$0.54/0.31$	0.45
H: High time of maintenance	$0.54 - 0.16/0.54$	0.9

Table 36. Obtained values using the prediction model.

	Greatest degree	Prototype		Results
Average		6 min. 30 sec.		5 min. 50 sec.
Maximum	**0.9**	10 min. 45 sec.	=	9 min. 40 sec.
Minimum		1 min. 50 sec.		1 min. 40 sec.

(2) The average of the normalised values is 0.54.

(3) The degrees of membership of the new class diagrams with the obtained prototypes (see Table 32) are obtained, as Table 35 shows. The most similar prototype is "High time of maintenance" with a degree of membership of 0.9. But there is also affinity with the prototype "Medium time of maintenance" too (0.45).

(4) Deforming the prototype with the greatest degree of affinity, we get the predicted values of the time of maintenance — average, minimum and maximum (see Table 36), which give us information about the range of time that could be necessary to maintain the new class diagram.

6.5. *Validation of the prediction model*

The techniques most commonly used to evaluate the accuracy of the prediction models are the following (Harrison et al., 2000):

- Magnitude of relative error (MRE) (Briand et al., 2001).
- Mean magnitude of relative error (MMRE) (Snedecor and Cochran, 1989).
- Median magnitude of relative error (MdMRE) (Briand et al., 2001).
- Prediction at level n (Pred(n)) (Kleinbaum and Kupper, 1987).

MRE is defined in this way:

$$MRE_i = \frac{|\text{Actual Maintenace Time} - \text{Predicted Maintenace Time}|}{\text{Actual Maintenace Time}}$$

where i represents each observation for which the maintenance time is predicted.

MMRE is calculated as the mean of the values of MRE:

$$MMRE = \frac{1}{n}\sum_{i=1}^{i=n} \frac{|\text{Actual Maintenance Time} - \text{Predicted Maintenace Time}|}{\text{Actual Maintenace Time}}.$$

The mean takes into account the numeric value of each observation in the distribution of the data and is sensitive to individual values of prediction with a very high MRE value. Therefore, another option is to use the median, which is also a measurement of the central tendency, but is less sensitive to extreme values. The median of the MRE values is called MdMRE.

Another commonly used indicator is the prediction at level n, also known as Pred(n). It measures the percentage of estimates within $n\%$ of the actual values. According to some suggestions 25% is a recommended value for n. This means that a good prediction model should have 75% precision.

In order to validate our prediction model we have used the data obtained in the second experiment. The value of MMRE is 0.145. The value of MdMRE is 0.0775. The value of Pred(25%) represents the percentage of estimates within 25% of the actual value. As the bibliography suggests, a good prediction model must offer at least 75% exactitude. The value obtained for Pred(25%) is 88%. From this we can say that the prediction

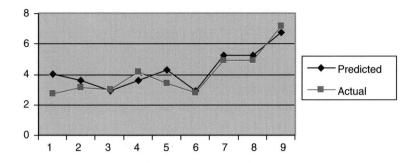

Fig. 6. Predicted vs actual values.

model obtained is valid since 88% of the values estimated have a precision of at least 75%. In Fig. 6, we can clearly see the predicted and the actual mean values.

7. Conclusions

UML class diagrams are commonly used in an early phase of software development as a conceptual representation of the application (domain) for which a software system is required. Because of the seamless nature of OO software development processes, the class diagram reflects both the structure of the problem and the structure of the software solution as it provides the foundation for the design of the software system. To guarantee the efficacy of the development processes, it is therefore crucial to control the quality of this early software development artefact. There are several factors which affect the quality of class diagrams such as, size, structural complexity, cohesion, coupling, etc. Quality assurance of early development artefacts requires the use of objective instruments to assess the level of quality in the artefact. These instruments are known as software metrics and quality prediction models.

In this chapter, first, a set of metrics is presented to measure the structural complexity of UML class diagrams. Although several metrics suites that can be used for measuring UML class diagrams have been proposed in the literature, a review of this work revealed that the structural complexity caused by the use of aggregation, association and dependency relationships was not addressed. Moreover, most of the previously proposed metrics suites have not been properly validated. Above all, there is a lack of theoretical validation (i.e. demonstrating that the metrics really measure structural complexity) and thoroughly executed and sufficiently replicated empirical validation (i.e. demonstrating the usefulness of the metrics in a well-defined quality assurance context).

The new metrics suite presented in this chapter addresses both issues. On the one hand, metrics are included that quantify the use that is made of all kinds of relationships between the classes in a UML class diagram. These metrics have been defined using the DISTANCE framework for software measure construction (Poels, 1999; Poels and Dedene, 2000a), which ensures a formal, set-theoretic and hence unambiguous and precise metric definition, and their theoretical validity. Moreover, by using this framework it can be shown that the metrics are defined on the ratio scale level, which means that they are a (statistically) powerful instrument of investigation for the researcher. On the other hand, the usefulness of the new metrics has been demonstrated through a series of three controlled experiments.

The aim of the experiments was two-fold. The previously proposed metrics suites that can be applied to UML class diagrams for measuring structural complexity due to size (in terms of number of classes, number of attributes, number of methods) and the use of the generalisation (or specialisation) mechanism. We wished to show empirically that structural complexity is also caused by the use of other types of relationships between classes. To this end, PCA was used. Although the rotated principal components extracted in each of the three experiments were not exactly the same, it was shown that the use of aggregation and the use of association present dimensions of structural complexity different from the complexity caused by generalisation. The results for dependency relationships are less conclusive as this mechanism was not distinguished (in terms of structural complexity caused) from generalisation in one experiment and association in another experiment.

Another result from the PCA was that size metrics do not provide additional information on structural complexity, except for the number of attributes, which was in one case (an important) part of the same principal component as association and in another case aggregation. This result might perhaps be explained by the choice that exists between modelling association and aggregation by means of relationships between classes or as attributes of a class. The most significant result from the PCAs is, however, that metrics that assess the use of other relationships than generalisation are not redundant in a metrics suite for the structural complexity of UML class diagrams.

But even when these metrics are non-redundant, the question remains whether it makes sense to assess these structural complexity aspects from a quality assurance point of view. Another aim of the experiments was therefore to demonstrate the relationship that exists between these (and other) structural complexity aspects and maintainability (in the sense of ease of understanding, ease of analysing, ease of modifying), which is a major quality attribute of conceptual models. In the first experiment, the structural complexity caused by the use of the generalisation mechanism was shown to be significantly related to the maintainability of the class diagrams, as perceived by the experimental subjects. This result is in line with the state-of-the-art research in empirical software engineering research. But also a significant relationship with the extent of using aggregation was found (albeit less explicit than in the case of generalisation). The results of the other two experiments, however, suggested that the use of aggregation and association might affect maintainability even more than generalisation. So, the overall conclusion of the experiments was that metrics for capturing all types of relationships in UML class diagrams result in, not only a non-redundant metrics suite, but in a more complete instrument to investigate the effect of structural complexity on maintainability.

Apart from the metrics suite, the chapter also discussed and demonstrated a method for building a metrics-based prediction model for the maintainability of UML class diagrams. This method is based on the FPKD process and the Fuzzy Deformables Prototypes (Olivas, 2000) that was used with success in other domains. The prediction results obtained are encouraging as predicted maintainability rates are close to the actual ones, even when applying the prediction model to new cases.

The empirical results that have been presented in this chapter must be interpreted with caution. Throughout the chapter several threats to the study's validity have been outlined and discussed. It is our belief that it is necessary to make a family of experiments to increase the external validity of the results to the extent that the conclusions currently presented can be generalised. Such a family of experiments should also use professionals as subjects and data about real projects. Besides we are conscious of the necessity to make laboratory packages with the information of the empirical studies, to encourage their external and independent replication and obtain a body of knowledge about the utility of metrics. This will eventually contribute to building a set of UML class diagram metrics and quality prediction models that allow software designers to make better decisions in the early phases of software development. After all, this is the most important goal for any measurement proposal to pursue if it aims to be useful (Brito e Abreu and Melo, 1996a).

Acknowledgements

This work has been partially funded by the TAMANSI project financed by "Consejería de Ciencia y Tecnología, Junta de Comunidades de Castilla-La Mancha" of Spain (project reference PBC-02-001) and the DOLMEN project financed by "Subdirección General de Proyectos de Investigación — Ministerio de Ciencia y Tecnología (Spain)" (project reference TIC 2000-1673-C06-06).

References

Anderson, T. and Rubin, H. (1956). Statistical Inference in Factor Analysis. *Proceedings of the Third Berkeley Symposium on Mathematical Statistics and Probability*, University of California Press, Vol. 5, pp. 345–357.

Bandi, R., Vaishnavi, V. and Turk, D. (2003). Predicting Maintenance Performance Using Object-Oriented Design Complexity Metrics. *IEEE Transactions on Software Engineering*, Vol. 29, No. 1, pp. 77–87.

Bansiya, J., Etzkorn, L., Davis, C. and Li, W. (1999). A Class Cohesion Metric For Object-Oriented designs. *The Journal of Object-Oriented Programming*, Vol. 11, No. 8, pp. 47–52.

Bansiya, J. and Davis, C. (2002). A Hierarchical Model for Object-Oriented Design Quality Assessment. *IEEE Transactions on Software Engineering*, Vol. 28, No. 1, pp. 4–17.

Basili, V. and Rombach, H. (1988). The TAME Project: Towards Improvement-Oriented Software Environments. *IEEE Transactions on Software Engineering*, Vol. 14, No. 6, pp. 728–738.

Basili, V. and Weiss, D. (1984). A Methodology for Collecting Valid Software Engineering Data. *IEEE Transactions on Software Engineering*, Vol. 10, pp. 728–738.

Basili, V., Briand, L. and Melo, W. (1996). A Validation of Object-Oriented Design Metrics as Quality Indicators. *IEEE Transactions of Software Engineering*, Vol. 22, No. 10, pp. 751–761.

Briand, L., El Emam, K. and Morasca, S. (1995). Theoretical and empirical validation of software product measures. *Technical Report ISERN-95-03*, International Software Engineering Research Network.

Briand, L., Morasca, S. and Basili, V. (1996). Property-Based Software Engineering Measurement. *IEEE Transactions on Software Engineering*, Vol. 22, No. 6, pp. 68–86.

Briand, L., Devanbu, W. and Melo, W. (1997). An Investigation into Coupling Measures for C++. *Proceedings of 19th International Conference on Software Engineering (ICSE 97)*, Boston, USA, pp. 412–421.

Briand, L., Wüst, J. and Lounis, H. (1998). Replicated Case Studies for Investigating Quality Factors in Object-oriented Designs. *Technical report ISERN 98-29 (version 3)*, International Software Engineering Research Network.

Basili, V., Shull, F. and Lanubile, F. (1999a). Building Knowledge through Families of Experiment. *IEEE Transactions on Software Engineering*, Vol. 25, No. 4, pp. 435–437.

Bonissone, P. (1982). *Approximate Reasoning in Decision Analysis*. Chapter: A Fuzzy Sets Based Linguistic Approach: Theory and Applications. Eds. Gupta, M. and Sanchez E., North-Holland Publishing Company, pp. 329–339.

Briand, L., Daly, J. and Wüst, J. (1999b). A Unified Framework for Coupling Measurement in Object-Oriented Systems. *IEEE Transactions on Software Engineering*, Vol. 25, No. 1, pp. 91–121.

Briand, L., Arisholm, S., Counsell, F., Houdek, F. and Thévenod-Fosse, P. (2000a). Empirical Studies of Object-Oriented Artefacts, Methods, and Processes: State of the Art and Future Directions. *Empirical Software Engineering*, Vol. 4, No. 4, pp. 387–404.

Briand, L., Wüst, J., Daly, J. and Porter, V. (2000b). Exploring the Relationships between Design Measures and Software Quality in Object-Oriented Systems. *The Journal of Systems and Software*, Vol. 51, pp. 245–273.

Briand, L., Bunse, C. and Daly, J. (2001). A Controlled Experiment for Evaluating Quality Guidelines on the Maintainability of Object-Oriented Designs. *IEEE Transactions on Software Engineering*, Vol. 27, No. 6, pp. 513–530.

Briand, L., Melo, W. and Wüst, J. (2002). Assessing the Applicability of Fault-Proneness Models Across Object-Oriented Software Projects. *IEEE Transactions on Software Engineering*, Vol. 28, No. 7, pp. 706–720.

Briand, L. and Wüst, J. (2002). Empirical Studies of Quality Models. *Advances in Computers*, Academic Press, Ed. Zelkowitz, M., Vol. 59, pp. 97–166.

Brito e Abreu, F. and Carapuça, R. (1994). Object-Oriented Software Engineering: Measuring and Controlling the Development Process. *Proceedings of 4th International Conference on Software Quality*, Mc Lean, VA, USA.

Brito e Abreu, F., Goulao, M. and Esteves, R. (1995). Towards the Design Quality Evaluation of Object-Oriented Software System, *Proceedings of the 5th International Conference on Software Quality*, Austin, Texas, USA.

Brito e Abreu, F. and Melo, W. (1996a). Evaluating the Impact of Object-Oriented Design on Software Quality. *3rd International Metric Symposium*, pp. 90–99.

Brito e Abreu, F., Esteves, R. and Goulao, M. (1996b). The Design of Eiffel programs: Quantitative Evaluation Using the MOOD Metrics. *Proceedings of TOOLS USA '96 (Technology of Object Oriented Languages and Systems)*, Santa Barbara, California, USA.

Brito e Abreu, F., Zuse, H., Sahraoui, H. and Melo, W. (1999). Quantitative Approaches in Object-Oriented Software Engineering. Object-Oriented technology — ECOOP'99 Workshop Reader, *Lecture Notes in Computer Science 1743*, Springer-Verlag, pp. 326–337.

Brito e Abreu, F., Poels, G., Sahraoui, H. and Zuse, H. (2000). Quantitative Approaches in Object-Oriented Software Engineering. Object-Oriented technology — ECOOP'00 Workshop Reader, *Lecture Notes in Computer Science*, 1964, Springer-Verlag, pp. 326–337.

Brito e Abreu, F., Henderson-Sellers, B., Piattini, M., Poels, G. and Sahraoui, H. (2001). Quantitative Approaches in Object-Oriented Software Engineering. Object-Oriented technology — ECOOP'01 Workshop Reader, *Lecture Notes in Computer Science 2323*, Springer-Verlag, pp. 174–183.

Brooks, A., Daly, J., Miller, J., Roper, M. and Wood, M. (1996). Replication of Experimental Results in Software Engineering. *Technical Report ISERN-96-10*, International Software Engineering Research Network.

Calero, C., Piattini, M. and Genero, M. (2001). Empirical Validation of Referential Integrity Metrics. *Information and Software Technology*, Vol. 43, pp. 949–957.

Cantone, G. and Donzelli, P. (2000). Production and Maintenance of Software Measurement Models. *Journal of Software Engineering and Knowledge Engineering*, Vol. 5, pp. 605–626.

Cartwright, M. (1998). An Empirical View of Inheritance. *Information and Software Technology*, Vol. 40, No. 4, pp. 795–799.

Chidamber, S. and Kemerer, C. (1991). Towards a Metric Suite for Object Oriented Design. *OOPSLA'91, Sigplan Notices*, Vol. 26, No. 11, pp. 197–211.

Chidamber, S. and Kemerer, C. (1994). A Metrics Suite for Object Oriented Design. *IEEE Transactions on Software Engineering*, Vol. 20, No. 6, pp. 476–493.

Chidamber, S., Darcy, D. and Kemerer, C. (1998). Managerial Use of Metrics for Object-Oriented Software: An Exploratory Analysis. *IEEE Transactions on Software Engineering*, Vol. 24, No. 8, pp. 629–639.

CUHK- Chinese University of Hong Kong — Department of Obstetrics and Gynaecology — Available: http://department.obg.cuhk.edu.hk/ ResearchSupport/Minimum_correlation.asp (Last visited on July 22nd, 2002).

Daly, J., Brooks, A., Miller, J., Roper, M. and Wood, M. (1996). An Empirical Study Evaluating Depth of Inheritance on Maintainability of Object-Oriented Software. *Empirical Software Engineering*, Vol. 1, No. 2, pp. 109–132.

Deligiannis, I., Shepperd, M., Webster, S. and Roumeliotis, M. (2002). A Review of Experimental into Investigations into Object-Oriented Technology. *Empirical Software Engineering*, Vol. 7, No. 3, pp. 193–231.

El-Emam, K., Benlarbi, S., Goel, N. and Rai, S. (1999). A Validation of Object-Oriented Metrics. *NRC/ERB 1074*, National Research Council Canada.

Fenton, N. (1994). Software Measurement: A Necessary Scientific Basis. *IEEE Transactions on Software Engineering*, Vol. 20, No. 3, pp. 199–206.

Fenton, N. and Pfleeger, S. (1997). *Software Metrics: A Rigorous Approach*, 2nd edition. London, Chapman & Hall.

Fenton, N. and Neil, M. (2000). *Future of Software Engineering*. Chapter: Software Metrics: a Roadmap, Ed. Finkelstein, A., *ACM*, pp. 359–370.

Fowler, M. and Scott, K. (1999). *UML Distilled: A Brief Guide to the Standard Object Modelling Language*. The Addison-Wesley Object Technology Series.

Galsberg, D., El-Emam, K., Melo, W., Machado, J. and Madhavji, N. (2000). Empirical Validation of Object-Oriented Design Measures (submitted for publication).

Genero, M., Piattini, M. and Calero, C. (2000). Early Measures For UML Class Diagrams. *L'Objet*, Vol. 6, No. 4, Hermes Science Publications, pp. 489–515.

Genero, M., Olivas, J., Piattini, M. and Romero, F. (2001a). Using Metrics to Predict OO Information Systems Maintainability. *13th International Conference* on *Advanced Information Systems Engineering (CAiSE'01)*, Eds. Dittrich, K., Geppert, A. and Norrie, M.C., *Lecture Notes in Computer Science 2068*, Interlaken, Switzerland, pp. 388–401.

Genero, M., Jiménez, L. and Piattini, M. (2001b). Empirical Validation of Class Diagram Complexity Metrics. Proceedings of *SCCC XXI International Conference of the Chilean Computer Science Society (SCCC'2001)*, Chile, IEEE Computer Society, pp. 95–104.

Genero, M., (2002). Defining and Validating Metrics for Conceptual Models. Ph.D. Thesis, University of Castilla-La Mancha.

Genero M., Romero, F., Olivas J. and Piattini M. Construcción de un Modelo Borroso de Predicción del Tiempo de Mantenimiento de Diagramas de Clases UML. *Proceedings of 6th Workshop Iberoamericano de Ingeniería de Requisitos y Ambientes Software (IDEAS 2003)*, pp. 249–260. (In Spanish).

Godo, L., López de Mántaras, R., Sierra, C. and Verdaguer, A. (1989). MILORD: The Architecture and Management of Linguistically Expressed Uncertainty. *International Journal of Intelligent Systems*, Vol. 4, pp. 471–501.

Hanebutte, N., Taylor, C. and Reiner, D. (2003). Techniques of Successful Application of Factor Analysis in Software Measurement. *Empirical Software Engineering*, Vol. 8, pp. 43–57.

Harrison, R., Counsell, S. and Nithi, R. (1998). Coupling Metrics for Object-Oriented Design Metrics, *Proceedings of the Sixth IEEE International Symposium on Software Metrics (METRICS 1998)*, pp. 150–156.

Harrison, R., Counsell, S. and Nithi, R. (1999). An Evaluation of the MOOD Set of Object-Oriented Software Metrics. *IEEE Transactions on Software Engineering*, Vol. 24, No. 6, pp. 491–496.

Harrison, R., Counsell, S. and Nithi, R. (2000). Experimental Assessment of the Effect of Inheritance on the Maintainability of Object-Oriented Systems. *The Journal of Systems and Software*, Vol. 52, pp. 173–179.

ISO/IEC 9126-1.2 (2001). Information technology — Software Product Quality — Part 1: Quality Model.

Jhonson, D. (1998). *Applied Multivariant Methods for Data Analysis*. Duxbury Press, Brooks/Cole Publishing Company.

Juristo, N. and Moreno, A. (2001). *Basics of Software Engineering Experimentation*. Kluwer Academic Publishers.

Kitchenham, B., Pfleeger, S. and Fenton, N. (1995). Towards a Framework for Software Measurement Validation. *IEEE Transactions of Software Engineering*, Vol. 21, No. 12, pp. 929–943.

Kitchenham, B. and Stell, J. (1997). The Danger of Using Axioms in Software Metrics. *IEE Proceedings — Software Engineering*, Vol. 144, No (5–6), pp. 279–285.

Kitchenham, B., Pfleeger, S., Pickard, L., Jones, P., Hoaglin, D., El Emam, K. and Rosenberg, J. (2002). Preliminary Guidelines for Empirical Research in Software Engineering. *IEEE Transactions on Software Engineering*, Vol. 28, No. 8, pp. 721–734.

Kleinbaum, D., Kupper, L. and Muller, K. (1987). *Applied Regression Analysis and Other Multivariate Methods*. Duxbury Press.

Krantz, D., Luce, R., Suppes P. and Tversky, A. (1971). *Foundations of Measurement*, Vol. 1, Academic Press, New York.

Li, W. and Henry, S. (1993). Object-Oriented Metrics That Predict Maintainability. *Journal of Systems and Software*, Vol. 23, No. 2, pp.111–122.

Lorenz, M., and Kidd, J. (1994). *Object-Oriented Software Metrics: A Practical Guide*. Prentice Hall, Englewood Cliffs, New Jersey.

Manso, M., Crespo, Y. and Dolado, J. (2002). Caracterización de Productos Software con Métricas no Redundantes. *Proceedings of the VII Jornadas de Ingeniería del Software y Bases de Datos (JISBD'02)*, pp. 177–188. (In Spanish).

Marchesi, M. (1998). OOA Metrics for the Unified Modeling Language. *Proceedings of the 2nd Euromicro Conference on Software Maintenance and Reengineering*, pp. 67–73.

Maxwell, K. (2002). *Applied Statistics for Software Managers*. Software Quality Institute Series. Prentice Hall.

MDA — The OMG Model Driven Architecture, 2002. Available: http://www.omg.org./mda/, August 1st, 2002.

Miller, J. (2000). Applying Meta-Analytical Procedures to Software Engineering Experiments. *Journal of Systems and Software*, Vol. 54, pp. 29–39.

Olivas, J. (2000). Contribución al Estudio Experimental de la Predicción basada en Categorías Deformables Borrosas. Ph.D. Thesis, University of Castilla-La Mancha, Spain.

Olivas, J. and Romero, F. (2000). FPKD. Fuzzy Prototypical Knowledge Discovery. Application to Forest Fire Prediction. *Proceedings of the SEKE'2000*, Knowledge Systems Institute, Chicago, Ill. USA, pp. 47–54.

Olivas, J., Garcés, P. and Romero, F. (2002). FISS: Application of Fuzzy Technologies to an Internet Meta-Searcher. *Proceedings of the 2002 Annual Meeting of the North American Fuzzy Information Processing Society (NAFIPS)*, pp. 140–145.

OMG (2001). Unified Modeling Language (UML) Specification, Version 1.4: Object Management Group (OMG).

Perry, D., Porter, A. and Votta, L. (2000). *Future of Software Engineering.* Chapter: Empirical Studies of Software Engineering: A Roadmap. Future of Software Engineering, *ACM*, Ed. Finkelstein, A., pp. 345–355.

Pflegeer, S. (1994–1995). Experimental Design and Analysis in Software Engineering Part 1–5, ACM Sigsoft, *Software Engineering Notes*, Vol. 19, No. 4, pp. 16–20; Vol. 20, No. 1, pp. 22–26; Vol. 20, No. 2, pp. 14–16; Vol. 20, No. 3, pp. 13–15; Vol. 20, No. 4, pp. 14–17.

Pigoski, T. (1997). *Practical Software Maintenance.* Wiley Computer Publishing, New York, USA.

Poels, G. (1999). On the Formal Aspects of the Measurement of Object-Oriented Software Specifications. Ph.D. Thesis, Faculty of Economics and Business Administration. Katholieke Universiteit Leuven, Belgium.

Poels, G. and Dedene, G. (2000a). Distance-Based Software Measurement: Necessary and Sufficient Properties for Software Measures. *Information and Software Technology*, Vol. 42, No. 1, pp. 35–46.

Poels, G. and Dedene, G. (2000b). Measures for Assessing Dynamic Complexity Aspects of Object-Oriented Conceptual Schemes. *19th International Conference on Conceptual Modeling (ER 2000)*, Salt Lake City, *Lecture Notes in Computer Science 1920*, Springer-Verlag, pp. 499–512.

Poels, G. and Dedene, G. (2001). Evaluating the Effect of Inheritance on the Modifiability of Object-Oriented Business Domain Models. *Proceedings of the 5th European Conference on Software Maintenance and Reengineering (CSMR 2001)*, Lisbon, Portugal, pp. 20–29.

Roberts, F. (1979). *Measurement Theory with Applications to Decision Making, Utility and the Social Sciences.* Addison-Wesley, Reading, MA, USA.

Robson, C. (1993). *Real world research: A Resource for Social Scientists and Practitioners-Researchers.* Blackwell.

Schneidewind, N. (1992). Methodology For Validating Software Metrics. *IEEE Transactions of Software Engineering*, Vol. 18, No. 5, pp. 410–422.

Schneidewind, N. (2002). Body of Knowledge for Software Quality Measurement. *IEEE Computer*, Vol. 35, No. 2, pp. 77–83.

Shull, F., Carver, J., Travassos, G., Maldonado, J., Conradi, R. and Basili, V. (2003). *Lecture Notes on Empirical Software Engineering.* Chapter: Replicated

Studies: Building a Body of Knowledge about Software Reading Techniques. Eds. Juristo, N. and Moreno, A. World Scientific, Singapore, pp. 9–84.

Siegel, S. and Castellan, N. (1988). *Statistics for the Behavioral Sciences*. New York, McGraw Hill.

Snedecor, G. and Cochran, G. (1989). *Statistical Methods* (8th edition). Iowa State University Press.

Stake, R. (1995). *The Art of Case Study Research*. Sage publications.

Subramanyan, R. and Krishnan, M. (2003). Empirical Analysis of CK metrics for Object-Oriented Design Complexity: Implications for Software defects. *IEEE Transactions of Software Engineering*, Vol. 29, No. 4, pp. 297–310.

Suppes, P., Krantz, M., Luce, R. and Tversky, A. (1989). Foundations of Measurement, Vol. 2, Academic Press, New York.

Tang, M., Kao, M. and Chen, M. (1999). An Empirical Study on Object-Oriented Metrics. *Proceedings of the Sixth IEEE International Symposium on Software Metrics*, pp. 242–249.

Unger, B. and Prechelt, L. (1998). The Impact of Inheritance Depth on Maintenance Tasks — Detailed Description and Evaluation of Two Experimental Replications. *Technical Report*, Karlsruhe University, Karlsruhe, Germany.

Van Solingen, R. and Berghout, E. (1999). *The Goal/Question/Metric Method: A Practical Guide for Quality Improvement of Software Development*. McGraw-Hill.

Westland, J., (2002). The Cost of Errors in Software Development: Evidence from Industry, *The Journal of Systems and Software*, Vol. 62, pp. 1–9.

Weyuker, E. (1998). Evaluating Software Complexity Metrics. *IEEE Transactions on Software Engineering*, Vol. 14, No. 9, pp. 357–1365.

Wohlin, C., Runeson, P., Höst, M., Ohlson, M., Regnell, B. and Wesslén, A. (2000). *Experimentation in Software Engineering: An Introduction*, Kluwer Academic Publishers.

Yin, R. (1994). *Case Study Research Design and Methods*. Sage Publications, Beverly Hills, California.

Zuse, H. (1998). *A Framework of Software Measurement*. Berlin, Walter de Gruyter.

Chapter 5

MEASURING OCL EXPRESSIONS: AN APPROACH BASED ON COGNITIVE TECHNIQUES

LUIS REYNOSO*, MARCELA GENERO[†,a] and MARIO PIATTINI[†,b]

*National University of Comahue, Department of Computer Science
Neuquén – Argentina
lreynoso@uncoma.edu.ar

[†]Alarcos Research Group, Department of Computer Science
University of Castilla La Mancha, Ciudad Real – Spain
[a]Marcela.Genero@uclm.es
[b]Mario.Piattini@uclm.es

1. Introduction

Class diagram quality is clearly a crucial issue that must be evaluated (and improved if necessary) in order to get quality OO software. This fact is corroborated by the huge amount of metrics that can be applied to UML (OMG, 2003c) class diagrams at a high level design stage, that have been recorded in relevant literature. Most of these studies are focused on the measurement of internal quality attributes such as structural complexity, coupling, size, etc. However, none of the proposed metrics take into account the added complexity involved when class diagrams are complemented by expressions written in Object Constraint Language (OCL).

OCL, defined by OMG (2003b), has became a fundamental language in developing OO software using UML, as it allows complete and consistent

161

UML modelling. A model specified in a combination of the UML and OCL languages is mentioned in Warmer and Kleppe (2003), as a UML/OCL combined model, or just a UML/OCL model. OCL enriches, for example, UML class diagrams with expressions that specify semantic properties of a model (Gogolla and Richters, 2001). The OCL expressions are unambiguous and make the model more precise and more detailed (Warmer and Kleppe, 2003) improving its understandability at early stages of OO software development. Moreover OCL is essential in building consistent and coherent platform-independent models (PIM) and helping to raise the level of maturity of the software process (Warmer and Kleppe, 2003).

Even though applying OCL to software specification has great potential for improving software quality and software correctness (Hennicker et al., 2001), there are no metrics for OCL expressions.

The theoretical basis for developing quantitative models relating to structural properties and external quality attributes has been provided by Briand and Wüst (2001). In this work, we assume that a similar representation holds for OCL expressions. We implement the relationship between the structural properties on one hand, and external quality attributes on the other hand (see Fig. 1).

We hypothesise that the structural properties (such as coupling, size, length, etc.) of an OCL expression have an impact on its cognitive complexity. By cognitive complexity we mean the mental burden of the persons who have to deal with the artifact (e.g. modellers, designers, maintainers). High cognitive complexity leads to a reduction in the understandability of an artifact, and this leads to undesirable external qualities, such as decreased maintainability.

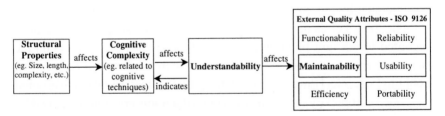

Fig. 1. Relationship between structural properties, cognitive complexity, understandability and external quality attributes (based on Briand and Wüst (2001) and ISO/IEC 9126, (2001)).

We suppose that OCL expression structural properties have an impact on the cognitive complexity of modellers. From a cognitive point of view, Cant et al. (1994) argue that measuring complexity should affect attributes of human comprehension since complexity is relative to human cognitive characteristics. Therefore, we have considered the cognitive techniques applied by modellers when they try to understand an OCL expression. These techniques are: "chunking" and "tracing" (Cant et al., 1994; Cant et al., 1992; El-Eman, 2001).

Therefore, this chapter pursues two main goals:

(1) To propose, in a methodological way, a set of metrics for measuring structural properties of OCL expressions, considering those OCL concepts specified in its metamodel (OMG, 2003b) which involve the use of two cognitive techniques — "chunking" and "tracing".
(2) To assure that the proposed metrics measure what they purport to measure through their theoretical validation, following a property-based framework proposed by Briand et al. (1996), (1997) and (1999).

In relation to our first aim we start in the following section by describing some concepts of the cognitive model of Cant et al. (1992), which we have used as a basis to define the metrics. Section 3 presents OCL and its concepts related to "tracing" and "chunking". The proper definition of the metrics is presented in Sec. 4, whilst their theoretical validation is presented in Sec. 5. Finally, in the last section some conclusions are drawn and future work is described.

2. Cognitive Techniques for Software Comprehension

The Cognitive Complexity Model (CCM) defined by Cant et al. (1992) gives a general cognitive theory of software complexity that elaborates on the impact of structure on understandability (El-Eman, 2001). Although the study of Cant et al. (1992) has been considered a reasonable point of departure for understanding the impact of structural properties "on understandability of code and the coding process", we believe that this model can also be applied to UML developers when they try to understand OCL expressions. The underlying rationale for the CCM argues that comprehension consists of two techniques or processes — "chunking" and "tracing", that are concurrently and synergistically applied in problem solving. Cant el al. (1992) argue that both techniques have implication for software complexity:

- "Chunking" technique — a capacity of short term memory, involves recognising groups of statements (not necessarily sequential) and extracting information from them which is remembered as a single mental abstraction — a "chunk" (Cant et al., 1992).
- "Tracing" technique — involves scanning, either forward or backward, in order to identify relevant "chunks" (El-Eman, 2001), resolving some dependencies.

Cant et al. (1992) argue that it is difficult to determine what constitutes a "chunk" since it is a product of semantic knowledge. For our purposes, we will consider an OCL expression as a "chunk" unit, whilst the comprehension of an operation, an attribute or a relationship with their associated OCL expressions are also considered "chunks". Henderson-Sellers (1996) notes that "tracing" disrupts the process of "chunking".

The comprehension of a particular "chunk" is the sum of three components: (1) the difficulty of understanding the "chunk" itself; (2) the difficulty of understanding all the dependencies on the "chunks" upon which a particular "chunk" depends, and (3) the difficulty of "tracing" these dependencies to those "chunks" (El-Eman, 2001). "Tracing" is applied when a method calls for another method to be used in a different class, or when an inherited property needs to be understood (El-Eman, 2001). UML modellers or developers also commonly perform these cognitive techniques during the understandability of OCL specifications.

3. OCL

As our intention is to define metrics for OCL expressions which are specified attached to a UML class diagrams, it is important to introduce OCL and its concepts as used in the definition of our metrics. Firstly, we will briefly describe OCL and its main elements in Sec. 3.1. In Sec. 3.2., we will structure the presentation of the OCL concepts in terms of their relation to the cognitive techniques mentioned in the previous section.

3.1. OCL characteristics

OCL is a textual specification language defined to solve different problems:

- UML is limited in its expressiveness, and many constraints cannot be defined using only UML graphical features (Cook et al., 2001), (Warmer and Kleppe, 2003).
- Frequently the system properties and constraints that cannot be defined using UML diagrams are defined using natural languages and this leads to misinterpretations, misunderstanding (Warmer and Kleppe, 1999), and ambiguities (OMG, 2003b).
- The use of formal methods can help to alleviate this problem, in order to specify correctly the system behaviour, but the use of formal methods by the object technology community' members requires a strong mathematical background, and formal methods are not a subject with which the average business or system modeller are familiar (OMG, 2003b).
- To provide precise information in the definition of standards, like the UML standard itself, use of a precise language is required.

OCL was defined as a textual add-on to the UML diagrams (Cook et al., 2001). Its main elements are OCL expressions that represent declarative and side-effect-free textual descriptions that are associated to different features of UML diagrams. OCL expressions add precision to UML models beyond the capabilities of the graphical diagrams of UML. Although OCL is considered in OMG (2003b) to be a formal language easy to read and write, the misuse of the language can lead to complicated written OCL expressions. Warmer and Kleppe (1999) give some tips and hints in writing OCL expressions (these recommendations are still valid although OCL has been modified through different versions); Furthermore, they recognise that the way OCL expressions are defined has a large impact on readability, maintainability and the complexity of the associated diagrams.

As previously mentioned, we will consider an OCL expression as a "chunk". An OCL expression is a suitable chunk unit, which modellers should understand as a whole declaration constraining an aspect of the system being modelled. It is therefore important to describe several concepts related to an OCL expression:

- Each OCL expression is written in the context of an instance of a specific type. This instance, *self*, provides a point of reference for interpretation of the expression, and is commonly referred to as the contextual instance.

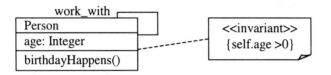

Fig. 2. Example of an invariant.

- The context in which an expression is written is introduced through the keyword *context*. Any OCL expression starts with the definition of the context, that involves the keyword *context* followed by the name of a type, then any specification of *self* within the OCL expression will be associated with the type declared in the context declaration.
- OCL expressions in UML class diagrams are used most importantly: to specify invariants[1] on classes and types in the class diagram, to specify constraints on operations and methods, to describe pre- and post conditions on operations, to specify initial values and derivation rules for attributes, to specify query operations, and to introduce new attributes and operations (OMG, 2003b).
- Invariants, preconditions and postconditions are constraints stereotyped respectively by ≪invariant≫, ≪precondition≫ and ≪postcondition≫. Although it is common for stereotypes to be attached to a UML feature using a graphical notation such as a note box, as shown in Fig. 2, the quantity of OCL expressions defined for a class diagram is significantly higher and this clutters the understandability of the UML diagram. For that reason all the OCL expressions shown in this chapter will be written in textual form and will not be shown using a note box.

Example 1:

An invariant definition for the Person class is:

context Person inv:
self.age > 0

The keyword *inv* means that the OCL expression, which comes after the colon, is an invariant expression. In fact, the *inv* keyword denotes

---

[1]An invariant is a constraint that must hold true anytime in the system, whereas pre- or post-conditions represent respectively a true condition that must be true just before/after the execution of an operation.

the stereotype ≪invariant≫. This expression means that all the values of any instance of the class Person must not be zero or lower. *self.age* uses a dot notation to refer to a property *age* of the object represented by *self*, however it is possible that *self* will be implicit in the expression (in the example is possible to simply write *age* instead of *self.age*). In general, whenever a property called *property* is specified without the object to which it applies — in the form of *"property"* instead of *"object.property"* —, the object is left out, or it is implicit in the specification of the *property* property.

Example 2 introduces a postcondition restriction for the *Birthday-Happens* operation of Person class. It is a postcondition as the post keyword is used, which in turn refers to a ≪postcondition≫ stereotype. This postcondition means that the *age* of a person is incremented by one when the birthday of a person had happened (age@pre is used to refer to the previous value of *age* just before the execution of BirthdayHappens).

Example 2:

context Person::BirthdayHappens()
post: age = age@pre + 1

Before giving more examples, we will introduce two important concepts used in the following sections:

- Properties: an attribute, an association-end, and side-effect-free operation or method are considered properties on an object (OMG, 2003b). The way an object property is specified in an OCL expression is by using a dot notation. *Object.property 1* refers to a *property 1* property of *object* wherever *object* is a valid reference to an object. To illustrate this concept, see Example 3.

Example 3:

In the following expression the *work_with* property is used in an expression, meaning that a person cannot work with himself or herself. In this case work_with represents an association-end property.

context Person inv:
not self.work_with.exists(self)

- Classifier: a classifier is a UML metaclass which represents a type, a class, an interface, an association (acting as types) and datatypes (OMG, 2003b). Each classifier defined within a UML model represents a distinct OCL type (OMG, 2003b).

3.2. *OCL concepts related to cognitive techniques*

The understanding of an OCL expression as a "chunk" involves a strong intertwining of "tracing" and "chunking" techniques. We need to understand which OCL concepts, specified in its metamodel (OMG, 2003b), are relevant to these techniques. Analysis of each of these techniques in turn leads to the identification of structural properties, which can be measured.

In order to describe the OCL concepts which involve "chunking" we have basically considered those concepts which belong to one expression (the chunk) and which do not require solving dependencies to other chunks. In order to analyse "tracing", however, we have considered those OCL concepts that imply solving dependencies to other chunks. *Self* is used as the main concept related to the OCL expression itself, i.e. to the "chunking" technique. Other instances (object or object collections), whose types are different to the type represented by the contextual instance, are commonly accessed by "tracing" techniques.

Table 1 shows the main OCL concepts involved in these cognitive techniques.

3.2.1. *OCL concepts related to the "Chunking" technique (group 1)*

In this section, we will describe the OCL concepts related to the "chunking" cognitive technique of group 1 (mentioned in Table 1).

In this group, we have included those OCL concepts that are intrinsic to the language itself, allowing the modellers:

- To specify a variable definition.
- To use conditional expressions.
- To use predefined iterator expressions.
- To use literals, boolean operations, etc.

Table 1. OCL concepts which involve "tracing" or "chunking".

Cognitive technique	OCL concepts related to the cognitive technique		Common characteristics of the group of OCL concepts
Chunking	Group 1	Variable definitions through *let* expression, *if* expression condition, predefined iterator variables, literals, etc.	OCL facilities related to the language itself.
	Group 2	Reference to attributes or operations of the contextual instance, values postfixed by @pre, variables defined through ≪definition≫ constraints.	OCL concepts related to the contextual instance and some of its properties, values before the execution of an operation (that is, properties postfixed by @pre) of the contextual instance, variables defined through ≪definition≫ constraints in the type represented by the contextual instance, etc.
Tracing	Navigation and collection operation, parameter whose type are classifiers defined in the class diagram, Messaging, etc.		OCL concepts which allow an expression to use properties belonging to other classes or interfaces, different to the type of the contextual instance

The concepts are:

- **Let expressions**

  The *let* expression allows the definition of a variable to stand for a subexpression, and wherever the subexpression needs to be specified it is possible to reuse the variable instead, as a shorthand. The variable declared through a *let* definition is allowed to be used only inside the OCL expression which defines it (see Example 4).

  Example 4:

  In the following expression taken from OMG (2003b) a variable called *income* is defined to represent the function self.job.salary−>sum().

> *context Person inv:*
> *let income : Integer = self.job.salary−> sum() in*
> *if isUnemployed then income < 100*
> *else income ≥ 100 endif*

- **If-expressions**

  The *if, then, else* and *endif* keywords allow one to write a conditional expression, this kind of expression should always have a value. The *if* expression takes the form of "*if b then e1 else e2 endif*". Both OCL expressions, *e1* and *e2*, should be of compatible types and neither *e1* nor *e2* can be omitted from the expression (OMG, 2003b) (see Example 5).

  Example 5:

  The following example is taken from Warmer and Kleppe (1999):

  > *context customer inv:*
  > *title = (if isMale = true*
  >   *then 'Mr.'*
  >   *else 'Ms.'*
  >   *endif)*

- **Collection literals**

  OCL provides four specific collection types: set, bag, orderedset and sequence[2]. The simplest way to define a collection is through collection literals. The syntax used is to define the collection elements inside curly brackets and separated by commas. Also collection literals can be specified by means of interval declaration. Another kind of literal that can be specified is a tuple[3] (see Example 6).

  Example 6:

  > *Set {'apple', 'strawberry', 'orange'},*
  > *Sequence {'apple, 'orange' },*
  > *Bag {1,3,4,3,2},*
  > *Tuple {name: String = 'John ', age: Integer = 10}*

---

[2] A set is a collection of different elements whereas a bag can contain duplicated elements. An OrderedSet is a set in which the element are ordered. A sequence is a bag but their elements are ordered.

[3] A tuple consists of named parts, each of which can have a distinct type.

Table 2. Predefined iterator expressions.

Collection		Set	Bag	Sequence
exists	any	select	select	select
forAll	one	reject	reject	reject
isUnique	collect	collectNested	collectNested	collectNested
		sortedBy	sortedBy	sortedBy

- **Logical operators**

  The Boolean type is a predefined type composed of two values: true and false. OCL defines the following logical operators for Boolean: *or*, *xor*, *and*, *not* and *implies*. It is common to use logical operators in OCL expression because they represent general connectors of subexpressions.

- **Predefined iterator expressions**

  The semantic of predefined iterator expressions is defined in terms of an *iterate* expression. The set of standard iterator expressions defined in OCL (OMG, 2003b) is included in Table 2. The *reject* operation shown in Example 7, allows us to obtain a subset from a collection, its syntax is specified using the arrow-syntax: *collection−>reject(Boolean-expression)*. The subset obtained from the collection using *reject*, is composed of all the elements of the collection from which the expression evaluates to *false*. However, the operation can adopt three different forms (sse Example 7). The last two include an iterator variable, being the iterator, in the last form, specified by its type. The iterator variable is used to refer explicitly to the collection elements. The use of these predefined expressions involves dealing with collections and iterators.

Example 7:

> *collection−>reject(Boolean-expression)*
> *collection−>reject(v | Boolean-expression-with-v)*
> *collection−>reject(v: Type | Boolean-expression-with-v)*

3.2.2. *OCL concepts related to the "Chunking" technique (group 2)*

In this section, we will describe the OCL concepts related to the "chunking" cognitive technique of group 2 (mentioned in Table 1).

Due to the fact that OCL expressions are textual add-on to UML class diagrams there should be OCL mechanisms for refering, for example, to class diagram elements. Implicitly, an OCL expression is associated to a specific element (of a class diagram) through the contextual instance *self*, because *self* is the main point of reference for the comprehension of the OCL expression. In this group, we have included those OCL concepts that allow one to refer to some properties of the Classifier:

- Attributes and operations of the Classifier (which is represented by *self*).
- Variable definitions known in the context of the Classifier (which is represented by *self*).
- Some OCL predefined operations which relate the Classifier (which is represented by *self*) with other supertypes of this Classifier.

The concepts are:

- **Accessing attributes and operations belonging to the Classifier represented by *self***
  As was previously mentioned, an OCL expression can refer to a Classifier and its properties. Using the contextual instance and the dot notation it is possible to refer to attributes and operations defined in the Classifier represented by *self*. Considering the OCL expression shown in the Example 8, two properties are referred:

  – The *level* attribute belonging to Person, and
  – The *age()* operation belonging to the same type.

  Example 8:

  > *context Person inv:*
  > *self.level = "Senior" implies self.age() = 21*

- **≪definition≫ constraints**
  To allow the reuse of a variable and/or operation over multiple OCL expressions is possible to define a ≪definition≫ constraint, using the keyword *def*. In fact, this OCL expression means a stereotype ≪definition≫, and the constraint is attached to a Classifier. The keyword *def*, can be used after the attribute or operation definition. The

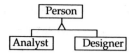

Fig. 3. An example of a class diagram.

constraint is exemplified as follows:

Example 9:

In the next OCL expression a variable called *income is defined*.

> *context Person*
> *def: income: Integer = self.job.salary−> sum( )*

The *income* variable is known in the same context as any property of Person. For example in:

> *context Person inv:*
> *if self.isUnemployee then*
> *sueldo < 100 else*
> *sueldo ≥ 100 endif*

- **Predefined properties that can be applied to any object**
  The following predefined operations can be applied to all objects[4]:

  - **oclIsTypeOf (t :OclType): Boolean:** The operation returns true if its argument (*t*) is equal to the type of *self*.
  - **oclIsKindOf (t :OclType): Boolean:** The operation determines whether *t* is either the direct type or one of the supertypes of an object.

  Example 10:

  According to the class diagram shown in Fig. 3, the following examples are defined in the context of the Designer class:

  > *self.oclIsTypeOf(Person) = false*
  > *self.oclIsKindOf(Person) = true*
  > *self.oclIsTypeOf(Designer) = true*
  > *self.oclIsKindOf(Designer) = true*

---

[4]Not all the predefined properties on all objects are included in this section, only those related to "chunking" — group 2.

- **oclAsType (t :OclType): instance of OclType:** Property of super-types when they are overridden within a type can be accessed through oclAsType().

Example 11:

If B is supertype of A then it is possible to write:

context B inv:
self.oclAsType(A).p1

in order to refer to the *p1* property of A.

The three properties are included in this group as they are commonly used with inheritance concepts of the Classifier represented by *self.*

- **Accessing previous values in postconditions**
  Whenever a property is postfixed with the keyword "@pre" in a post-condition, the value accessed is the property value before the execution of the operation (where the postcondition is defined).

Example 12:

In the following example taken from Cook et al. (2001) the *usage* prop-erty refers to the property of Bathroom whereas *usage@pre* refers to the value of *usage* of Bathroom before the execution of the *uses* operation.

context Bathroom::uses (g: Guest)
pre: ....
post: usage = usage@pre + 1

3.2.3. *OCL concepts related to the "Tracing" technique*

In this section, we will describe the OCL concepts related to the "trac-ing" cognitive technique. This technique was defined in Sec. 2. The OCL concepts related to "tracing" techniques allow the modeller to write an expression using properties belonging to other classes or interfaces, differ-ent to the Classifier that self represents, such as:

- **Navigations**
  Starting from a specific object, it is possible to navigate an association in the class diagram, to refer to other objects and their properties (OMG, 2003b). A relation is navigated when we use the rolename of the opposite association-end of a relation, that links the class where the expression is

defined with another class in the diagram class (when the association-end is missing we can use the name of the type at the association-end as the rolename). The result of a navigation is a single object or a collection of objects depending on the multiplicity of the association-end (Richters, 2002). The syntax uses the dot notation followed by an association-end property. It is possible to navigate many relationships in order to access as many properties as needed in an expression.

Example 13:

The following expression is specified for the class diagram of Fig. 4.

> *context LoyaltyProgram inv:*
> *membership.card −> forAll (goodThru = Date::fromYMD*
> *(2007,1, 1))*
> *and self.customer−>forAll (age()>30)*

membership.card used in the expression represents a navigation from LoyaltyProgram to CustomerCard. It navigates two relationships: one from LoyaltyProgram to Membership (an association class), and another from Membership to CustomerClass. In the former relationship there is no rolename attached to the association-end where Membership is the sink class, and for that reason the name of the class is used. Meanwhile, in the latter relationship, the navigation is represented by its rolename "card". The expression also contains another navigation self.customer.

- **In, Out and In/Out Parameters, and Return Values**
  Operations may have *in, out, in/out* parameters. If the operation has *out* or *in/out* parameters, the result of this operation is a tuple containing all *out, in/out* parameters and the return value (OMG, 2003b).
- **Collection Operations**
  OCL defines many operations for handling the elements in a collection. The operations allow the modeler to project new collections from the existing one. Operations like *select, reject, iterate, forAll* and *exists*, take each element in a collection and evaluate an expression for them. The expression evaluated for each collection can be defined in terms of new navigations. We will take into account those expressions of collection operations which are defined in terms of other navigations.

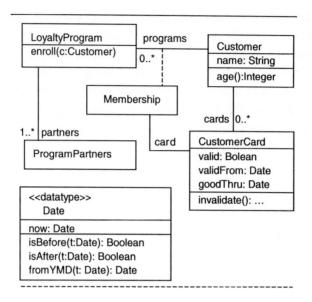

Fig. 4. Part of the Loyal and Royal class diagram of Warmer and Kleppe (2003).

Example 14:

self.customer of Example 13 specifies a *forAll* collection operation to express that all customer' ages of a LoyaltyProgram should be more than 30 years old.

- **Messages**
  OCL message expressions are used to specify the fact that an object has, or will send some message to another object at some moment in time (Kleppe and Warmer, 2000), (OMG, 2003b).

Example 15:

The following expression broadcasts a message called update to the observers of a subject.

> *context Subject:: haschanged()*
> *post: observer ^ update(?:Integer, ?:Integer)*

- **User-Defined DataType**
  "A data type is a special kind of classifier, similar to a class, whose instances are pure values (not objects). Usually, a data type is used for

specification of the type of an attribute. A data type is denoted using the rectangle symbol with keyword ≪dataType≫ or, when it is referenced by e.g. an attribute, denoted by a string containing the name of the data type." (OMG, 2003a)

Example 16:

A user-defined data type called Date is included in the class diagram of Fig. 4. The expression of the Example 13 uses it and access to its property (the *fromYMD* property).

4. Metrics Definition for OCL Expressions

Using the GQM (Basili and Rombach, 1998; Van Solingen and Berghout, 1999) template for goal definition, the goal pursued for the definition of the metrics for OCL expression is:

Analyze	*OCL expression structure related to cognitive techniques*
for the purpose of	*Evaluating*
with respect to	*Their Understandability*
from the point of view of	*the OO Software modellers*
in the context of	*OO software organisations*

Although our objective is to evaluate OCL expression understandability we are conscious that understandability is an external quality attribute and therefore it is influenced by structural properties of the OCL expressions. Therefore, we will focus the metrics on the structural properties of OCL expressions, and afterwards will ascertain through experimentation if these metrics could be used as early understandability indicators.

As Fenton and Pfleeger (1997) suggest that it is not advisable to define a single measure for capturing different structural properties, we will define a set of metrics, each of which captures different structural properties of an OCL expression related to a specific cognitive technique, considering those groups of elements presented in the previous section.

In order to define valid and reliable metrics we have applied a method based on (Calero et al., 2001; Cantone and Donzelli, 2000), which is composed of many steps beginning with the definition of the metrics goals and finishing with the acceptance of these metrics in real projects. Even though all the steps are equally important, in this chapter we only address the definition of the metrics goals, the definition of the metrics and their theoretical validation. It is advisable to perform the theoretical validation of the metrics before the empirical validation. In the context of an empirical study, the theoretical validation of metrics demonstrates their construct validity, i.e. it "proves" that they are valid measures to be used as variables in the empirical study. The rest of the steps will be tackled in future studies.

4.1. *Metrics for "chunking" (group 1)*

In this section, we present the first set of metrics for OCL expressions considering those elements which involve "chunking" grouped as "group 1" in Table 1. For each metric, we provide its proper definition, its goals and an example to illustrate its calculus.

- **Number of OCL KeyWords (NKW)**
  DEFINITION: This metric counts the total number of OCL keywords used in an expression. The OCL keywords are: *and, attr, context, def, else, endif, endpackage, if, implies, in, inv, let, not, oper, or, package, post, pre, then,* and *xor.* Each occurrence of these keywords will increment by one the value of NKW, with the exception of the groups:

  - *if, then, else* and *endif* keywords,
  - *package* and *endpackage* keywords,
  - *let* and *in* keywords

  that will be counted as only one keyword, because they are used together to represent a single subexpression.
  GOAL: The number of keywords is an indicator of the complexity of an OCL expression, in terms of its size. A higher number of keywords used in an OCL expression the greater its complexity.

  Example 17:

  In the Expression of Example 5 the value of NKW is 3, the keywords used are: *context, inv, if, then, else,* and *endif.*

- **Number of Explicit *Self* (NES)**
DEFINITION: This metric counts the number of times *self* is used in an explicit form in an OCL expression.
GOAL: *Self*, as explained in Sec. 3.1, provides a point of reference for the interpretation of an OCL expression. By using it in an explicit or implicit form it is possible to access different properties (attributes, operations, and associations-end). The greater the number of times *self* is used may indicate the greater the difficulty of the context to be understood.

Example 18:

The expression of Example 3 contains a navigation of a reflexive association written as *self.work_with.exists(self);* in this example the first *self* could be written in implicit form but the last *self* must be explicitly declared because *self* is sent as a parameter. The value of NSE is 2, as *self* was used in explicit form twice.

- **Number of Implicit *Self* (NIS)**
DEFINITION: This metric counts the number of times S*elf* is used in an implicit form in an expression.
GOAL: The goal of NES is also valid for the NIS metric; however, as *self* (and iterator variables in operation collections) can be left implicit, the number of times *self* is left implicit introduces a difficulty for modellers, because they have to evaluate to which object a property is applied. This evaluation will interrupt the process of chunking an expression.

Example 19:

In the following expression, the value of NIS is 1, *self* is implicit when the property *work_with* is referred.

> *context Person inv:*
> *not work_with.exists(self)*

- **Number of Variables defined by *Let* expressions (NVL)**
DEFINITION: This metric counts the total number of variables defined by *Let* expressions in an expression. This metric does not take into account the number of times a variable is reused, but the quantity of different defined variables.

GOAL: NVL metric is related to the degree of reuse of the variables within an OCL expression. Although a low use of *let* expressions can improve the readability of an OCL expression, we believe that a higher number of variables defined through *let* can indicate that the OCL expression is reasonably complex.

Example 20:

In Example 4, a variable called *income* is defined to represent the expression: *self.job.salary−>sum()*. The value of NVL is 1, as there is only one variable defined through a *let*-expression.

- **Number of *If* Expressions (NIE)**
  DEFINITION: This metric counts the total number of *if* expressions used in an expression.
  GOAL: A high number of *if*-expressions can increase the complexity of an OCL expression, in terms of conditional situations to be understood.

Example 21:

The value of NIE in the expression of Example 4 is 1, there is only one if-expression specified.

- **Number of *Set*, *OrderedSet*, *Bags*, *Sequence* or *Tuple* literals**
  DEFINITION: The total number of *set*, *orderedset*, *bags*, *sequence* or *tuple* literals used in an OCL expression are considered respectively by NSL, NOSL, NBL, NSQL, NTL metrics.
  GOAL: A high number of collection literals used in an expression could reduce its simplicity.

Example 22:

The value of NSQL is 1 in the following expression, as a sequence literal is specified:

$$= (s : Sequence(T)):Boolean$$
$$post: result = Sequence\{1 ...self−>size()\}−>$$
$$forAll(index :Integer \ |self−>at(index) = s−>at(index)) \ and$$
$$self−>size() = s−>size()$$

- **Number of Boolean Operators (NBO)**
  DEFINITION: This metric counts the total number of boolean operators used in an expression.
  GOAL: We believe that the number of boolean operators is an indicator of the complexity of an OCL expression, in the same way as the number of keywords used in it. In Warmer and Kleppe (1999, 2003) is also recommended to split a constraint with many boolean *and* operator, as a correct style for writing less complex (and easier to read and write) expressions. Those expressions with a high number of boolean operators can be candidates to be evaluated in order to be rewritten.

  Example 23:

  NBO $= 2$ in the following expression:

  context ProgramPartner inv:
  partners.deliveredServices−>forAll(pointsEarned = 0) and
  membership.card−>forAll(goodThru = Date::fromYMD(2000,1,1))
  and customer−>forAll(age() >55)

  NBO $= 2$ because two *and* operators are used in the expression. This expression taken from Warmer and Kleppe (2003), is an example of an invariant that can be rewritten splitting it into three different invariants. Each of the new invariants will be composed of an operand of the *and* logical operator.

- **Number of Comparison Operators (NCO)**
  DEFINITION: This metric counts the number of times an operator like: $<, \leq, >, \geq, = $ y $<>$[5] is used in an expression. If an operator is used many times the metrics take into account each occurrence of it.
  GOAL: It is common to use a comparison operator as a way of expressing a constraint. The goal is similar to that of the previous metric.

---

[5] Some operators are overloaded = is defined for OclAny, OclModelElement, OclType and OclState.

Example 24:

The value of NCO metric is 4 in the following expression:

> *context Person inv:*
> *age( ) > 30 and*
> *Person.allinstances( )−>forAll(p1, p2 | p1 <>p2*
>   *implies p1.dni <> p2.dni) and*
> *work_with−>size( ) ≤ 5*

- **Number of Explicit/Implicit Iterator variables (NEI, NII)**
  DEFINITION: These metrics count the total number of iterator variables specified in explicit or implicit form respectively. The way to determine the values of the NEI and NII metrics is similar to NSE and NSI metrics. NEI is the number of times an iterator variable appears in an expression (except in the way it is declared), whilst the way to compute the value of the NII metric involves the evaluation of each property with an implicit object in order to determine the object to which the property applies. If the property belongs to an object represented by an iterator variable, the metric is incremented by one. In OMG (2003b) there is a clear example of the resolution of ambiguities for an implicit object.
  GOAL: As already mentioned, the use of implicit objects and the determination of which object a property is applied to, leads to the interruption of the understandability of the expression as a chunk and could also reduce its understandability, as it is not always easy to know immediately which is the target object.

Example 25:

Given the class diagram of Fig. 5 and the following expression:

> *context Person inv:*
> *self.employer−>forAll (iter1 | iter1.employee−>*
>   *exists (lastname = name))*

Fig. 5. An example of class diagram.

The value of NEI is 1 due to *iter1* is an explicit iterator variable for the *forAll* operation (*iter1* is an explicit variable whose type is Company), and it is used in an explicit form when iter1.employee is used.

The value of NII is 2 due to:

- *exists* operation does not have an explicit iterator variable (an iterator variable whose type is Person), and *lastname* refers to this implicit variable.
- The *name* attribute is a property of *self* and *iter1,* and this constitutes an ambiguity. To determine to which object *name* is applied, the most inner scope is used. The result is: *name* attribute refers to *iter1.*

4.2. Metrics for "chunking" (group 2)

In this section, we define a set of metrics for OCL expressions considering those elements which involve "chunking" grouped as "group 2" in Table 1. For each metric, we provide its proper definition, its goals and an example to illustrate its calculus.

- **Number of Attributes belonging to the classifier that *Self* represents (NAS)**
  DEFINITION: This metric counts the total number of attributes belonging to the classifier that *Self* represents. The attributes are directly referred using the notation *self.attributename.*
  GOAL: A higher number of this kind of attributes will increase the complexity of the expression. The comprehension of attributes used in an expression not only involves the meaning of them as a constituent of a class diagram but also the different OCL expressions that declare restriction on them.

Example 26:

In Example 5, two attributes of Person are used, *title* and *isMale*, the former has an implicit *self* instance, while in the latter it is explicit, thus the value of NAS is 2.

- **Number of Operations belonging to the classifier that *Self* represents (NOS)**

  DEFINITION: This metric counts the total number of Operations belonging to the classifier that *self* represents. These operations are directly referred using the notation *self.operationname.*

  GOAL: The same goal as NAS but considering operations instead of attributes. The comprehension of an operation involves the comprehension of its meaning as a class diagram constituent and also the pre and postconditions associated to it.

  Example 27:

  The value of NOS in the OCL expression of Example 8 is 1, only one operation is used: age().

- **Number of Variables defined through ≪Definition≫ constraints**

  DEFINITION: This metric counts the total number of variables used in an expression which are defined through ≪definition≫ constraints. If a variable is reused many times in an expression the variable is counted only once.

  GOAL: A high number of variables reused in an expression can interrupt the meaning of the expression itself.

  Example 28:

  The value of NVD in Example 9 is 1 as the *income* variable is used in the expression and this variable has been defined through a ≪definition≫ constraint.

- **Number of oclIsTypeOf, oclIsKindOf or oclAsType Operations (NIO)**

  DEFINITION: This metric counts the number of times an oclIsTypeOf, oclIsKindOf or oclAsType operation is used in an expression (NIO). These are some predefined properties. We are conscious that NIO does not only use the type represented by *self*, which identifies the metrics of group 2, but also uses other types connected by *self* through inheritance (a characteristic of group 1). Despite this, we prefer to leave this metrics in this group. This is an example where "chunking" and "tracing" are performed sinergically.

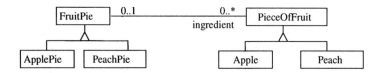

Fig. 6. Example for illustrating NIO.

GOAL: A high number of this kind of predefined operations can increase the complexity of the expression, as the modelers have to deal with inheritance concepts. The complexity will also depend on the complexity of the inheritance tree in which the classifier represented by *self* is included.

Example 29:

Given the class diagram of Fig. 6 and the following expression of the *ApplePie* class:

> *context ApplePie inv:*
> *self.ingredient−>forAll(oclIsKindOf(Apple))*

The value of NIO is 1, because the expression uses oclIsKindOf().

- **Number of properties postfixed by @Pre (N@P)**
  DEFINITION: This metric represents the number of different properties postfixed by @pre. This metric can be used exclusively for postconditions.
  GOAL: A high number of variables postfixed by @pre could increase the complexity of an OCL expression.

Example 30:

In the expression of Example 12 the value of N@P is 1, as the postfix @pre is used with the *usage* property.

4.3. *Metrics for "tracing"*

In this section, we propose a set of metrics for OCL expressions considering those elements which involve "tracing" (see Table 1). The definition of each metric is accompanied by the goals and an example to illustrate its calculus.

- **Number of Navigated Relationships (NNR)**
  DEFINITION: This metric counts the total number of relationships that are navigated in an expression. If a relationship is navigated twice, for example using different properties of a class or interface, this relationship is counted only once. Whenever an *association class* is navigated we will consider the association to which the association class is attached.
  GOAL: As Warmer and Kleppe (2003) remark: An "argument against complex navigation expressions is that writing, reading and understanding invariants becomes very difficult". The meaning of each relationship involves the understanding of how the objects are coupled to each other. The larger the set of relationships to be navigated, the greater is the context to be understood.

Example 31:

In the following expression (valid for Fig. 4 and defined for the LoyaltyProgram, class) two different relationships are navigated: (1) the relationship between LoyaltyProgram and Customer (it is navigated from LoyaltyProgram to Membership, and from LoyaltyProgram to Customer), (2) the relationship between Membership and CustomerCard.

> *context LoyaltyProgram inv:*
> *membership.card −> forAll (*
>   *goodThru = Date::fromYMD (2007,1, 1)*
>   *and self.customer−>forAll (age()>30)*

thus NNR = 2 because two relationships were navigated.

- **Number of Attributes referred through Navigations (NAN)**
  DEFINITION: This metric counts the total number of attributes referred through navigations in an expression.
  GOAL: NAN measures the extent of usage of attributes of other classes by the class where the expression is defined. The larger the set of attributes referred through navigations, the greater is the context to be understood. The understanding of attributes belonging to other classes involves the comprehension of them as a chunk, i.e. their meaning and the OCL specification associated to them.

Table 3. WNON metric definition.

$\sum(1 + |\text{Par}(m)|)(1 + R + |P_{\text{out, in/out}}(m)|)\ m \in N(\text{expression})$
$N(\text{expression})$: Set of different[6] operations referred through navigations.
$|\text{Par}(m)|$: quantity of actual parameters of m
R stands for the m operation result and represents the value of 1.
$|P_{\text{out, in/out}}(m)|$: quantity of *out* and *in/out* parameters of the m operation. Through a navigation it is possible to exclusively access one result as a time (OMG, 2003b), this weighted formula giving a higher weight to those operations used many times to access different results.

Example 32:

In the following expression, valid for Fig. 4 and defined for the LoyaltyProgram class, only the *goodThru* attribute is used, thus NAN = 1:

> *context LoyaltyProgram inv:*
> *membership.card —> forAll (goodThru = Date::fromYMD*
> *(2007,1, 1)) and self.customer—>forAll (age()>30)*

- **Weighted Number of referred Operations through Navigations (WNON)**

  DEFINITION: The metric is defined as the sum of weighted operations (operations which are referred through navigations). For that reason we must consider the operation calls. The operations are weighted by the number of actual parameters (only the values of all *in* or *in/out* parameters are necessary to specify in the operation call (OMG, 2003b)) and the number of *out* parameters used (also considering the return type of the operation). The definition of the WNON metric is defined as it is shown in Table 3.

  GOAL: WNON measures the extent of usage of operations of other classes by the class where the expression is defined. The larger the set of operations (referred through navigations) and its parameters, the greater is the context to be understood.

---

[6]We will consider the actual parameter of the operation call in order to analyse if two operations (referred through navigations) are different elements in the N(expression)-set. Having two operation calls they will be different if they have different operation names or different actual parameters (their parameter names or/and the quantity of actual parameter are not equal).

Example 33:

The following operation "income" has a result of type Integer, an *in* parameter (d) and an *out* parameter (bonus):

> *context Person::income(d: Date, bonus: Integer): Integer*
> *post: result = type { bonus = ...,*
>   *result = ... }*

Now, consider an expression in which we navigate to the Person class, and we operate with the two returned values of income:

> *context Salary::calculate()*
> *post: person.income(aDate).bonus + person.income(aDate).result*

Applying the metric WNON to the postcondition expression of the *calculate* operations we obtain: WNON $= (1 + 1)(1 + 1 + 1) = 6$.

- **Number of Navigated Classes (NNC)**
  DEFINITION: This metric counts the total number of classes, association classes or interfaces to which an expression navigates. If a class contains a reflexive relation and an expression navigates it, the class will be considered only once in the metric. Also, as a class might be reachable from a starting class/interface from different forms of navigations (i.e. following different relationships) we must consider this situation as a special case: If a class is used in two (or more) different navigations the class is counted only once .
  GOAL: Warmer and Kleppe (1999) argue that "any navigation that traverses the whole class model creates a coupling between the object involved". A high number of navigated classes will increase the coupling between the objects.

Example 34:

In the expression of Example 32, the value of NNC $= 3$, because the classes Membership, Customer and CustomerCard are used.

- **Weighted Number of Messages (WNM)**
  DEFINITION: This metric counts the total number of messages defined in an expression weighted by its actual parameters. The weighted operation is carried out according to Table 4.

Table 4. WNM metric definition.

$\sum(1 + \|Par(m)\|)\ m \in M(\text{expression})$
M(expression): Set of different operations[7] used through messaging in an expression.
$\|Par(m)\|$: quantity of actual parameter of the m operation.

GOAL: The modeller should consider that a communication has taken place (OMG, 2003b) whenever a message is specified in an OCL expression. A high number of operations called — through messaging — could reduce the understandability of the expression. The understanding of each message involves the understanding of its parameters and its semantics (OCL expressions associated with them).

Example 35:

If we apply WNM metric to the following expression (an expression valid for the class diagram of Fig. 4) the value of WNM is 1, because there is only one message, without parameters, in the expression.

context CustomerCard inv:
validFrom.isBefore(goodThru) or
goodThru.isAfter(Date::now) implies self ^ invalidate()

- **Number of Parameters whose Types are classes defined in a class diagram (NPT)**
  DEFINITION: This metric is specially used in pre and postcondition expressions and it counts the method parameters, and the return type (also called result) used in an expression, each parameter/result having a type representing a class or interface defined in the class diagram.
  GOAL: In an object oriented system a typical method of communication is by using an object as a parameter (Gamma et al., 1995). Parameters can be used in the specification of an OCL constraint. However if the quantity of parameters whose types are classes in the class diagram is high, the context of the object involved will affect the understanding of the OCL expression.

---

[7]In order to analyse if two messages are different we will consider the object to which the message is sent and its operation call as we describe in WNO metric.

Example 36:

In the following expressions (both, pre- and post-conditions, are valid expressions for the LoyaltyProgram class of Fig. 4), the value of NPT = 1 because only one parameter (c), whose type is a class in the class diagram (Customer), is used in the expression.

> *LoyaltyProgram::enroll(c: Customer)*
> *pre: not customer−>includes(c)*
> *post: customer = customer @ pre−> including (c)*

- **Number of User-Defined Data Type Attributes (NUDTA)**
  DEFINITION: This metric counts the total NUMBER of attributes belonging to a user-defined data type used in an expression. Attributes are counted once if they belong to the data type class, even if they are used more than once.
  GOAL: NUDTA is a measure of the potential reuse of user-defined data type attributes.

Example 37:

In the expression of Example 35, the value of NUDTA = 1 because only one class attribute (*now*) of a data type (*Date*) is used.

- **Number of User-Defined Data Type Operations (NUDTO)**
  DEFINITION: The definition of this metric is analogous to the NUDTA metric, but considering operations instead of attributes.
  GOAL: NUDTO is a measure of the potential reuse of user-defined data type operations.

Example 38:

In the expression of Example 35, NUDTO = 2 because the *isBefore* and *isAfter* operations (belonging to the data type Date) are used.

- **Weighted Number of Navigations (WNN)**
  DEFINITION: As we explain in the Sec. 3.2.3 an operation collection is composed of an expression which is evaluated for each collection element, and if the evaluated expression involves a new navigation (or many) we will give a higher weight to the new navigation used inside the

definition of the outermost expression. As the collection operation can be defined in terms of a new navigation and its collection operations, i.e. in a recursive way, we will refer to the different compositions of navigation as "level". In the case that navigation B is used in the immediate definition of an operation collection for navigation A, we would say that B is in level 2 and A in level 1.

The weight associated with each level is equal to the level number. Therefore the definition of the WNN metric is:

$$WNN = \sum \text{weight of the level} * \text{number of navigations of the level.}$$

GOAL: This metric is an estimate of overall coupling among objects (those involved through relationships) in the specification of an OCL expression. The value of WNN will provide an indicator of how the relationships are used together for specifying semantics of an expression in terms of a coupling set of objects. A high number of WNN will indicate an intertwining specification of relationships and this could reduce the understandability of an OCL expression.

Example 39:

In the precondition expression of Example 36, the value of WNN is 1, and there is only one navigation (self.customer). Now, we will show how the WNN is obtained in the following expression:

> *context LoyaltyProgram inv:*
> *self.customer —>forAll(age() <= 30) and*
> *self.customer —>forAll (c1 | self.customer —>*
> *forAll (c2| c1 <> c2 implies c1.name <> c2.name)*

Two subexpressions are connected by an *and* operator. Each subexpression involves navigations. Whilst the navigation of the first subexpression does not include a new navigation in its evaluation, the second one uses a collection operation defined in terms of another, and the value of WNN is obtained in the following way: $\mathbf{1} * 2 + \mathbf{2} * 1 = 4$.

The number shown in bold print font represents the applied weight, and the number shown in normal font indicates the **number of navigations**.

- **Depth of Navigations (DN)**

  DEFINITION: Given that in an OCL expression there can be many navigations regarding its definition, we build a tree of navigation using the class
  name to which we navigates. We will only consider navigations starting
  from the contextual instance (from *self*). The root of the tree is the class
  name which *self* represents. Then we build a branch for each navigation,
  where each class we navigate to is a node in the branch. Nodes are connected by "navigation relations". DN is defined as the maximum depth
  of the tree.

  When a navigation includes a collection operation expression defined
  in terms of a new navigation(s), we will build a new tree for the navigation
  used in the collection operation expression, using the same method, then
  we will connect both trees using a "definition connection". A dashed
  line will represents a definition connection. When we obtain the depth
  of the tree, we will apply the following rule: "Navigation connection is
  counted once, and definition connection twice".

  GOAL: A high depth of navigations may involve a complicated navigation. Warmer et al. (2003) suggest avoiding complex navigation expressions, they also argue that: "using long navigation makes details of distant
  objects known to the object where we started the navigation".

  This metric was proposed as a measure of class complexity and
  design complexity. It is based on the idea that a high value of the metrics
  will be an indicator of how distant are the objects known by the Classifier
  (where the expression is defined).

Example 40:

A tree built for the expression of Example 32, using the method described
above, is shown in Fig. 7(a). In this example the value of DN is 2.

Example 41:

According to the expression of Example 39, the tree built is shown in
Fig. 7(b), where a dashed line represents a definition connection. The
DN value for the expression of Fig. 7(b) is equal to 4.

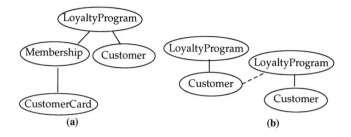

Fig. 7. Examples of navigation.

- **Weighted Number of Collection Operations (WNCO)**

  DEFINITION: The collection operations used in the expression definition are weighted according to the level in which they are defined, so the metric is defined thus:

  $$\text{WNCO} = \sum \text{weight of the level}$$
  $$* \text{number of collection operations of the level.}$$

  GOAL: The value of WCO will provide an indicator of how the operation collections are specified using a sort of composition. A high number of WNCO will indicate an intertwining specification of operation collections and this could reduce the understandability of an OCL expression.

Example 42:

In the expression of Example 39 WNCO = 4, and the value is obtained in the following way: $1 * 2 + 2 * 1 = 4$. The number shown in bold font represents the weight, and the number shown in normal font indicates the number of operation collections. Three operation collections are used in the specification of the expression, two of them are used in the same subexpression at different levels.

5. Theoretical Validation of the Proposed Metrics

To develop the theoretical validation of metrics we have used the property-based framework of Briand et al. (1996) and (1997) and its adaptation for interaction-based metrics for coupling and cohesion (Briand et al., 1999).

The framework and its adaptation, before being used, are explained in Sec. 5.1. Then they are applied for the validation of the metrics defined in Sec. 4. We will only show one example of the theoretical validation for each kind of measure proposed.

5.1. *Briand et al.'s frameworks*

Property-based approaches (also called axiomatic approaches) such as the Briand et al.'s frameworks, formally define desirable properties of the measures for a given software attribute. These properties are properties of the numerical relation system of measures. They aim to formalise the empirical properties that a generic attribute of software or a system (e.g. the length or size) must satisfy in order for it to be used in the analysis of any measurement proposed for that attribute. Property-based approaches propose a measure property set that is necessary but not sufficient (Briand et al., 1996; Poels and Dedene, 2000). They can be used as a filter to reject proposed measures (Kitchenham and Stell, 1997), but they are not sufficient to prove the validity of the measure. The two best known approaches were proposed by Weyuker (1988) and Briand et al. (1996).

5.1.1. *The original framework of Briand et al. (1996)*

Briand et al. (1996) have provided a set of mathematical properties that characterise and formalise several important measurement concepts such as size, length, complexity, cohesion and coupling, related to internal software attributes. After some criticisms made by Poels and Dedene (1997), Briand et al. (1997) made some modifications to the definition of the properties they had initially proposed. Hereafter, we refer to the final framework, i.e. the modified version. This framework is based on a graph-theoretic model of a software artifact, which is seen as a set of elements linked by relationships. The idea is to characterise the properties for measurement of a given software attribute via a set of mathematical properties, based on this graph-theoretic model.

The properties they provide are generally enough to be applied not only to code, but also to other artifacts produced during the software process, for example for OCL expression metrics.

– **Systems, Modules and Modular Systems.** In this framework, a system is characterised by its elements and the relationships between them. The authors want the properties they define to be as independent as possible of any product abstraction. Thus, the framework does not reduce the number of possible system representations, as elements and relationships can be defined according to the needs.

A software artifact is modelled by a graph $S = \langle E, R \rangle$, called system, where E is the set of elements of S, and R is a binary relation among the elements of E($R \subseteq E \times E$). From this point, we say that m is a module of S if and only if $E_m \subseteq E$, $R_m \subseteq E_m \times E_m$ and $R_m \subseteq R$. A module is connected to the rest of the system by external relationships, whose set is defined as Outer$R(m) = \{\langle e_1, e_2 \rangle | (e_1 \in E_m \wedge e_2 \notin E_m) \vee (e_1 \notin E_m \wedge e_2 \in E_m)\}$. A modular system is one where all the elements of the system have been partitioned into different modules. Therefore the modules of a modular system do not share elements, but there may be relationships across modules. Figure 8 shows a modular system with three modules m_1, m_2 and m_3.

We will now introduce inclusion, union, intersection operations for modules and the definitions of empty and disjoint modules.

– **Inclusion.** Module $m_i = \langle E_{mi}, R_{mi} \rangle$ is said to be included in module $m_j = \langle E_{mj}, R_{mj} \rangle$ (notation: $m_i \subseteq m_j$) if $E_{mi} \subseteq E_{mj}$ and $R_{mi} \subseteq R_{mj}$.

MS

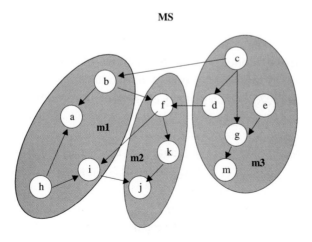

Fig. 8. A modular system.

- **Union.** The union of modules $m_i = \langle E_{mi}, R_{mi} \rangle$ and $m_j = \langle E_{mj}, R_{mj} \rangle$ (notation: $m_i \cup m_j$) is the module $\langle E_{mi} \cup E_{mj}, R_{mi} \cup R_{mj} \rangle$.
- **Intersection.** The intersection of modules $m_i = \langle E_{mi}, R_{mi} \rangle$ and $m_j = \langle E_{mj}, R_{mj} \rangle$ (notation: $m_i \cap m_j$) is the module $\langle E_{mi} \cap E_{mj}, R_{mi} \cap R_{mj} \rangle$.
- **Empty module.** Module $\langle \emptyset, \emptyset \rangle$ (denoted by $\emptyset$) is the empty module.
- **Disjoint modules.** Modules m_i and m_j are said to be disjoint if $m_i \cap m_j = \emptyset$.
- Since in this framework modules are just subsystems, all systems can theoretically be decomposed into modules. The definition of a module for a particular measure in a specific context is just a matter of convenience.

5.1.1.1. Properties for size and length

We will describe in this section only the properties for the internal attributes size and length, as only these two properties were applied in the theoretical validation. Both properties may be defined for entire systems or modules of entire systems.

- **Size.** The basic idea is that size depends on the elements of the system. The size of a system $S = \langle E, R \rangle$ is a function Size(S) that is characterised by the following properties:

  - Property 1. Nonnegativity. Size(S) ≥ 0
  - Property 2. Null value. The size of a system S is null if E is empty:

  $$E = \emptyset \Rightarrow \text{Size(S)} = 0$$

  - Property 3. Module additivity. The size of a system S is equal to the sum of the sizes of two of its modules $m_1 = \langle E_m1, R_m1 \rangle$ and $m_2 = \langle E_{m2}, R_{m2} \rangle$ such that any element of S is an element of either m_1 or m_2:

  $$(m_1 \subseteq S \text{ and } m_2 \subseteq S \text{ and } E = E_{m1} \cup E_{m2} \text{ and } E_{m1} \cap E_{m2} = \emptyset)$$
  $$\Rightarrow \text{Size}(S) = \text{Size}(m_1) + \text{Size}(m_2)$$

- **Length.** The length of a system $S = \langle E, R \rangle$ is a function Length (S) characterised by the following properties:

  - Property 1. Nonnegativity. Length (S) ≥ 0

– Property 2. Null value. The length of a system S is null if E is empty:

$$E = \emptyset \Rightarrow \text{Length}(S) = 0$$

– Property 3. Nonincreasing monotonicity for connected components. Let S be a system and m be a module of S such that m is represented by a connected component of the graph representing S. Adding relationships between elements of m does not increase the length of S:

$$(S = \langle E, R \rangle \text{ and } m = \langle E_m, R_m \rangle ym \subseteq Sym$$

"is a connected component of S" and

$$S' = \langle E, R' \rangle \text{ and } R' = R \cup \{\langle e_1, e_2 \rangle\} \text{ and } \langle e_1, e_2 \rangle \notin R \text{ and }$$

$$e_1 \in E_{m1}, \text{ and } e_2 \in E_{m1})$$

$$\text{Length}(S) \geq \text{Length}(S')$$

– Property 4. Nondecreasing monotonicity for non-connected components. Let S be a system and m_1 and m_2 be two modules of S such that m_1 and m_2 are represented by two separate connected components of the graph representing S. Adding relationships from elements of m_1 to elements of m_2 does not decrease the length of S.

$$(S = \langle E, R \rangle \text{ and } m_1 = \langle E_{m1}, R_{m1} \rangle ym_2 = \langle E_{m2}, R_{m2} \rangle \text{ and }$$

$$m_1 \subseteq S \text{ and } m_2 \subseteq S$$

"are separate connected components of S" and

$$S' = \langle E, R' \rangle \text{ and } R' = R \cup \{\langle e_1, e_2 \rangle\} \text{ and } \langle e_1, e_2 \rangle \notin R \text{ and }$$

$$e_1 \in E_{m1}, \text{ and } e_2 \in E_{m2})$$

$$\text{Length}(S') \geq \text{Length}(S)$$

– Property 5. Disjoint modules. The length of a system S made of two disjoint modules m_1, m_2 is equal to the maximum of the lengths of m_1 and m_2.

$$(S = m_1 \cup m_2 \text{ and } m_1 \cap m_2 = \emptyset \text{ and } E = E_{m1} \cup E_{m2})$$

$$\text{Length}(S) = \max\{\text{Length}(m_1), \text{Length}(m_2)\}$$

5.1.2. *An adaptation of Briand et al.'s framework*
       for interaction-based metrics for coupling

In the Briand et al.'s framework adaptation for interaction-based metrics (Briand et al., 1999) coupling is defined as a relation between an individual software part and its associated software system, rather than as a relation between two software parts. The interactions described in Briand et al. (1999) are directly related with the definition of a *high level design*. They use two kinds of interactions: *Interaction between data* (if a piece of data appears in the definition of other) and *interaction between data and function* (if a piece of data appears in the definition of a function). Most of the metrics defined for OCL for tracing techniques are interaction-based metrics, and for that reason in order to use a similar approach to Briand et al. (1999) we need to define what we consider a high level design, which kind of interaction we will use and how coupling is defined in terms of the interaction:

- *High level design*: A UML class diagram with the specification of OCL expression defining invariants, pre- and post-condition of operations (which only declares the effect of the operation but not how the operation is performed (Warmer and Kleppe, 1999)) will be considered a high level design.
- *Relation*: The relations are defined between a software individual part — in our context, an OCL expression — and its associated software system — mainly, attributes and operations which it is possible to access through messaging, navigations, etc.
- *DU-interaction/OU-interaction*: The interaction from Data declaration (or Operation declaration) to data Used (or operation used) in an OCL expression.
- *Import coupling*: Given a software part *sp*, import coupling of *sp* is the number of DU- or OU-interaction between data declaration (or operation declaration) external to *sp* and data used (or operation used) within *sp*.

We have only defined metrics related to import coupling.[8] Our hypothesis is similar to the ISP-hypothesis of Briand et al. (1999): The larger the

---

[8]The extent to which a software part depends on the rest of the software system.

number of imported software parts, the larger the context to be understood, the more likely the occurrence of a fault.

5.2. *NAN properties as coupling (interaction-based) metric*

We will make some definitions prior to the application of properties of interaction-based metrics for coupling to the NAN (the number of attributes referred through navigations in an expression) metric:

- Relation: The relations are defined between a software individual part- in our context, an OCL expression) and its associated software system (attributes which it is possible to access through navigations in the NAN metric).
- DU-interaction: The interaction from Data declaration to Data Used (attributes used through navigations) in an OCL expression.
- Import coupling: Given a software part *sp* (an OCL expression), the import coupling of *sp* is the number of DU-interactions between data declaration external to *sp* and data used within *sp*.

Our hypothesis is similar to the ISP-hypothesis of Briand et al. (1999): The larger the number of "used" software parts, the larger the context to be understood, the more likely the occurrence of a fault.

Following a similar approach applied in Briand et al. (1999) the proper- ties for interaction-based measures for coupling are instantiations, for our specific OCL context, of the properties defined in Briand et al. (1996) and (1997) for coupling.

- Nonnegativity: Is directly proven, and it is impossible to obtain a negative value. An expression *sp* without navigation (referring to attributes) in its definition has $NAN(sp) = 0$.
- Monotonicity: Is directly verified, adding import interactions — in this case, DU-interactions of navigations referring to attributes — to an OCL expression cannot decrease its import coupling. If we add a new nav- igation referring to an attribute in an expression *sp*, two possible situ- ations can happen: (1) the attribute referred to in the added navigation is an attribute already used by a DU-interaction. Thus the metric NAN applied to the new expression obtained, is equal to $NAN(sp)$. (2) If the

added navigation refers to a new attribute, then NAN applied to the new expression is greater than NAN(*sp*).

– Merging of Modules: This property can be expressed for our context in the following way: "the sum of the import coupling of two modules is no less than the coupling of the module which is composed of the data used of the two modules". The value of NAN for an expression which consists of the union of two original expressions, is equal to the NAN of each expression merged when the sets of attributes referred to in each original expression are disjointed, otherwise it is less than NAN of each expression merged.

In a similar way, it is possible to show that NNR, WNON, NNC, WNM, NPT, NUDTA, NUDTO, NAS, NOS, N@P and NIO are interaction-based measures for coupling.

5.3. *WNM as a size metric*

For our purpose and in accordance with the framework of Briand et al. (1996) and (1997), we consider that an OCL expression is a system composed of OCL messages (elements) and relationships are represented by the relation "belong to", which reflects that a message belongs to an OCL expression. A sub-expression will be considered a module. We will demonstrate that WNM fulfils all of the axioms that characterize size metrics, as follows:

– Nonnegativity: Is directly proven and it is impossible to obtain a negative value.
– Null value: An expression *e* without a message, has a $WNM(e) = 0$.
– Module Additivity: If we consider that an OCL expression is composed of modules with no message in common, the number of messages of an OCL expression will always be the sum of the number of messages of its modules. In other words, when two modules (sub-expression) without messages in common are merged then the new expression has as many messages as each of the merged expressions. But if the original merged modules (sub-expressions) have some message in common, then the WNM of the resulting expression should be less than adding the WNM

of the original expressions. In a similar way, it is possible to show that WNN, WCO are size metrics.

In a similar way, it is possible to show that WNN, WNCO, NKW, NES, NIS, NIE, NSL, NOSL, NBL, NSQL, NTL, NBO, NCO, NEI, NII, NVL and NVD are size metrics.

5.4. *DN as a length metric*

For our purpose and in accordance with the framework of Briand et al. (1996) and (1997), we consider that an OCL expression is a system. The elements are the classes (to which the expression navigates) and the relationships are the navigations of a UML relationship. We will demonstrate that DN fulfils all of the axioms that characterise length metrics, as follows:

– Nonnegativity and Null Value are straightforwardly satisfied, the depth of a tree can never be negative, and an expression without navigation has an empty tree, and DN is 0.
– Nonincreasing monotonocity for connected components: If we add relationships between elements of a tree (classes or interfaces) the depth does not vary.
– Nondecreasing monotonocity for non-connected components: Adding a relationship to two unconnected components (two trees) makes them connected, and its length is not less than the length of the two unconnected components.
– Disjoint modules: The depth of a tree is given by the component that has more levels from the root to the leaves.

6. Conclusions and Future Work

This chapter gives the definition of a set of metrics for OCL expressions to measure structural properties of OCL expressions, considering OCL concepts related to the cognitive techniques of "tracing" and "chunking".

After performing the theoretical validation of the proposed metrics using the original framework of Briand et al. (1996; 1997) and its adaptation

Table 5. Theoretical validation of metrics according to Briand et al. (1996), (1997) and (1999).

Metric classification	OCL expression metrics defined in terms of cognitive techniques					
	Chunking (group 1)	Chunking (group 2)		Tracing		
	NKW, NES, NIS, NVL, NIE, NSL, NOSL, NBL, NSQL, NTL, NBO, NCO, NEI, NII	NAS, NOS, NIO, N@P	NVD	NNR, NAN, WNON, NNC, WNM, NPT, NUDTA, NUDTO	WNM WNN WNCO	DN
Interaction-based metrics for coupling		X		X		
Length						X
Size	X		X		X	

to interaction-based metrics (Briand et al., 1999), the results are summarised in Table 5.

As Table 5 shows, most of the measures obtained for chunking techniques are size metrics, and most of the metrics defined for tracing techniques are interaction-based metrics for coupling. This correlation between a cognitive technique and some kinds of measures for internal attributes is significant, and the reason is because of the proper definition of the cognitive technique. In fact, Klemola (2000) argues that "some traditional complexity metrics can be supported by the fact they are clearly related to cognitive limitations".

We believe that measures obtained for tracing technique will be more important than measures obtained for chunking technique, as the former cognitive technique has been observed as a fundamental activity in program comprehension (Boehm-Davis, 1996; Klemola, 2000).

We are aware that it is necessary to provide comprehensive information about this set of metrics in order to perform the empirical validation of them. As many authors mentioned (Basili et al., 1998; Fenton and

Pfleeger, 1997; Kitchenham et al., 1995; Schneidewind, 1992) empirical validation employing experiments or case studies is fundamental to assure that the metrics are really significant and useful in practice. We are currently planning a controlled experiment for corroborating if the proposed metrics could be useful as early indicators of the OCL expression understandability. Moreover, once we have empirically validated these metrics at an expression level, we will be able to extend them at a class level.

Acknowledgements

This work has been partially funded by the MUML project financed by "University of Castilla-La Mancha" (011.100623), the network VII-J-RITOS2 financed by CYTED, and the UNComa 04/E048 project financed by "Subsecretaría de Investigación de la Universidad Nacional del Comahue". Luis Reynoso enjoys a postgraduate grant from the agreement between the Government of Neuquen Province (Argentina) and YPF-Repsol.

References

Basili, V. R. and Rombach, H. (1998). The TAME Project: Towards Improvement-Oriented Software Environments. *IEEE Transactions on Software Engineering*, Vol. 14, No. 6, pp. 758–773.

Basili, V., Shull, F. and Lanubile, F. (1999). Building Knowledge Through Families of Experiments. *IEEE Transactions on Software Engineering*, Vol. 25, No. 4, pp. 435–437.

Boehm-Davis, D. A., Fox, J. E. and Philips, B. (1996). Techniques for Exploring Program Comprehension. *Empirical Studies of Programmers, Sixth Workshop*. Eds. Gray W. and Boehm-Davis D. Norwood, NJ. Ablex, pp. 3–21.

Briand, L. C., Morasca, S. and Basili, V. (1999). Defining and Validating Measures for Object-Based High Level Design. *IEEE Transactions on Software Engineering*, Vol. 25, No. 5, pp. 722–743.

Briand, L., Morasca, S. and Basili, V. (1996). Property-Based Software Engineering Measurement. *IEEE Transactions on Software Engineering*, Vol. 22, No. 1, pp. 68–86.

Briand, L. C., Morasca S. and Basili, V. (1997). Response to: Comments 'Property-Based Software Engineering Measurement': Refining the Additivity Properties. *IEEE Transactions on Software Engineering*, Vol. 22, No. 3, pp. 196–197.

Briand, L. and Wüst, J. (2001). Modeling Development Effort in Object-Oriented Systems Using Design Properties. *IEEE Transactions on Software Engineering*, Vol. 27, No. 11, pp. 963–986.

Brito e Abreu, F. and Melo, W. (1996). Evaluating the Impact of Object-Oriented Design on Software Quality. *Proceedings of the 3rd International Metric Symposium*, pp. 90–99.

Calero, C., Piattini, M. and Genero, M. (2001). Method for Obtaining Correct Metrics. *Proceedings of the 3rd International Conference on Enterprise and Information Systems (ICEIS'2001)*, pp. 779–784.

Cant, S. N., Henderson-Sellers, B. and Jeffery, D. R. (1994). Application of Cognitive Complexity Metrics to Object-Oriented Programs. *Journal of Object-Oriented Programming*, Vol. 7, No. 4, pp. 52–63.

Cant, S. N., Jeffery, D. R. and Henderson-Seller, B. (1992). A Conceptual Model of Cognitive Complexity of Elements of the Programming Process. *Information and Software Technology*, Vol. 7, pp. 351–362.

Cantone, G. and Donzelli, P. (2000). Production and Maintenance of Software Measurement Models. *Journal of Software Engineering and Knowledge Engineering*, Vol. 5, pp. 605–626.

Cook, S., Kleepe, A., Mitchell, R., Rumpe, B., Warmer, J. and Wills, A. (2001). *The Amsterdam Manifiesto on OCL*. Eds. Clark T. and Warmer J. Advances in Object Modelling with the OCL. *Lecture Notes in Computer Science 2263*, Springer, Berlin, pp. 115–149.

El-Eman, K. (2001). *Object-Oriented Metrics: A Review of Theory and Practice*. National Research Council Canada. Institute for Information Technology.

Fenton, N. and Pfleeger, S. (1997). *Software Metrics: A Rigorous and Practical Approach*. Chapman & Hall, London, 2nd Edition. International Thomson Publishing Inc.

Gamma, E., Helm, R., Johnson, R. and Vlissides, J. (1995). *Design Patterns*. Addison Wesley. Massachusetts.

Gogolla, M. and Richters, M. (2001). *Expressing UML Class Diagrams properties with OCL*. Eds. Clark T. and Warmer J. Advances in Object Modelling with the OCL. *Lecture Notes in Computer Science 2263*, Springer, Berlin, pp. 85–114

Henderson-Sellers, B. (1996). *Object-Oriented Metrics: Measures of Complexity.* Prentice-Hall.

Hennicker, R., Hussmann, H. and Bidoit, M. (2001). *On the Precise Meaning of OCL Constraints.* Eds. Clark T. and Warmer J. Advances in Object Modelling with the OCL. *Lecture Notes in Computer Science 2263*, Springer, Berlin, pp. 69–84.

ISO/IEC 9126 (2001). *Software Product Evaluation-Quality Characteristics and Guidelines for their Use.* Geneva.

Kitchenham, B., Pflegger, S. and Fenton, N. (1995). Towards a Framework for Software Measurement Validation. *IEEE Transactions of Software Engineering*, Vol. 21, No. 12, pp. 929–943.

Kitchenham, B. and Stell, J. (1997). The Danger of Using Axioms in Software Metrics. *IEEE Proc.-Soft. Eng.*, Vol. 144, No. 5–6, pp. 279–285.

Klemola, T. (2000). A Cognitive Model for Complexity Metrics. *Proceedings of the 4th International ECOOP Workshop on Quantitative Approaches in Object-Oriented Software Engineering.* Sophia Antipolis and Cannes, France.

Kleppe, A. and Warmer, J. (2000). *Extending OCL to Include Actions.* UML 2000, York, UK, October 2000, Proceedings, *Lecture Notes in Computer Science*, Springer, pp. 440–450.

Object Management Group. (2003a). *UML 2.0 Infrastructure Final Adopted Specification. OMG Document* ptc/03-09-15. [On-line] Available http://www.omg.org/
cgi-bin/doc?ptc/2003-09-15.

Object Management Group. (2003b). *UML 2.0 OCL 2nd revised submission. OMG Document ad/2003-01-07.* [On-line] Available: http://www.omg.org/ cgi-bin/doc?ad/2003-01-07.

Object Management Group. (2003c). *UML Specification Version 1.5, OMG Document formal/03-03-01.* [On-line] Available: http://www.omg.org/cgi-bin/doc?formal/03-03-01.

Poels, G. and Dedene, G. (1997). Comments on "Property-Based Software Engineering Measurement": Refining the Additivity Properties. *IEEE Transactions on Software Engineering*, Vol. 23, No. 3, pp. 190–195.

Poels, G. and Dedene, G. (2000). Distance-Based Software Measurement: Necessary and Sufficient Properties for Software Measures. *Information and Software Technology*, Vol. 42, No. 1, pp. 35–46.

Richters, M. (2002). *A Precise Approach to Validating UML Models and OCL Constraints*. Biss Monographs Vol. 14. (Series Editors) Gogolla, M., Kreowski, H. J., Krieg-Brückner, B., Peleska, J., Schlingloff, B.H. Logos Verlag. Berlin.

Schneidewind, N. (1992). Methodology For Validating Software Metrics. *IEEE Transactions on Software Engineering*, Vol. 18, No. 5, pp. 410–422.

Van Solingen, R. and Berghout, E. (1999). *The Goal/Question/Metric Method: A Practical Guide for Quality Improvement of Software Development*. McGraw-Hill.

Warmer, J. and Kleppe, A. (1999). *The Object Constraint Language. Precise Modeling with UML*. Object Technology Series. Addison-Wesley. Massachusetts.

Warmer, J. and Kleppe, A. (2003). *The Object Constraint Language. Second Edition. Getting Your Models Ready for MDA*. Object Technology Series. Addison-Wesley. Massachusetts.

Weyuker, E. (1988). Evaluating Software Complexity Measures. *IEEE Transactions Software Engineering*, Vol. 14, No. 9, pp.1357–1365.

Chapter 6

METRICS FOR DATAWAREHOUSES
CONCEPTUAL MODELS

MANUEL SERRANO[*,a], CORAL CALERO[*,b], JUAN TRUJILLO[†,d],
SERGIO LUJÁN[†,e] and MARIO PIATTINI[*,c]

*Alarcos Research Group, Department of Computer Science
University of Castilla — La Mancha
Paseo de la Universidad, 4
13071 Ciudad Real
[a]Manuel.Serrano@uclm.es
[b]Coral.Calero@uclm.es
[c]Mario.Piattini@uclm.es

†Department of Computer Science
University of Alicante, Apto. Correos 99. E-03080
[d]jtrujillo@dlsi.ua.es
[e]slujan@dlsi.ua.es

1. Introduction

Datawarehouses have become the most important trend in business information technology and represent one of the most interesting areas within
the database industry (Chaudhuri and Dayal, 1997) as they provide relevant
and precise information enabling the improvement of strategic decisions
(Jarke et al., 2000) and as such the quality of the information that they
contain must be guaranteed (English, 1996). In fact, a lack of quality can

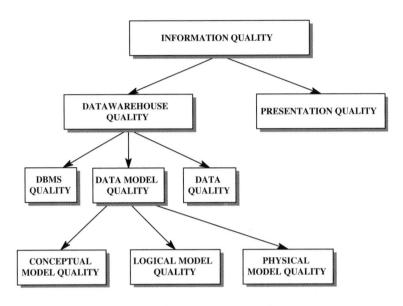

Fig. 1. Quality of the information and the datawarehouse.

have disastrous consequences from both a technical (Celko, 1995) and organisational point of view — loss of clients (Redman, 1996), important financial losses (Loshin, 2001) or discontent amongst employees (English, 1996).

The quality of the information of a datawarehouse is determined by the quality of the system itself as well as by the quality of the presentation of the data (see Fig. 1). Clearly it is important not only that the data of the datawarehouse correctly reflects the real world, but also that the data is interpreted correctly. As far as the quality of a datawarehouse is concerned, as with an operational database, three aspects must be considered — the quality of the relational or multidimensional DBMS (Database Management System) that supports it, the quality of the data model[1] (conceptual, logical and physical) and the quality of the data itself contained in the warehouse.

---

[1]We will use the term "model" without distinction to refer to both a modelling technique or language (eg. The E/R model) and the result ("schema") of applying this technique to a specific Universe of Discourse. The difference between the two concepts can be easily deduced from the context.

In order to guarantee the quality of the DBMS we can use an International Standard such as ISO/IEC 9126 (ISO, 2001) or one of the comparative studies of existing products. The quality of the data itself is mainly determined by the processes of extraction, filtering, cleaning, cleansing, synchronisation, aggregation and loading (Bouzeghoub et al., 2000), as well as by the level of maturity of these processes in the organisation.

Clearly the quality of the datawarehouse model also strongly influences information quality. The model can be considered at three levels: conceptual, logical — for which the use of "star design" has become universal (Kimball et al., 1998) — , and physical — which depends on each system, and consists of selecting the physical tables, indexes, data partitions, etc. (Bouzeghoub and Kedad, 2002; Harinarayan et al., 1996; Jarke et al., 2000; Labio et al., 1997).

At the logical level, several recommendations exist in order to create a "good" dimensional data model (Kimball et al., 1998; Adamson and Venerable, 1998; Inmon, 1997) and in recent years we have proposed (Serrano et al., 2001) and validated both formally (Calero et al., 2001) and empirically (Serrano et al., 2002; Serrano et al., 2003) several metrics that enable the evaluation of the complexity of star models.

Although conceptual modelling is not usually the object of much attention, there do currently exist various proposals for representing datawarehouse information from a conceptual perspective. Some approaches propose a new notation (Cabbibo and Torlone, 1998; Golfarelli et al., 1998; Golfarelli and Rizzi, 1999), others use extended E/R models (Sapia et al., 1998; Tryfona et al., 1999; Cavero et al., 2001) and finally others use the UML class model (Abelló et al., 2001; Abelló et al., 2002; Trujillo et al., 2001; Luján-Mora et al., 2002a). However, it is even more difficult to guarantee the quality of datawarehouse models, with the exception of the model proposed by Jarke et al. (Jarke et al., 2000), which is described in more depth in Vassiladis' Ph.D. thesis (Vassiliadis, 2000). Nevertheless, even this model does not propose metrics that allow us to replace the intuitive notions of "quality" with regards to the conceptual model of the datawarehouse with formal and quantitative measures that reduce subjectivity and bias in evaluation, and guide the designer in his work.

The final objective of our study is to define a set of metrics to guarantee the quality of the conceptual models of datawarehouses. In particular, we will focus on the complexity of the models obtained, which is one of the most important factors in relation to quality in datawarehouses — along with others such as completion, minimality and traceability (Vassiliadis, 2000) — and which affects comprehensibility, one of the most important dimensions in data quality (Redman, 1996).

In the next section, we summarise the extension of the UML (Trujillo et al., 2001; Luján-Mora et al., 2002a), which we will use as a base for the object-oriented conceptual modelling of datawarehouses. Sections 3–6 summarise the phases of the method we have followed for defining and validating metrics for datawarehouse conceptual models. Lastly, we draw conclusions and describe future investigation arising from this present chapter.

2. Object-Oriented Conceptual Modelling for Datawarehouses

In this section, we outline our approach to conceptual modelling based on UML for the representation of structural properties of multidimensional modelling.[2]

This approach has been specified by means of UML profiles[3] that contain the necessary stereotypes in order to carry out conceptual modelling successfully (Luján-Mora et al., 2002a). Tables 1 and 2 present in a summarised way the defined stereotypes along with a brief description and the corresponding icon in order to facilitate their use and interpretation. These stereotypes are classified as class stereotypes (Table 1) and attribute stereotypes (Table 2) as the metrics analysed in following sections will be performed based on this classification.

In our approach, the structural properties of multidimensional modelling are represented by means of a class diagram in which the information is organised in facts and dimensions. Some of the principal characteristics that can be represented in this model are the relations "many-to-many" between the facts and one specific dimension, the degenerated dimensions,

---

[2]Due to space limitations we will not look at the dynamic properties of multidimensional modelling in this article.

[3]A *profile* is a set of improvements that extend an existing UML type of diagram for a different use. These improvements are specified by means of extendibility mechanisms provided by UML (stereotypes, properties and restrictions) in order to be able to adapt it to a new method or model.

Table 1. Stereotypes of class.

Name	Description	Icon
Fact	Classes of this stereotype represent facts in a MD model	
Dimension	Classes of this stereotype represent dimensions in a MD model	
Base	Classes of this stereotype represent dimension hierarchy levels in a MD model	**B**

Table 2. Stereotypes of attribute.

Name	Description	Icon
OID	Attributes of this stereotype represent OID attributes of Fact, Dimension or Base classes in a MD model	OID
FactAttribute	Attibutes of this stereotype represent attributes of Fact classes in a MD model	FA
Descriptor	Attributes of this stereotype represent descriptor attributes of Dimension or Base classes in a MD model	D
DimensionAttribute	Attributes of this stereotype represent attributes of Dimension or Base classes in a MD model	DA

the multiple classification and alternative path hierarchies, and the non-strict and complete hierarchies.

Facts and dimensions are represented by means of fact classes (Fact stereotype) and dimension classes (Dimension stereotype) respectively. Fact classes are defined as compound classes in an aggregation relation of *n* dimension classes. The minimum cardinality in the role of the dimension classes is 1 to indicate that all the facts must always be related to all the dimensions. The relations "many-to-many" between a fact and a specific dimension are specified by means of the cardinality 1...* in the role of the corresponding dimension class. A fact is composed of measurements or fact attributes (stereotype FactAttribute) and it is on these that we wish to focus our analysis.

By default, all the measures in a class of facts are considered to be additive. The semi-additive and non-additive measures are specified by means of restrictions. Furthermore, derived measures can also be represented (by means of the restriction/) and their rules of derivation are specified in keys around the corresponding class of facts.

Our approach also allows the definition of identifying attributes (stereotype OID). In this way "degenerated dimensions" can be represented (Kimball, 1996), which provide the facts with other characteristics in addition to the defined measures.

As regards to dimensions (stereotype Dimension), each level of a classification hierarchy is represented by means of a base class (stereotype Base). An association of base classes specifies a relation between two levels of a classification hierarchy. The only prerequisite is that these classes should define a Directed Acyclic Graph (DAG) from the class of dimension (DAG restriction is defined in the stereotype Dimension). The DAG structure enables the representation of both multiple and alternative path hierarchies. Each base class must contain an identifying attribute (stereotype OID) and a descriptive attribute[4] (stereotype Descriptive) in addition to the additional attributes that characterise the instances of that class.

Due to the flexibility of UML, we can consider the peculiarities of classification hierarchies as non-strict hierarchies (an object of an inferior level belongs to more than one of a superior level) and as complete hierarchies (all the members belong to a single object of a superior class and that object is composed exclusively of those objects). These characteristics are specified by means of the cardinality of the roles of the associations and the restriction completeness respectively. Lastly, the categorisation of dimensions is considered by means of the generalisation/specialisation hierarchies belonging to UML.

3. Identification Phase

In order to define the metrics for datawarehouse conceptual models, we follow the method that is shown on Chapter 7. We begin this section with

---

[4]The identifying attribute is used in the OLAP tools in order to identify univocally the instances of one hierarchy level and the descriptive attribute as a label by default in the analysis of data.

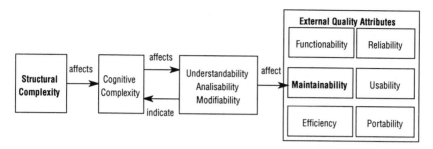

Fig. 2. Relationship between structural properties, cognitive complexity, understandability and external quality attributes (based on Briand et al. (1999)).

the first step of the method, where the goals of the metrics we want to define and the derived hypothesis are stated. In our case, the main goal is "Define a set of metrics to assess and control the quality of conceptual datawarehouse schemas."

As Briand et al. (1999) said, the structural properties (such as structural complexity) of a schema have an impact on its cognitive complexity (see Fig. 2). By cognitive complexity we mean the mental burden of the persons who have to deal with the artefact (e.g. developers, testers, maintainers). High cognitive complexity leads to an artefact reducing their understandability and this conduce undesirable external quality attributes, such as decreased maintainability (a characteristic of quality; ISO 9126 (ISO, 2001)).

So, we can state our hypothesis as: "Our metrics (defining for capturing the structural complexity of a datawarehouse conceptual schema) can be used for controlling and assessing the quality of a datawarehouse (through its maintainability)."

4. Metric Definition

Taking into account the metrics defined for datawarehouses at a logical level (Serrano et al., 2002) and the metrics defined for UML class diagrams (Genero, 2002; Genero et al., 2001; Genero et al., 2002) (see Chapter 4) we can propose an initial set of metrics for the model described in the previous section. When drawing up the proposal of metrics for datawarehouse models, we must take into account three different levels:

4.1. *Class-scope metrics*

The metrics we propose to be applied at class level are shown in Table 3.

4.2. *Star-scope metrics*

The following table (see Table 4) details the metrics proposed for the star level, one of the main elements of a datawarehouse, composed of a fact class together with all the dimensional classes and associated bases.

Table 3. Class-scope metrics.

Metrics	Description
NA(C)	Number of attributes FA, D or DA of the class C
NR(C)	Number of relationships (of any type) of the class C

Table 4. Star-scope metrics.

Metrics	Description
NDC(S)	Number of dimensional classes of the star S (equal to the number of aggregation relations)
NBC(S)	Number of base classes of the star S
NC (S)	Total number of classes of the star S $NC(S) = NDC(S) + NBC(S) + 1$
RBC(S)	Ratio of base classes. Number of base classes per dimensional class of the star S
NAFC(S)	Number of FA attributes of the fact class of the star S
NADC(S)	Number of D and DA attributes of the dimensional classes of the star S
NABC(S)	Number of D and DA attributes of the base classes of the star S
NA(S)	Total number of FA, D and DA attributes of the star S $NA(S) = NAFC(S) + NADC (S) + NABC(S)$
NH(S)	Number of hierarchy relationships of the star S
DHP(S)	Maximum depth of the hierarchy relationships of the star S
RSA(S)	Ratio of attributes of the star S. Number of attributes FA divided by the number of D and DA attributes

4.3. *Diagram-scope metrics*

Lastly in Table 5, we present metrics at diagram level of a complete datawarehouse which may contain one or more stars.

4.4. *Example*

Figure 3 gives an example of a datawarehouse, whilst Tables 6–8 summarise the values for the metrics. As the example has only one star, in Table 6, only those values of the metrics that are different at star and model level are shown.

5. Theoretical Validation

We have formally validated the metrics proposed using the DISTANCE framework (Poels and Dedene, 2000) (described in detail in Chapter 4).

Table 5. Diagram-scope metrics.

Metrics	Description
NFC	Number of fact classes
NDC	Number of dimensional classes
NBC	Number of base classes
NC	Total number of classes NC = NFC + NDC + NBC
RBC	Ratio of base classes. Number of base classes per dimensional class
NSDC	Number of dimensional classes shared by more than one star
NAFC	Number of FA attributes of the fact classes
NADC	Number of D and DA attributes of the dimensional Tables
NASDC	Number of D and DA attributes of the shared dimensional classes
NA	Number of FA, D and DA attributes
NH	Number of hierarchies
DHP	Maximum depth of the hierarchical relationships
RDC	Ratio of dimensional classes. Number of dimensional classes per fact class
RSA	Ratio of attributes. Number of FA attributes divided by the number of D and DA attributes

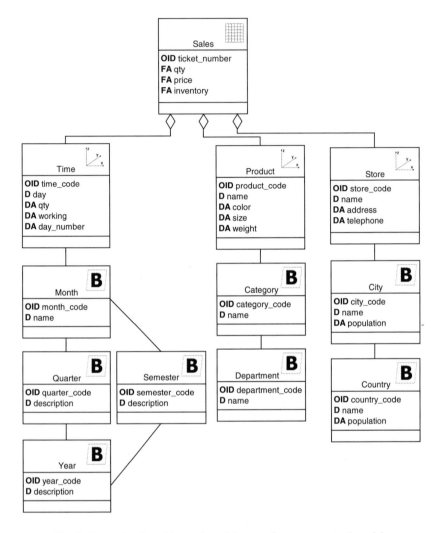

Fig. 3. Example of an object oriented datawarehouse conceptual model.

This framework is based on the measurement theory, and consequently enables the scale to which a metric belongs to be determined.

5.1. *Theoretical validation of NDC*

The Number of Dimensional Classes (NDC) measure is defined at the diagram level as the total number of dimensional classes of a datawarehouse conceptual model.

Table 6. Class-scope metrics values.

Classes	NA	NR
Sales	3	3
Time	4	2
Product	4	2
Store	3	2
Month	1	3
Quarter	1	2
Semester	1	2
Year	1	2
Category	1	2
Department	1	1
City	2	2
Country	2	1

Table 7. Star-scope metrics values.

Metrics	Value
NDC(S)	3
NBC(S)	8
NC(S)	12
RBC	8/3
NAFC(S)	3
NADC(S)	11
NABC(S)	10
NA(S)	24
NH(S)	3
DHP(S)	3
RSA(S)	3/21

In the following, we will present each of the steps for measure construction proposed in the DISTANCE framework. In order to exemplify the process we will use the models shown in Fig. 4.

- **Step 1. Find a measurement abstraction.** In our case, the set of software entities P is the Universe of datawarehouse conceptual models (UDCM) that is relevant for some Universe of Discourse (UoD) and p is a Datawarehouse Conceptual Model (DCM) (i.e. $p \in$ UDCM). The

Table 8. Diagram-scope level metrics values.

Metric	Value
NFC	1
NSDC	0
NASDC	0
RDC	3

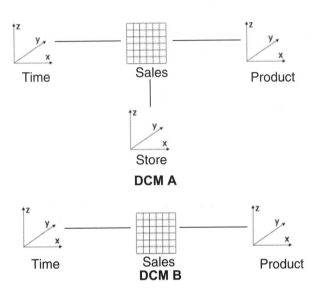

Fig. 4. Two examples of conceptual models of datawarehouse.

attribute of interest *attr* is the number of dimensional classes, i.e. a particular aspect of DCM structural complexity. Let UDC be the Universe of Dimensional Classes relevant to the UoD. The set of dimensional classes within a DCM, called SDC(DCM) is then a subset of UDC. All the sets of dimensional classes within the DCMs of UDCM are elements of the power set of UDC, denoted by $\wp$(UDC). As a consequence, we can equate the set of measurement abstractions M to $\wp$(UDC) and define the abstraction function as:

$$abs_{\text{NDC}} \colon \text{UDCM} \to \wp(\text{UDC}) \colon \text{DCM} \to \text{SDC(DCM)}.$$

This function simply maps a DCM onto its set of dimensional classes.

In our example, we have the set of dimensional classes of DCM A and of DCM B:

$$abs_{NDC}(\text{DCM } A) = \text{SDC}(\text{DCM } A) = \{\text{Time, Store, Product}\}$$
$$abs_{NDC}(\text{DCM } B) = \text{SDC}(\text{DCM } B) = \{\text{Time, Product}\}.$$

- **Step 2. Model distances between measurement abstractions.** The next step is to model distances between the elements of M. We need to find a set of elementary transformation types for the set of measurement abstractions $\wp(\text{UDC})$ such that any set of dimensional classes can be transformed into any other set of dimensional classes by means of a finite sequence of elementary transformations. Finding such a set is quite easy in case of a power set. Since the elements of $\wp(\text{UDC})$ are sets of dimensional classes, T_e must only contain two types of elementary transformations: one for adding a dimensional class to a set and one for removing a dimensional class from a set. Given two sets of dimensional classes $s_1 \in \wp(\text{UDC})$ and $s_2 \in \wp(\text{UDC})$, s_1 can always be transformed into s_2 by removing first all the dimensional classes from s_1 that are not in s_2, and then adding all the dimensional classes to s_1 that are in s_2, but were not in the original s_1. In the 'worst case scenario', s_1 must be transformed into s_2 via an empty set of attributes. Formally, $T_e = \{t_{0\text{-NDC}}, t_{1\text{-NDC}}\}$, where $t_{0\text{-NDC}}$ and $t_{1\text{-NDC}}$ are defined as:

$$t_{0\text{-NDC}}: \; \wp(\text{UDC}) \to \wp(\text{UDC}): \; s \to s \cup \{a\}, \quad \text{with } a \in \text{UDC}$$
$$t_{1\text{-NDC}}: \; \wp(\text{UDC}) \to \wp(\text{UDC}): \; s \to s - \{a\}, \quad \text{with } a \in \text{UDC}.$$

In our example, the distance between $abs_{NDC}(\text{DCM } A)$ and $abs_{NDC}(\text{DCM } B)$ can be modelled by a sequence of elementary transformations that does not remove any dimensional class from SDC(DCM A) and that adds Store to SDC(DCM A). This sequence of 1 elementary transformation is sufficient to transform SDC(DCM A) into SDC(DCM B). Of course, other sequences exist and can be used to model the distance in sets of dimensional classes between DCM A and DCM B. But it is obvious that no sequence can contain fewer than 1 elementary transformation if it is going to be used as a model of this distance. All 'shortest' sequences of elementary transformations qualify as models of distance.

- **Step 3. Quantify distances between measurement abstractions.** In this step, the distances in $\wp$ (UDC) that can be modelled by applying sequences of elementary transformations of the types contained in T_e, are quantified. A function δ_{NDC} that quantifies these distances is the metric (in the mathematical sense) that is defined by the symmetric difference model, i.e. a particular instance of the contrast model of Tversky (Suppes et al., 1989). It has been proven in Poels and Dedene (2000) that the symmetric difference model can always be used to define a metric when the set of measurement abstractions is a power set.

$$\delta_{NA}: \ \wp\,(UDC) \times \wp\,(UDC) \to \Re: \ (s, s') \to |s - s'| + |s' - s|.$$

This definition is equivalent to stating that the distance between two sets of dimensional classes, as modelled by a shortest sequence of elementary transformations between these sets, is measured by the count of elementary transformations in the sequence. Note that for any element in s but not in s' and for any element in s' but not in s, an elementary transformation is needed.

The symmetric difference model results in a value of 1 for the distance between the set of dimensional classes of DCM A and DCM B. Formally,

$$\delta_{NDC}(abs_{NDC}(DCM\ A), abs_{NDC}(DCM\ B))$$
$$= |\{Time, \ Store, \ Product\} - \{Time, \ Product\}|$$
$$+ \ |\{Time, \ Product\} - \{Time, \ Store, \ Product\}|$$
$$= |\{Store\}| + |\{\}| = 1.$$

- **Step 4. Find a reference abstraction.** In our example, the obvious reference point for measurement is the empty set of dimensional classes. It is desirable that an DCM without dimensional classes will have the lowest possible value for the NDC measure. So that we define the following function:

$$ref_{NDC}: \ UDCM \to \wp\,(UDC): DCM \to \emptyset.$$

- **Step 5. Define the software measure.** In our example, the number of dimensional classes of a Datawarehouse Conceptual Model DCM $\in$ UDCM can be defined as the distance between its set of attributes

SDC(DCM) and the empty set of dimensional classes $\emptyset$, as modelled by any shortest sequence of elementary transformations between SDC(DCM) and $\emptyset$. Hence, the NDC measure can be defined as a function that returns for any DCM $\in$ UDCM the value of the metric δ_{NDC} for the pair of sets SDC(DCM) and $\emptyset$:

$$\forall\, DCM \in UDCM: NDC(DCM) = \delta_{NDC}(SDC(DCM), \emptyset)$$
$$= |SDC(DCM) - \emptyset|$$
$$+ |\emptyset - SDC(DCM)|$$
$$= |SDC(DCM)|.$$

As a consequence, a measure that returns the count of dimensional classes in an Datawarehouse Conceptual Model qualifies as a number of dimensional classes measure. It must be noted here that, although this result seems trivial, other measurement theoretic approaches to software measure definition cannot be used to guarantee the ratio scale type of the NDC measure. The number of dimensional classes in a DCM can, for instance, not be described by means of a modified extensive structure, as advocated in the approach of Zuse (1998), which is the best-known way to arrive at ratio scales in software measurement.

5.2. *Theoretical validation of the rest of metrics*

Due to space constraints we cannot present the measure construction process for the other proposed metrics for datawarehouse conceptual models. However, the process is analogous and we have obtained that the metrics proposed are on a ratio scale. That means that they are formally valid software metrics because they are in the ordinal or in a superior scale, as remarked by Zuse (1998), and are therefore perfectly usable.

6. Empirical Validation

Hereafter, we present a controlled experiment we carried out to empirically validate the proposed metrics.

The goal definition of the experiment using the GQM template (Basili and Weiss, 1984) can be summarised as:

> *To analyse* the metrics for conceptual models of datawarehouse
> *for the purpose* of evaluating if they can be used as useful mechanisms
> *with respect of* the datawarehouse maintainability
> from the designer's *point of view*
> *in the context of* Professionals

6.1. Subjects

Ten Professionals participated in the experiment (see Table 9). The subjects work at a Spanish software factory that specially works on information systems development. All the subjects were men with an average age of 27.60 years. With respect to the experience of the subjects, they have an average experience of 4 years on computers, 3 years on databases, but little knowledge working with UML (only 2.25 years on average).

Table 9. Subjects of the experiment.

Subject#	Sex	Age	Computers	Databases	UML
1	M	24	3	1	0
2	M	23	5	4	0
3	M	27	5	4	1
4	M	30	2	0	0
5	M	28	8	4	4
6	M	25	5	3	3
7	M	34	6	4	1
8	M	23	1	1	0
9	M	32	4	3	0
10	M	30	1	0	0
Mean		27.60	4.00	3.00	2.25
Minimun		23	1	0	0
Maximun		34	8	4	4
Standard Deviation		3.86	2.26	1.71	1.45

6.2. Hypotheses formulation

The hypotheses of our experiment are:

Null hypothesis, H_0: There is not a statistically significant correlation between metrics and the maintainability of the schemas.
Alternative hypothesis, H_1: There is a statistically significant correlation between metrics and the maintainability of the schemas.

Alternative hypothesis H_1 is stated to determine if there is any kind of interaction between the metrics and the understandability of a dataware-house schema, based on the fact that the metrics are defined in an attempt to acquire all the characteristics of a conceptual datawarehouse model.

6.3. Variables in the study

- **Independent variables.** The independent variables are the variables for which the effects should be evaluated. In our experiment these variables correspond with the metrics being researched. Table 10 presents the values for each metric in each schema.
- **Dependent variables.** The maintainability of the tests was measured as the time each subject used to perform the tasks of each experimental test. The experimental tasks consisted of two different tasks. The first one involves understanding the models to count the number of classes

Table 10. Values of the metrics for the experiment schemas.

	NDC	NBC	NC	RBC	NAFC	NADC	NABC	NA	NH	DHP	RSA
S01	6	16	23	2.67	2	13	18	33	6	4	0.06
S02	5	19	25	3.8	2	16	36	54	9	4	0.04
S03	2	5	8	2.5	5	6	11	22	3	2	0.29
S04	4	17	22	4.25	5	10	34	49	9	3	0.11
S05	3	21	25	7	5	11	35	51	7	4	0.11
S06	5	13	19	2.6	4	0	31	35	5	4	0.13
S07	3	6	10	2	4	10	4	18	5	2	0.29
S08	4	5	10	1.25	4	17	10	31	2	3	0.15
S09	3	5	9	1.67	3	15	10	28	2	3	0.12
S10	2	4	7	2	2	9	4	15	3	2	0.15

that must visit to access to a concrete information. The second type of tasks involves modifying the models to fit new design requisites. For each schema we record separately the understanding time (including analysis of the model and the answering time to the first type of tasks) and the modification time that includes the time spent in performing the second type of tasks.

6.4. *Material design and experiment running*

Ten conceptual datawarehouse models were used for performing the experiment. Although the domain of the schemas was different, we tried to select examples representatives of real cases in such a way that the results obtained were due to the difficulty of the schema not to the complexity of the domain problem. We tried to have schemas with different complexity and different metrics values (see Table 10).

We selected a within-subject design experiment (i.e. all the tests had to be solved by each of the subjects). The documentation, for each design, included a datawarehouse schema and a questions form. The questions form included the tasks that had to be performed and a space for the answers. For each design, the subjects had to analyse the schema, answer some questions about the design and perform some modifications on it.

Before starting the experiment, we explained to the subjects the kind of exercises that they must perform, the material that they would be given, what kind of answers they had to provide and how they had to record the time spent solving the problems. We also explained to them that before studying each schema they must annotate the start time (hour, minutes and seconds), after that they could analyse the design and answer the given question. Once the answer to the question was written they must annotate the final time (again in hour, minutes and seconds). After that they must repeat the process with the modifications of the schema.

Tests were performed in distinct order by different subjects for avoiding learning and fatigue effects. The way we ordered the tests was using a randomisation function. To obtain the results of the experiment we used the number of seconds needed by each subject for each task on each schema.

6.5. *Data validation*

After marking the test we obtained all the times for each schema and subject (Tables 11 and 12). We notice that subject 2 did not answer to the modification tasks on schema 8 and that subject 10 did not answer to the modification tasks on schema 9. The times for these subjects in these exercises were considered as null values.

We decided to study the outliers before working with the average data. In order to find the outliers we made a box plot (Figs. 5 and 6) with the collected data (Tables 11 and 12). Observing these box plots (Figs. 5 and 6)

Table 11. Collected data from the experiment (understanding time).

Subject#	S01	S02	S03	S04	S05	S06	S07	S08	S09	S10
1	60	60	30	75	128	60	35	30	96	45
2	60	89	35	120	55	85	55	75	45	48
3	45	110	30	50	45	105	40	45	70	40
4	60	30	60	90	60	60	30	60	300	150
5	65	50	30	62	50	60	30	45	40	15
6	80	55	30	240	82	85	80	45	27	27
7	125	75	30	270	70	60	60	50	45	80
8	70	64	70	180	90	90	45	45	50	30
9	65	60	50	85	100	60	65	45	65	30
10	105	82	51	89	90	48	35	101	36	38

Table 12. Collected data from the experiment (modification time).

Subject#	S01	S02	S03	S04	S05	S06	S07	S08	S09	S10
1	109	65	45	58	55	60	57	91	75	70
2	150	90	63	80	130	70	140	—	50	238
3	115	145	65	120	125	255	105	155	145	75
4	120	120	50	85	110	180	90	50	120	300
5	240	200	45	95	100	135	65	185	130	120
6	180	190	250	160	95	185	180	150	80	119
7	270	91	25	355	115	205	205	135	120	95
8	180	240	120	175	180	95	125	145	130	135
9	110	155	90	105	100	210	300	55	130	190
10	111	138	72	70	74	100	395	92	—	220

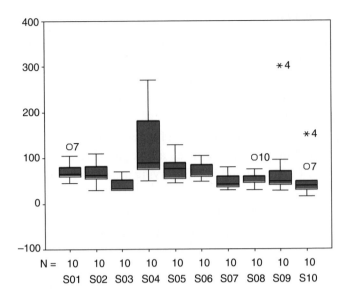

Fig. 5. Box plot of the understanting time.

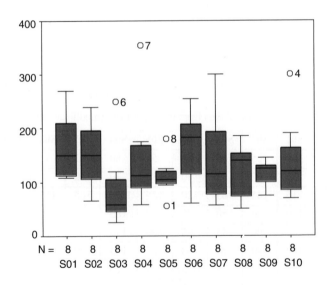

Fig. 6. Box plot of the modification time.

we can observe that there are several outliers (shown in Tables 13 and 15). The outliers values were eliminated from the collected data. The eliminated values are shown in Tables 11 and 12 in italic font. The descriptive statistics of the final set of data can be found in Tables 14 and 16. With this data we perform the analysis.

6.6. *Validity of results*

As we know, different threats to the validity of the results of an experiment exist. In this section, we are going to discuss threats to construct, internal, external and conclusion validity.

Table 13. Outliers.

Schema	Subject Outliers
S01	7
S02	
S03	
S04	
S05	
S06	
S07	
S08	10
S09	4
S10	4.7

Table 14. Descriptive statistics of the understanding time.

	S01	S02	S03	S04	S05
Mean	67.78	67.50	41.60	12610	77.00
Minimum	45	30	30	50	45
Maximum	105	110	70	270	128
Deviation	16.8	22.4	14.98	77.1	26
	S06	S07	S08	S09	S10
Mean	71.30	47.50	48.89	52.67	34.13
Minimum	48	30	30	27	15
Maximum	105	80	75	96	48
Deviation	18.4	16.87	12.4	21.1	10.76

Table 15. Outliers.

Schema	Subject Outliers
S01	
S02	
S03	6
S04	7
S05	1,8
S06	
S07	
S08	
S09	
S10	4

Table 16. Descriptive statistics of the modification time.

	S01	S02	S03	S04	S05
Mean	158.50	143.40	63.89	105.33	106.13
Minimum	109	65	25	58	74
Maximum	270	240	120	175	130
Deviation	58.22	54.94	28.1	39.86	17.93
	S06	S07	S08	S09	S10
Mean	149.50	166.20	117.56	108.89	140.22
Minimum	60	57	50	50	70
Maximum	255	395	185	145	238
Deviation	66.68	108.55	47.3	32.28	61.77

6.6.1. *Construct validity*

The construct validity is the degree to which the independent and the dependent variables are accurately measured by the measurement instruments used in the study. The dependent variables we used are understanding and modification time, i.e. the time each subject spent performing these tasks, so we consider this variable constructively valid. The construct validity of the metrics used for the independent variables is guaranteed by Poels and Dedene's framework (2000) used for their theoretical validation.

6.6.2. *Internal validity*

Regarding internal validity, the following issues should be considered:

- **Differences among subjects.** Within-subject experiments reduce variability among subjects.
- **Differences among schemas.** The domain of the schemas were different and this could influence the results obtained in some way.
- **Precision in the time values.** The subjects were responsible for recording the start and finish times of each test. We think this method is more effective than having a supervisor who records the time of each subject. However, we are aware that the subject could introduce some imprecision.
- **Learning effects.** Using a randomisation function, tests were ordered and given in a distinct order for different subjects. So, each subject answered the tests in the given order. This way we tried to minimise learning effects.
- **Fatigue effects.** The average time for completing the experiment was 31 minutes varying from a minimum of approximately 19 minutes and a maximum of about 35 minutes. With this range of times we think that fatigue effects hardly exist at all. Also, the different order of the tests helped to avoid these fatigue effects.
- **Persistence effects.** In our case persistence effects are not present because the subjects had never participated in a similar experiment.
- **Subject motivation.** Subjects were volunteers and they were convinced that the exercises they were doing are useful for developing metrics for datawarehouses. We think that subjects were motivated during the experiment.
- **Plagiarism and influence among subjects.** In order to avoid these effects, a supervisor was present during the experiment. Subjects were informed that they should not talk to or share answers with other subjects.

6.6.3. *External validity*

Regarding external validity, the following issues should be considered:

- **Materials and tasks used.** We tried to use schemas and operations representative of real cases in the experiments although more experiments with larger and more complex schemas are necessary.

- **Subjects.** Although this experiment was run by professionals we are aware that the number of subjects (10) could be insufficient to generalise the results. We are aware that more experiments with practitioners and professionals must be carried out in order to better generalise the results.

6.6.4. *Conclusion validity*

The conclusion validity defines the extent to which conclusions are statistically valid. The only issue that could affect the statistical validity of this study is the size of the sample data (10 values), which perhaps are not enough for both parametric and non-parametric statistic test (Briand et al., 1995). We are aware of this, so we will try to obtain bigger sample data through more experimentation.

6.7. *Analysis and interpretation*

We used the data collected in order to test the hypotheses formulated previously. As we cannot assure the data we collected follows a common statistical distribution (mainly because we have a very small group of subjects), we decided to apply a non-parametric correlational analysis, avoiding assumptions about the data normality. In this way, we made a correlation statistical analysis using the Spearman's Rho statistic. We used a level of significance, $\alpha = 0.05$.

Table 17 shows the results obtained for the correlation between each of the metrics and the time each subject used to perform the task of understanding each schema. Table 18 shows the same data for the modification tasks.

Analysing Table 17, we can conclude that there is a high correlation between the understanding time used (understandability of the schemas)

Table 17. Results of the experiment (understanding time).

Metrics	NDC	NBC	NC	RBC	NAFC	
Correlation	0.43	0.72	0.72	0.57	0.36	
Significance	0.21	**0.02**	**0.02**	**0.08**	0.31	
Metrics	NADC	NABC	NA	NH	DHP	RSA
Correlation	−0.06	0.77	0.75	0.77	0.47	−0.45
Significance	0.88	**0.01**	**0.01**	**0.01**	0.17	0.19

Table 18. Results of the experiment (modification time).

Metric	NDC	NBC	NC	RBC	NAFC	
Correlation	0.53	0.13	0.21	−0.21	−0.60	
Significance	0.12	0.72	0.56	0.57	0.07	
Metric	NADC	NABC	NA	NH	DHP	RSA
Correlation	0.03	−0.05	−0.09	0.20	0.25	−0.28
Significance	0.94	0.90	0.81	0.57	0.49	0.44

and the metrics NBC, NC, NABC, NA and NH (the value of significance is lower than $\alpha = 0.05$). The other metrics do not seem to be correlated with time. On the other hand, there is no correlation at all between the modification time and the metrics.

Seeing these results, it seems that analysability is closely related to metrics that capture in some sense the "complexity" of the schemas. This complexity is captured by the number of classes of the schemas (size of the schema) and the number of hierarchy relationships in the stars. The modification time is not related with the metrics, perhaps because the modification tasks affects in great manner the modification time.

Pending are the rest of phases of the method for metric definition (see Chapter 7). We consider that further empirical validation is needed before continuing with the rest of the phases. However, we look forward to go further with the method and reach the acceptance phase, obtaining a set of good and valid metrics for datawarehouse conceptual schemas.

7. Conclusions and Future Research

Businesses must manage information as an important product, capitalise on knowledge as a principal asset and by so doing survive and prosper in the digital economy (Huang et al., 1999) in which datawarehouses play an essential role. Consequently, one of the main obligations of information technology professionals is to ensure the quality of the datawarehouses.

We believe that a key factor in relation to quality in datawarehouses is the quality of the conceptual model. Using UML extensions for modelling datawarehouses at a conceptual level, we have proposed a set of metrics for measuring the quality of the conceptual models obtained in the design of the datawarehouses, and these will help designers to choose the best option between several alternative designs (semantically equivalent).

Although we have theoretically validated the metrics used, this is only the first step in the complete definition process of the metrics. By means of experiments, we are currently validating empirically all the metrics presented, which will enable us to discard or refine these metrics. In this chapter, we have presented the first experiment we have made with the metrics for datawarehouse conceptual models. This experiment is the first approach to a complete empirical validation of the metrics.

It would also be advisable to study the influence of the different analysis dimensions (Abelló et al., 2001) on the cognitive complexity of the object-oriented model; as well as the repercussion of using packages in the conceptual modelling of complex and extensive datawarehouses in order to simplify their design (Luján-Mora et al., 2002b).

Acknowledgements

This research is part of the CALIPO project, supported by "Dirección General de Investigación of the Ministerio de Ciencia y Tecnologia" (TIC2003-07804-C05-03). This research is also part of the MESSENGER project, supported by "Consejeria de Ciencia y Tecnología de la Junta de Comunidades de Castilla-La Mancha" (PCC-03-003-1).

We would like to thank all the people in Cronos Iberica who kindly volunteered to take part in this experiment.

References

Abelló, A., Samos, J. and Saltor, F. (2001). Understanding Analysis Dimensions in a Multidimensional Object-Oriented Model. *3rd International Workshop on Design and Management of Data Warehouses (DMDW'2001)*. Interlaken (Switzerland).

Abelló, A., Samos, J. and Saltor, F. (2002). YAM2 (Yet Another Multidimensional Model): An extension of UML. *International Database Engineering & Applications Symposium (IDEAS'02)* July, pp. 172–181.

Adamson, C. and Venerable, M. (1998). *Data Warehouse Design Solutions.* John Wiley and Sons, USA.

Basili, V. and Weiss, D. (1984). A Methodology for Collecting Valid Software Engineering Data. *IEEE Transactions on Software Engineering*, Vol. 10, pp. 728–738.

Briand, L., El Emam, K. and Morasca, S. (1995). Theoretical and Empirical Validation of Software Product Measures. *Technical Report ISERN-95-03*, International Software Engineering Research Network.

Briand, L., Wüst, J. and Lounis, H. (1999). A Comprehensive Investigation of Quality Factors in Object-Oriented Designs: An Industrial Case Study. *21st Int. Conf. Software Engineering*, Los Angeles, pp. 345–354

Bouzeghoub, M., Fabret, F. and Galhardas, H. (2000). Datawarehouse Refreshment. Capitulo 4 in *Fundamentals of Data Warehouses.* Springer.

Bouzeghoub, M. and Kedad, Z. (2002). Quality in Data Warehousing. En: Information and Database Quality. Kluwer Academic Publishers.

Cabbibo, L. and Torlone, R. (1998). A Logical Approach to Multidimensional Databases. *6th International Conference on Extending Database Technology (EDBT'98).* Valencia. Spain. *Lecture Notes in Computer Science 1377*, Springer-Verlag, pp. 183–197.

Calero, C., Piattini, M., Pascual, C. and Serrano, M.A. (2001). Towards Data Warehouse Quality Metrics. *Workshop on Design and Management of Data Warehouses (DMDW'01).*

Cavero, J. M., Piattini, M., Marcos, E. and Sánchez, A. (2001). A Methodology for Datawarehouse Design: Conceptual Modeling. *12th International Conference of the Information Resources Management Association* (IRMA2001). Toronto, Ontario, Canada.

Celko, J. (1995). Don't Warehouse Dirty Data. *Datamation*, 15 October, pp. 42–52.

Chaudhuri, S. and Dayal, U. (1997). An Overview of Data Warehousing and OLAP Technology. *ACM SIGMOD Record*, Vol. 26, No. 1.

English, L. (1996). *Information Quality Improvement: Principles, Methods and Management, Seminar*, 5th Ed. Brentwood, TN: Information Impact International, Inc.

Genero, M. (2002). Defining and Validating Metrics for Conceptual Models. Ph.D. Thesis, University of Castilla-La Mancha.

Genero, M., Olivas, J., Piattini, M. and Romero, F. (2001). Using Metrics to Predict OO Information Systems Maintainability. *Proc. of 13th International Conference on Advanced Information Systems Engineering (CAiSE'01). Lecture Notes in Computer Science 2068*, pp. 388–401.

Genero, M., Jiménez, L. and Piattini, M. (2002). A Controlled Experiment for Validating Class Diagram Structural Complexity Metrics. *Proc. of the 8th International Conference on Object-Oriented Information Systems (OOIS'2002). Lecture Notes in Computer Science 2425*, pp. 372–383.

Golfarelli, M., Maio, D. and Rizzi, S. (1998). Conceptual Design of Data Warehouses from E/R Schemes. *31st Hawaii International Conference on System Sciences.*

Golfarelli, M. and Rizzi, S. (1999). Designing the Data Warehouse: Key Steps and Crucial Issues. *Journal of Computer Science and Information Management*, Vol. 2, No. 3.

Harinarayan, V., Rajaraman, A. and Ullman, J. D. (1996). Implementing Data Cubes Efficiently. *Proc. of the 1996 ACM SIGMOD International Conference on Management of Data*, Eds. Jagadish, H. V. and Mumick, I. S., pp. 205–216.

Huang, K-T., Lee, Y.W. and Wang, R.Y. (1999). *Quality Information and Knowledge*. Prentice-Hall, Upper Saddle River.

Inmon, W.H. (1997). Building the Data Warehouse, 2nd edition. John Wiley and Sons, USA.

ISO (2001). ISO International Standard ISO/IEC 9126. Information Technology — Software Product Evaluation. ISO, Geneve.

Jarke, M., Lenzerini, M., Vassiliou, Y. and Vassiliadis, P. (2000). *Fundamentals of Data Warehouses*. Springer.

Kimball, R. (1996). *The Data Warehouse Toolkit*. John Wiley & Sons.

Kimball, R., Reeves, L., Ross, M. and Thornthwaite, W. (1998). *The Data Warehouse Lifecycle Toolkit*, John Wiley and Sons, USA.

Labio, W., Quass, D. and Adelberg, B. (1997). Physical Database Design for Data Warehouses. *13th International Conference on Data Engineering*. IEEE Computer Society, Birmingham, UK, pp. 277–288.

Loshin, D. (2001). *Enterprises Knowledge Management: The Data Quality Approach*. Morgan Kauffman, San Francisco (California).

Luján-Mora, S., Trujillo, J. and Song, I.-Y. (2002a). Extending UML for Multidimensional Modeling. *5th International Conference on the Unified Modeling Language* (UML 2002). *Lecture Notes in Computer Science 2460*, pp. 290–304.

Luján-Mora, S., Trujillo, J. and Song, I.-Y. (2002b). Multidimensional Modeling with UML Package Diagrams. *21st International Conference on Conceptual Modeling* (ER 2002). *Lecture Notes in Computer Science 2503*, pp. 199–213.

Piattini, M., Calero, C. and Genero, M. (2002). *Information and Database Quality*, EEUU, Kluwer Academic Publishers.

Poels, G. and Dedene, G. (2000). Distance-Based Software Measurement: Necessary and Sufficient Properties for Software Measures. *Information and Software Technology*, Vol. 42, No. 1, pp. 35–46.

Redman, T.C. (1996). *Data Quality for the Information Age.* Artech House Publishers, Boston.

Sapia, C., Blaschka, M., Höfling, G. and Dinter, B. (1998). Extending the E/R Model for the Multidimensional Paradigm. *ER Workshops 1998*, Singapore, *Lecture Notes in Computer Science (LNCS) 1552*, pp. 105–116.

Serrano, M., Calero, C., Coimbra, C. and Piattini, M. (2001). Métricas de calidad para almacenes de datos. *Proceedings of the VI Jornadas de Ingeniería del Software y Bases de Datos (JISBD'2001)*, Eds. Ciudad Real, Díaz, O., Illarramendi, A. y Piattini, M., pp. 537–548.

Serrano, M., Calero, C. and Piattini, M. (2002). Validating Metrics for Datawarehouses. *IEE Proceedings SOFTWARE*, Vol. 149, No. 5, pp. 161–166.

Serrano, M., Calero, C. and Piattini, M. (2003). Experimental Validation of Multidimensional Data Models Metrics, *Proc of the Hawaii International Conference on System Sciences* (HICSS'36), IEEE Computer Society.

Suppes, P., Krantz, D., Luce, R. and Tversky A. (1989). *Foundations of Measurement: Geometrical, Threshold, and Probabilistic Representations*, 2, San Diego, Calif., Academic Press.

Tryfona, N., Busborg, F. and Christiansen, G.B. (1999) starER: A Conceptual Model for Data Warehouse Design. *Proceedings of the ACM Second International Workshop on Data Warehousing and OLAP (DOLAP'99)*, Kansas City, USA, pp. 3–8.

Trujillo, J., Palomar, M., Gómez, J. and Song, I.-Y. (2001). Designing Data Warehouses with OO Conceptual Models. *IEEE Computer*, Special issue on Data Warehouses, Vol. 34, No. 12, pp. 66–75.

Vassiliadis, P. (2000). *Data Warehouse Modeling and Quality Issues.* Ph.D. Thesis. National Technical University of Athens.

Zuse, H. (1998). *A Framework of Software Measurement.* Berlin. Walter de Gruyter.

Chapter 7

METRICS FOR UML STATECHART
DIAGRAMS

JOSÉ ANTONIO CRUZ-LEMUS[*,a], MARCELA GENERO[†,c]
and MARIO PIATTINI[‡,c]

*Department of Computer Science, University of Castilla La Mancha
Ciudad Real – Spain
[a]jacruz@proyectos.inf-cr.uclm.es
[b]Marcela.Genero@uclm.es
[c]Mario.Piattini@uclm.es

1. Introduction

When modelling OO software with UML (Object Management Group, 1999) the static aspects at conceptual level are mainly represented in structural diagrams such as class diagrams, whilst dynamic aspects are represented in behavioural diagrams such as use case diagrams, statechart diagrams, activity diagrams, sequence diagrams and collaboration diagrams.

In software engineering, it is widely recognised that the structural properties of conceptual models, i.e. those models obtained at early phases of the development have a great influence on the quality of the software product that is finally implemented. For this reason, as Chapter 4 reveals, several proposals of metrics exists for structural diagrams, such as proposals of metrics that can be applied to measure the size, structural complexity, coupling, etc. of UML class diagrams. The behavioural diagrams have been slightly disregarded in the software measurement field. Since the late 90's, some proposals of metrics for use cases diagrams have appeared (see Chapter 3). However, there is little reference to metrics for behavioural diagrams such as UML statechart diagrams, sequence diagrams, activity diagrams and collaboration diagrams in the existing literature (see Sec. 2).

Despite this situation, several authors such as Poels and Dedene (2000b) and Brito e Abreu et al. (2000; 2002) among others, pointed out that the definition of metrics for diagrams that capture dynamics aspects of OO software is an interesting topic for investigation. This fact motivated us to start working on metrics for UML behavioural diagrams, starting with UML statechart diagrams and this chapter is the fruit of the research we have been doing for the last three years.

The goal of this chapter is two-fold:

(1) To present an overview of the existing metrics that can be applied to statechart diagrams.
(2) To define a new set of valid metrics for the structural complexity and size of UML statechart diagrams in a methodogical way. To achieve this purpose, we will follow a process for metric definition, which has emerged as an integration of two main proposals — Calero et al. (2001) and Cantone and Donzelli (2000). This process assures to some extent that the proposed metrics are valid in two senses — theoretical and empirical.

The rest of the chapter is organised as follows: Section 2 addresses the first goal of the chapter, which is to show the state-of-the-art for metrics for statechart diagrams. Section 3 briefly introduces the process we have followed to obtain valid metrics. Section 4 identifies the metric goals. From Sec. 5 to Sec. 7, our own set of metrics is defined and also validated. Finally, Sec. 8 provides some concluding remarks and points out some topics that should be considered in the near future.

2. State-of-the-Art About Metrics for UML Statechart Diagrams

After having thoroughly reviewed existing works about metrics which measure quality aspects, there is little reference to metrics for behavioural diagrams such as UML statechart diagrams in the existing literature. In any case, in this section we will go over the metrics proposals for diagrams that cover dynamic aspects of OO software systems.

2.1. *Derr's metrics*

One of the first approaches towards the definition of metrics for behavioural diagrams can be found in (Derr, 1995), where a group of metrics (see Table 1) were applied to statechart diagrams developed with OMT (Rumbaugh et al., 1991).

Derr only defined these metrics but he did not provide any theoretical or empirical validation of them.

2.2. *Poels and Dedene's metrics*

Poels and Dedene (2000b) defined structural complexity metrics for event-driven OO conceptual models using MERODE (Snoeck, 1995).

They consider that objects in a certain domain are affected by the occurrence of events and that all objects identified during conceptual modelling are persistent, i.e. they have a state, represented at any moment by the values of their attributes.

The dynamic perspective on conceptual modelling is captured in a *object type — event type* association matrix. Each conceptual schema has one object type — event type association matrix composed of a series of associations that relate one event type with one object type. Each event has two attributes — the type of involvement (creation (C), ending (E) or modification (M) of an event state) and the type of provenance of the association (inheritance (I), propagation (A) or new definition (O)).

The proposed metrics relate several aspects of the complexity with the size and the structure of the conceptual schema under a dynamic viewpoint. Many measurements are obtained by looking directly at the object type — event type association matrix. Nevertheless, if this matrix is too simple,

Table 1. Derr's metrics.

Attribute measured	Metrics
Transition Complexity	Number of States Number of Transitions

Table 2. Poels and Dedene's metrics.

Type	Metrics	Description
Size	Level of Event Participation (LEP)	$LEP(S) = \sum_{P \in t} \#\{E \in A \mid \tau(e, P) \neq \text{"/"}\}$
Structure	Level of Object Type Coupling (LOTC)	$LOTC(S) = \sum_{P \in T} \#\{Q \in T - \{P\} \mid \exists e \in A : \tau(e, P) \neq \text{"/"} \wedge \tau(e, Q) \neq \text{"/"}\}$
	Degree of Object Type Coupling (DOTC)	$DOTC(S) = LOTC(S)/(\#T.(\#T - 1))$
	Level of Inheritance of Event Participation (LIEP)	$LIEP(S) = \sum_{P \in T} \#\{e \in A \mid \tau_P(e, P) = I\}$
	Level of Propagation of Event Participation (LPEP)	$LPEP(S) = \sum_{P \in T} \#\{e \in A \mid \tau_P(e, P) = A\}$
	Degree of Inheritance of Event Participation (DIEP)	$DIEP(S) = LIEP(S)/LEP(S)$
	Degree of Propagation of Event Participation (DIEP)	$DPEP(S) = LPEP(S)/LEP(S)$
Dynamic Behaviour Complexity	Level of Synchronisation-based Coupling (LSC)	$LSC(S) = \sum_{P \in T} \#\{Q \in T - \{P\} \mid \exists e \in A : (\tau_I(e, P) = C \wedge \tau_I(e, Q) = E) \vee (\tau_I(e, P) = E \wedge \tau_I(e, Q) = C)\}$
	Degree of Synchronisation-based Coupling (DSC)	$DSC(S) = LSC(S)/LOTC(S)$
Distance	Object Life Cycle Complexity (OLCC)	The greatest distance between the actual life cycle specifications and the default life cycle specifications.

some additional information is needed and should be fetched from the specifications of the object life cycle.

A series of metrics are proposed (see Table 2) based on the size, the structure, the dynamic behaviour complexity and the distance. They are defined and theoretically validated using the DISTANCE framework. The authors state that there is no empirical confirmation of the usefulness of the metrics yet, although it is a goal for future research.

2.3. *Cartwright and Shepperd's metrics*

Cartwright and Shepperd (2000) carried out an empirical investigation in the system of a telecommunication company, certificated by ISO 9000, using 13 metrics (9 internal for the analysis phase, and other 4 external) that can be seen in Table 3.

The authors were searching for a relationship between the values obtained for both internal and external metrics in order to build prediction models for the external attributes, such as the system size or the defects number.

They concluded that using straightforward techniques based upon linear regression is possible to build accurate prediction systems both for size and defects. This could be achieved using a small number of measures that are all readily available early in the analysis and design stage.

Also, the patterns in the distribution of defects may enable software managers to better allocate resources.

There is no theoretical validation presented for any of the metrics.

2.4. *Carbone and Santucci's metrics*

Carbone and Santucci (2002) present a method for estimating the complexity of a class in a software project developed under the OO paradigm. This

Table 3. Cartwright and Shepperd's metrics.

Metrics	Description
ATTRIB	Count of attributes per class from the information model
STATES	Count of states per class in the state model
EVNT	Count of events per class in the state model
READS	Count of all read accesses by a class contained in the CASE tool
WRITES	Count of all write accesses by a class contained in the CASE tool
DELS	Count of all delete accesses by a class contained in the CASE tool
RWD	Count of synchronous accesses (i.e. the sum of READS, WRITES and DELS) per class from the CASE tool
DIT	Depth of a class in the inheritance tree where the root class is zero
NOC	Number of child classes
LOC	Lines of code per class
LOC_B	Body file lines of code per class
LOC_H	Header file lines of code per class
DFCT	Count of defects per class

Table 4. Carbone and Santucci's metrics for UML statechart diagrams.

Metrics	Name
totSta(c)	Total amount of states for the class c
totAction(c)	Total amount of actions for the class c

method receives information from different UML diagrams and applies a
group of metrics defined for class diagrams. This way, a CP (Class Point)
coefficient is obtained and it can be used for determining the complexity
of the final system by applying it to the interaction, use case and statechart
diagrams of the design.

We are interested in metrics proposed for statechart diagrams (see
Table 4). We will take them into account when facing the definition of our
own metrics for calculating the structural complexity of UML statechart
diagrams.

The use of these metrics is limited to the calculation of the CP coefficient, without worrying about their theoretical or empirical validation.

2.5. *Conclusions of the state-of-the-art*

Looking at Table 5, which summarises the metrics proposals previously
outlined, we can conclude that:

- Most of these proposals of metrics have not gone beyond the definition
  step.
- There are no metrics defined to UML statechart diagrams (except
  Carbone and Santucci's proposal).
- The work related to their empirical and theoretical validation is scarce.

The state-of-the-art reveals what was said in the introduction, that the
behavioural diagrams have been disregarded in the software measurement
arena. To contribute to this deficiency, we will present in the following
sections the process we have followed to define some metrics for UML
statechart diagrams structural complexity and size, their definition and their
validation.

Table 5. Proposals of metrics for behavioural diagrams.

Proposal authors	Scope	Goal	Theoretical validation	Empirical validation
Derr (1995)	OMT	Model and Statechart Diagrams Complexity	No	No
Poels and Dedene (2000b)	MERODE	Conceptual Schema Complexity	Yes	No
Cartwright and Shepperd (2000)	Shlaer and Mellor	Size and Number of Defects	No	Partial
Carbone and Santucci (2002)	UML	Class Complexity	No	No

3. Process for Metric Definition

In this section, we briefly introduce the method we have followed for obtaining valid metrics for UML statechart diagrams maintainability. The method shown in Fig. 1, has been developed using the method proposed by Calero et al. (2001) and the Measure Model Life Cycle proposed by Cantone and Donzelli (2000). In this figure, continuous lines show the metric flow and dotted lines show the information flow. This approach is based both on measurement theory and on an experimental research methodology, stemming mainly from current research in the field of empirical software engineering.

This method has five main steps going from the identification of goals and hypotheses to the metric application and retirement:

- **Identification.** Goals of the metric are defined and measuring of hypotheses are planned. All the following phases will be based upon these goals and hypotheses. As a result of this phase we should obtain the metric requirements.
- **Creation.** This is the main phase, in which the metric is defined and validated formally and empirically. This phase is divided into three subphases:
  - *Metrics definition.* The first step is the proposal of metrics. This definition should be made taking into account the specific characteristics of the software artefact we want to measure, in our case the UML

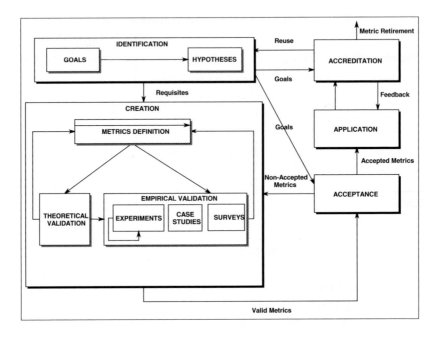

Fig. 1. Process for metric definition.

statechart diagrams and the experience of the OO modellers and OO designers. It is also advisable to use the Goal-Question-Metric (GQM) template (Basili and Weiss, 1984; Basili and Rombach, 1988; Van Solingen and Berghout, 1999) for goal definition, to define the metrics goals.

– *Theoretical validation.* The theoretical validation should be carried out in order to discover whether the metric we propose really measures the attribute it purports to measure. Moreover theoretical validation provides knowledge about metric scales, for which it is important to know which are the suitable statistical tests we have to apply to metrics values when we carry out empirical studies.

Work on theoretical validation has followed two paths:

• Measurement-theory-based approaches such as those proposed by Zuse (1998) and Poels and Dedene (2000b).
• Property-based approaches (also called axiomatic approaches), such as those proposed by Weyuker (1988) and Briand et al. (1996).

In this work, the theoretical validation of the UML statechart diagrams structural complexity and size metrics is presented using a measurement-theory-based approach such as, Poels and Dedene's framework (2000b) and a property-based approach, such us, Briand et al.'s framework (Briand et al., 1996).

- *Empirical validation.* The goal of this step is to prove the practical utility of the proposed metrics. Although there are various ways of performing this step, basically we can divide the empirical validation into experiments, case studies and surveys.

This creation step is evolutionary and iterative, and as a result of the feedback, the metric could be redefined or discarded depending on its theoretical and empirical validation. As a result of this phase, we should obtain a valid metric.

- **Acceptance.** The aim of this step is the systematic experimentation of the metric. This is applied to a context suitable for the reproduction of the characteristics of the application environment, with real projects and real users, to verify its performance against the initial goals and stated requirements.

- **Application.** The accepted metric is used in real projects.

- **Accreditation.** This is the final step of the process. It is a dynamic step that proceeds simultaneously with the application phase. The goal of this step is the maintenance of the metric, so it can be adapted to application changing environment. As a result of this step the metric can be retired or reused for a new metric definition process.

4. Identification of Metric Goals

The main goal is to define a set of valid metrics for the structural complexity and size of UML statechart diagrams in a methodological way and investigate through experimentation if they are related to the understandability of UML statechart diagrams.[1] If such a relationship exists and is confirmed

---

[1]The theoretical basis for developing quantitative models relating to structural properties (size and structural complexity) and external quality attributes (understandability, maintainability) is based on the model provided by Briand et al. (1998) and the standard ISO 9126 (2001).

by empirical studies, we will have really obtained early indicators of UML statechart diagram understandability. We consider the understandability because it is an external quality attribute which directly influences several quality characteristics (ISO, 2001), among others maintainability.[2]

5. Definition of Metrics for UML Statechart Diagrams Strcutural Complexity

The structural complexity and size of a statechart diagram is determined by the different elements that compose it, such as states, transitions, activities, etc. It is not advisable to define a single measure for the structural complexity and size of UML statechart diagrams, since a single measure cannot capture all possible aspects or viewpoints of complexity and size (Fenton, 1994). Instead several measures are needed, each one focusing on a different UML statechart diagram's elements. Therefore, before explaining our proposal, we will briefly go over the main elements of a UML statechart diagram.

5.1. *Statechart diagrams elements*

Based on the UML metamodel (Object Management Group, 2001), our measurement experience, what UML elements could have more influence on UML statechart diagram structural complexity and size, and looking to the statechart diagrams that are most commonly modelled, we consider the following UML constructs:

- **Action.** An action is a specification of an executable statement that forms an abstraction of a computational procedure that results in a change in the state of the model, and can be carried out by sending a message to an object or modifying a link or a value of an attribute. In a state, we can find several types of actions: *entry actions*, *exit actions* and *do/Activity actions*, i.e. sequences of actions that are executed consecutively while staying in the state.

---

[2]There exists a lot of work related to software measurement, that consider understandability to be a factor that influences maintainability (Fenton and Pflegeer, 1997; Harrison et al., 2001).

- **State.** A state is an abstract metaclass that models a situation during which some invariant condition holds. This invariant may represent a static situation such as an object waiting for some external event to occur. However, it can also model dynamic conditions such as the process of performing some activity; that is, the model element under consideration enters the state when the activity commences and leaves it as soon as the activity is completed.
- **Composite State.** A composite state is a state that contains other states vertices (states, pseudostates, etc.). The association between the composite and the contained vertices is a composition association. Hence, a state vertex can be a part of at most one composite state.
- **Simple State.** A simple state is a state that does not have substates.
- **Event.** An event is the specification of a type of observable occurrence. The occurrence that generates an event instance is assumed to take place at an instant in time with no duration. Strictly speaking, the term 'event' is used to refer to the type and not to an instance of the type. However, on occasion, where the meaning is clear from the context, the term is also used to refer to an event instance. An event can have the association *parameter,* that specifies the list of parameters defined for the event.
- **Guard.** A guard is a boolean expression that is attached to a transition as a fine-grained control over its firing. The guard is evaluated when an event instance is dispatched by the state machine. If the guard is true at that time, the transition is enabled, otherwise, it is disabled. Guards should be pure expressions without side effects and have the attribute *expression,* which is the boolean expression that specifies the guard.
- **Transition.** A transition is a directed relationship between a source state vertex and a target state vertex. It may be part of a compound transition, which takes the state machine from one state configuration to another, representing the complete response of the state machine to a particular event instance.

5.2. *Proposal of metrics*

Once we identified the UML statechart diagram elements, we proceed to define the metrics, which are shown in Table 6.

Table 6. Metrics for UML statechart diagrams.

	Metric name	Metric definition
Size metrics	NEntryA (Number of entry actions)	The total number of entry actions, i.e. the actions performed each time a state is entered
	NexitA (Number of exit actions)	The total number of exit actions, i.e. the actions performed each time a state is left
	NA (Number of activities)	The total number of activities (do/activity)
	NSS (Number of simple states)	The total number of states considering also the simple states within the composites states
	NCS (Number of composite states)	The total number of composite states
	NE (Number of events)	The total number of events
	NG (Number of guards)	The total numbers of guard conditions
Structural complexity metrics	McCabe (Cyclomatic Number of McCabe [29].[3]	It is defined as $|NSS|-|NT| + 2$
	NT (Number of transitions)	The total number of transitions, considering common transitions (the source and the target states are different), the initial and final transitions, self-transitions (the source and the target states are the same) and internal transitions (transitions inside a state that responds to an event but without leaving the state)

The ISO 9126 (2001) requires certain properties for metrics used for comparison. The metrics we propose accomplish those properties, because:

- They are objective, i.e. there is an agreed procedure for assigning values to the metrics.
- They are empirical, i.e. the data is obtained by observation.

---

[3]Even tough the Cyclomatic Number of McCabe was defined to calculate single module complexity and entire system complexity, we adapted it for measuring the structural complexity of UML statechart diagrams.

• They are repeatable, i.e. the procedures for measurement result in the same measures being obtained by different persons making the same measurement of the same UML statechart diagram on different occasions.

The ISO 9126 (2001) also proposes that the metrics shall be characterised in an interval or higher scale. This property is evaluated by the theoretical validation, presented in Sec. 6. Moreover, as the ISO 9126 (2001) demand the metrics have predictive validity. This fact can be evaluated by the empirical validation discussed in Sec. 7.

Another relevant property is that the proposed metrics are simple, which as Fenton and Neil (2000) remark in a work related to the future of software metrics, is a desirable property for software metrics in general.

5.3. *An example*

In order to clarify how to calculate the metric values, Table 7 presents the metrics values calculated on the statechart diagrams of Fig. 2.

Table 7. Metric values.

Metrics	Value	Explanation
NEntryA	1	*Emit message* in INVALID state
NExitA	0	There are no exit actions in this diagram
NA	4	*Dial tone* (GET TONE), *Check* (*Number complete*) (DIALING), *Start occupied tone* (OCCUPIED), *Emit ring* (RINGING)
NSS	9	IDLE, GET TONE, DIALING, DISCONNECTING, OCCUPIED, TALKING, INVALID, CONNECTING, RINGING
NCS	1	ACTIVE
NE	11	One for each labelled arrow connecting two states in the diagram
NG	4	*Number non complete* (DIALING-DIALING), *Number non complete* (DIALING-OCCUPIED), *Number complete and invalid* (DIALING-INVALID), *Number complete and valid* (DIALING-CONNECTING)
NT	13	One for each arrow connecting two states in the diagram
McCabe	2	$|NSS - NT + 2| = |9 - 13 + 2| = |-2| = 2$

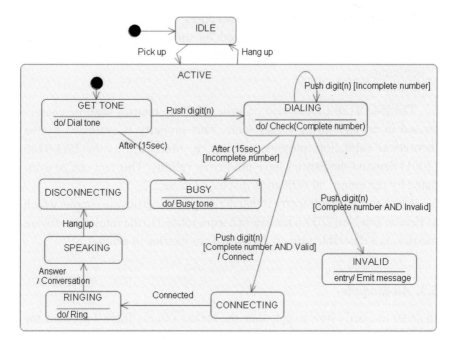

Fig. 2. Statechart diagram of a phone call.

6. Theoretical Validation of the Proposed Metrics

For the theoretical validation of the proposed metrics we followed Briand et al.'s framework (1996) as a property-based framework and Poels and Dedene's framework (Poels and Dedene, 2000a) as a measurement-theory-based framework.

6.1. *Theoretical validation using Briand et al.'s framework*

Briand et al.'s framework (1996) provides a set of mathematical properties that characterise and formalise several important measurement concepts such as size, length, complexity, cohesion and coupling, related to internal software attributes (see Chapter 5 for a further explanation of the foundation of this framework).

6.1.1. *Theoretical validation of NSS metric*

For our purpose and in accordance with Briand et al.'s framework (1996), we consider that a statechart diagram is a system composed of states (elements) and transitions (relations). A module is composed of a subset of the states and transitions. We will demonstrate that NSS fulfils all of the axioms that characterise size metrics, as follows:

- *Nonnegativity.* The number of states in a statechart diagram is always greater than zero, so that NSS can never be negative.
- *Null value.* If we have no states, NSS $= 0$.
- *Module additivity.* If we consider that a statechart diagram is composed of modules with no states in common, the number of states of an statechart diagram will always be the sum of the number of states of its modules.

Following an analogous reasoning used for NSS metric, it can be proved that the other metrics related to internal transitions, such as NCS and NE are also size metrics.

6.1.2. *Theoretical validation of NT metric*

Following the same explanation given in the previous section, we will demonstrate that NT fulfils all of the axioms that characterise complexity metrics, as follows:

- *Nonnegativity.* It is obvious that there is always a null or positive value of transitions. Then, NT ≥ 0.
- *Null value.* If there are no transitions within an statechart diagram, then NT $= 0$.
- *Symmetry.* The number of transitions does not depend on the convention used to represent the transitions.
- *Module monotonicity.* According to the definition of this property, it is obvious that being m_1 and m_2, any two modules of the statechart diagram with no transitions in common, have the value of NT(SD) $\geq$ NT(m_1) + NT(m_2).
- *Disjoint module additivity.* Let m_1 and m_2 be any two disjoint modules such that SD $= m_1 \cup m_2$. Let NT$_1$ and NT$_2$ be the number of transitions in the m_1 and m_2 modules. Obviously: NT $=$ NT$_1$ + NT$_2$, because m_1 and m_2 are disjoint modules.

6.1.3. *Theoretical validation of NA metric*

In this case, we consider that states are system modules, the activities are the elements and relationships are represented by the relation "belong to", which reflects that each activity belongs to a state. We will demonstrate that NA fulfils all of the axioms that characterise size metrics, as follows:

- *Nonnegativity.* One state can or cannot have activities, i.e. it could happen that NA = 0 or NA > 0, but never NA < 0.
- *Null value.* If we have no activities then NA = 0.
- *Module additivity.* If we consider that a state is composed of substates (modules) with no activities in common, the NA of a state will always be the sum of the NA of all its substates, because each activity of a substate is an activity of the state.

A similar reasoning can be used to prove that other metrics related to internal transitions, such as NEntryA, NExitA and NG are also size metrics.

Table 8 summarises the proposed metrics and the properties of Briand et al.'s framework:

6.2. *Theoretical validation using the DISTANCE framework*

A property-based approach such as Briand et al.'s framework proposes a measure property set that is necessary but not sufficient (Briand et al., 1996;

Table 8. Metrics for UML statechart diagrams and the properties of Briand et al.'s framework.

Properties	NSS, NCS, NE, NEntryA, ExitA, NG	NT
Nonnegativity	×	×
Null value	×	×
Module additivity	×	
Disjoint modules Additivity		×
Symmetry		×
Module monotonicity		×
	Size	Complexity

Poels and Dedene, 2000a). They can be used as a filter to reject proposed measures (Kitchenham and Stell, 1997), but they are not sufficient to prove the validity of the measure.

Measurement theory-based approaches to software metric validation, like DISTANCE (Poels and Dedene, 2000a), propose methods to verify whether these conditions hold for software metrics. Their use of measurement theory as the reference theory for measurement distinguishes these approaches from property-based approaches to metric validation, like Briand et al.'s framework, which is based on argumentation, subjective experience or even intuition, instead of having a well-established theoretical base (Poels and Dedene, 1997).

The DISTANCE framework offers a measure construction procedure to model properties of software artefacts and define the corresponding software metrics. An important pragmatic consequence of the explicit link with measurement theory is that the resulting measures define ratio scales (see Chapter 4 for a deeper explanation of this framework).

6.2.1. *Theoretical validation of NSS metric*

In this section, we will follow each of the steps for measure construction proposed in the DISTANCE framework for the metric NSS. In order to exemplify the process we will use the UML statechart diagrams shown in Fig. 3.

Step 1: Find a measurement abstraction. In our case the set of software entities is the Universe of Statechart Diagrams (USD) that are relevant to some application domains where p is an SD (i.e. $p \in$ USD). The attribute of interest is the number of simple states, i.e. a particular aspect of statechart diagrams size. Let US be the Universe of States relevant to an application domain. The set of states within an SD, denoted by $S(SD)$, is a subset of USD. All the sets of states within the statechart diagrams of USD are elements of the power set of US, denoted by $\wp(US)$. We can therefore equate the set of measurement abstractions to $\wp(US)$ and define the abstraction function as:

$$abs_{NS} \colon USD \to \wp(UAS) \colon SD \to S(SD),$$

where SD is a function that projects a statechart diagram upon its set of states.

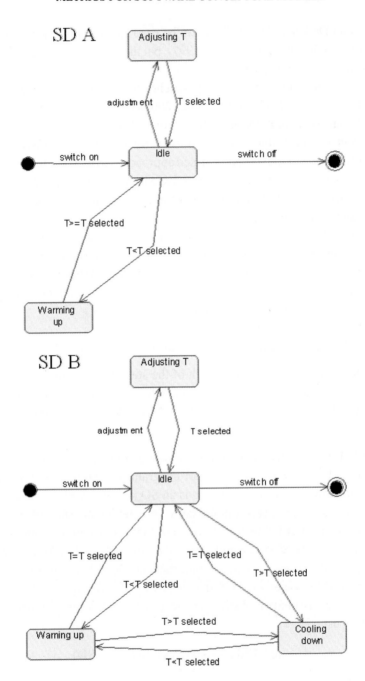

Fig. 3. An example of an UML statechart diagram.

Example:

$$abs_{NS}(\text{SD } A) = S(\text{SD } A) = \{A, B, C\}$$
$$abs_{NS}(\text{SD } B) = S(\text{SD } B) = \{A, B, D\}.$$

Step 2: Model distances between measurement abstractions. The next step is to model distances between the elements of $\wp(US)$. We need to find a set of elementary transformation types for the set of measurement abstractions $\wp(US)$ so that any set of simple states can be transformed into any other set of simple states by means of a finite sequence of elementary transformations. Finding such a set in the case of a power set is a trivial task. Since the elements of $\wp(US)$ are sets of states, T_e must only contain two types of elementary transformations: one for adding a state to a set and one for removing a state from a set. Given two sets of associations $s_1 \in \wp(US)$ and $s_2 \in \wp(US)$, s_1 can always be transformed into s_2 by removing first all states from s_1 that are not in s_2, and then adding all states to s_1 that are in s_2, but not in the original s_1. In the 'worst case scenario', s_1 must be transformed into s_2 via an empty set of associations. Formally, $T_e = \{t_{0\text{-NSS}}, t_{1\text{-NSS}}\}$, where $t_{0\text{-NSS}}$ and $t_{1\text{-NSS}}$ are defined as:

$$t_{0\text{-NSS}}: \wp(US) \rightarrow \wp(US): s \rightarrow s \cup \{a\}, \quad \text{with } a \in US$$
$$t_{1\text{-NSS}}: \wp(US) \rightarrow \wp(US): s \rightarrow s - \{a\}, \quad \text{with } a \in US.$$

In our example, the distance between $abs_{NSS}(\text{SD } A)$ and $abs_{NSS}(\text{SD } B)$ can be modelled by a sequence of elementary transformations that remove the state C from $S(\text{SD } A)$ and add the state D to $S(\text{SD } A)$. This sequence of two elementary transformations is sufficient to transform $S(\text{SD } A)$ into $S(\text{SD } B)$. All the 'shortest' sequences of elementary transformations qualify as models of distance.

Step 3: Quantify distances between measurement abstractions. In this step the distances in $\wp(US)$ that can be modelled by applying sequences of elementary transformations of the types contained in T_e are quantified. A function δ_{NSS} of these distances is a metric (in a mathematical sense) that is defined by the symmetric difference model, i.e. a particular instance of the contrast model of Tversky (Suppes et al., 1989). It has been proven in Poels (1999) that the symmetric difference model can always be used to define a metric when the set of measurement abstractions is a power set:

$$\delta_{\text{NSS}}: \wp(\text{US}) \times \wp(\text{US}) \to \mathfrak{R}: (s, s') \to (|s - s'| + |s' - s|).$$

This definition is equivalent to stating that the distance between two sets of associations, as modelled by a shortest sequence of elementary transformations between them, is measured by the count of elementary transformations in the sequence. Note that for any element in s but not in s' and for any element in s' but not in s, an elementary transformation is needed.

The symmetric difference model results in a value of 2 for the distance between the set of associations of SD A and SD B.

$$\delta_{\text{NSS}}(abs_{\text{NSS}}(\text{SD } A), abs_{\text{NSS}}(\text{SD } B))$$
$$= |\{A, B, C\} - \{A, B, D\}| + \{A, B, D\} - \{A, B, C\}|$$
$$= |\{C\}| + |\{D\}| = 2.$$

Step 4: Find a reference abstraction. In our example, the obvious reference point for measurement is the empty set of associations. It is desirable that a statechart diagram without states should have the lowest possible value for the NSS measure. So we define the following function:

$$ref_{\text{NSS}}: \text{USD} \to \wp(\text{US}): \text{SD} \to \emptyset$$

Step 5: Define the software measure. In our example, the number of states of a statechart diagram SD $\in$ USD can be defined as the distance between its set of states $S(\text{SD})$ and the empty set of states $\emptyset$. Hence, the NSS measure can be defined as a function that returns the value of the metric δ_{NSS} for the pair of sets $S(\text{SD})$ and $\emptyset$ for any statechart diagram:

$$\forall \text{SD} \in \text{USD}: \text{NSS}(\text{SD}) = \delta_{\text{NSS}}(S(\text{SD}), \emptyset)$$
$$= |S(\text{SD}) - \emptyset| + |\emptyset - S(\text{SD})| = |S(\text{SD})|.$$

Consequently, a measure that returns the count of states within a statechart diagram qualifies as a number of states measure.

The rest of the proposed statechart diagram metrics can be modelled by means of a set abstraction (see Table 9) and as a consequence all the measures take the form of a simple count, so their process construction is analogous followed by the metric NSS.

Table 9. Abstract functions for the rest of UML class diagram metrics.

Metric	Abstraction function
NSS	*abs*NSS: USD → $\wp$ (USS): SD → SSS(SD) where USS is the Universe of Simple States relevant to an UoD, SSS(SD) ⊆ USS is the set of simple states within an SD
NCS	*abs*NCS: USD → $\wp$ (UCS): SD → SCS(CD) where US is the Universe of Composite States relevant to an UoD, SCS(SD) ⊆ US is the set of Composite States within a SD
NE	*abs*NE: USD → $\wp$ (UE): SD → SE(SD) where UE is the Universe of Events relevant to an UoD, SE(SD) ⊆ UE is the set of events within an SD
NA	*abs*NA: USD → $\wp$ (UA): SD → SA(SD) where UA is the Universe of Activities relevant to an UoD, SA(SD) ⊆ UA is the set of activities within an SD
NEntryA	*abs*NEntryA: USD → $\wp$ (UEntryA): SD → SEntryA(SD) where UEntryA is the Universe of Entry Actions relevant to an UoD, SentryA(SD) ⊆ UEntryA is the set of entry actions within an SD
NExitA	*abs*NExitA: USD → $\wp$ (UExitA): SD → SExitA(SD) where UExitA is the Universe of Exit Actions relevant to an UoD, SExitA(SD) ⊆ UExitA is the set of exit actions within an SD
NG	*abs*NG: USD → $\wp$ (UG): SD → SG(SD) where US is the Universe of Guards relevant to an UoD, SG(SD) ⊆ UG is the set of guards within an SD
NT	*abs*NT: USD → $\wp$ (UT): SD → ST(SD) where US is the Universe of Transitions relevant to an UoD, ST(SD) ⊆ UT is the set of transitions within an SD

7. Empirical Validation of the Proposed Metrics

In this section, we describe an experiment and its replication, which we carried out to empirically validate the proposed metrics as early understandability indicators.

7.1. *Description of the experiment*

We have followed some suggestions provided in Briand et al. (1999); Kitchenham et al. (2002); Perry et al. (2000) and Wohlin et al. (2000)

on how to perform controlled experiments and have used (with only minor changes) the format proposed by Wohlin et al. (2000) to describe it.

7.1.1. Definition

Using the Goal-Question-Metric (GQM) template for goal definition, the goal of the experiment is the following:

Analyse	*UML statechart diagrams metrics*
for the purpose of	*Evaluating*
with respect to	*The capability of being used as understandability indicators of UML statechart diagrams*
from the point of view of the	*OO software modellers, OO software deisgners*
in the context of	*Undergraduate students in the final year of computer science and teachers in software engineering in the Department of Computer Science at the University of Castilla-La Mancha*

7.1.2. Planning

After defining the experiment (why the experiment is conducted), planning took place. It explains how the experiment is conducted and includes the following activities:

- **Context selection.** The context of the experiment is a group related to the area of software engineering at the university, and hence the experiment is a run-off line (not in an industrial software development environment).

  The subjects include eight teachers and eleven students. Students were enrolled in the final-year of computer science in the Department of Computer Science at the University of Castilla-La Mancha in Spain. All the teachers belong to the software engineering segment.

  The experiment is specific since it focuses on UML statechart diagram structural complexity and size metrics. The ability to generalise from this specific context is further elaborated below when we discuss threats to the experiment. The experiment addresses a real problem, i.e. which indicators can be used to assess the understandability of UML statechart diagram? To this end, it investigates the correlation between metrics and understandability.

- **Selection of subjects.** The subjects are chosen for convenience, i.e. the subjects are students that have medium experience in the design and development of OOSS.
- **Variables selection.** The independent variables are UML statechart diagram structural complexity and size. The dependent variable is UML statechart diagram understandability.
- **Instrumentation.** The objects used in the experiment were 20 UML statechart diagrams. The independent variables were measured by the metrics presented in Sec. 5.2. The dependent variable was measured by the time the subject spent answering the questionnaire attached to each diagram. We called that time "understandability time".
- **Hypothesis formulation.** An important aspect of experiments is to know and to state in a clear and formal way what we intend to evaluate in the experiment. This leads us to the formulation of the following hypotheses:
  - *Null hypothesis*, H_0: There is no significant correlation between the UML statechart diagrams structural complexity and size metrics and the understandability time.
  - *Alternative hypothesis*, H_1: There is a significant correlation between the UML statechart diagrams structural complexity and size metrics and the understandability time.
- **Experiment design.** We selected a within-subject design experiment, i.e. all the questionnaires had to be solved by each of the subjects. The subjects were given tests in different order.

7.1.3. *Operation*

It is in this phase where measurements are collected, including the following activities:

- **Preparation.** At the time the experiment was done all the students had taken a course in software engineering, in which they learnt in depth how to design OOSS using UML. Moreover, the subjects were given an intensive training session before the experiment took place. However, the subjects were not aware of what aspects we intended to study. Neither were they informed about the actual hypotheses stated. We handed the material to the subjects, which consisted of a guide explaining the UML statechart notation and 20 UML statechart diagrams. These diagrams were related to different universes of discourse that were easy enough to understand by each of the subjects. The structural complexity and size of each diagram is different, covering a broad range of the metrics values (see Table 10). Each diagram had a test enclosed, which included a questionnaire in order to evaluate whether the subjects really understood the content of the UML statechart diagrams. Each questionnaire contained exactly the same number of questions (four) and the questions were conceptually similar and were written in identical order. Each subject had to write down the time he started answering the questionnaire and at the time he finished. The difference between the two is what we called the understandability time (expressed in seconds). In Appendix A, there is an example of the material we gave out to the subjects.

- **Execution.** The subjects were given all of the material described in the previous paragraph. We explained to them how to carry out the experiment. We allowed them one week to do the experiment, i.e. each subject had to carry out the test alone, and could use unlimited time to solve it. We collected all of the data with the understandability time calculated from the responses of the experiments.

- **Data Validation.** Once the data was collected, we controlled whether the tests were completed and whether the questions have been answered correctly. All the tests were considered valid because all the questions were correctly answered.

7.1.4. Analysis and interpretation

First we summarised the data collected for each diagram. We had the metric values and we calculated the mean of the subjects' understandability time for each statechart diagram (see Table 11). We want to analyse this data and the data shown in Table 10 in order to test the hypotheses formulated above.[4]

---

[4]To analyse the empirical data we used the Statistical Package for Social Science (SPSS, 2001).

Table 10. Metrics values for each UML statechart diagram used in the experiment.

Diagram	NEntryA	NExitA	NA	NSS	NCS	NT	NE	NG	McCabe
1	1	1	0	3	0	7	6	2	5
2	1	0	3	4	0	7	6	0	4
3	2	0	2	4	1	7	4	3	1
4	0	0	2	4	0	11	11	2	7
5	3	2	2	4	0	13	11	0	9
6	6	6	0	6	1	13	12	1	5
7	1	0	1	5	2	11	6	3	2
8	1	0	3	5	0	13	12	4	9
9	0	1	4	5	0	10	7	1	7
10	2	1	0	4	0	6	6	0	4
11	1	2	1	6	3	17	12	0	3
12	1	1	1	3	0	5	5	2	3
13	2	1	0	2	0	4	4	0	2
14	1	1	2	3	0	8	8	0	5
15	1	0	4	9	1	13	11	4	3
16	0	0	5	9	0	24	22	1	16
17	2	0	1	5	1	8	6	2	2
18	2	0	1	12	0	24	23	2	13
19	0	1	0	2	0	6	5	0	4
20	0	0	0	5	1	12	11	0	7

7.1.4.1. Correlational analysis

First, we applied the Kolmogrov–Smirnov test to ascertain if the distribution of the data collected was normal. As the data were non-normal, we decided to use a non-parametric test like Spearman's correlation coefficient, with a level of significance $\alpha = 0.05$, which means the level of confidence is 95% (i.e. the probability that we reject H_0 when H_0 is false is at least 95%, which is statistically acceptable). Each of the metrics was correlated separately to the mean of the subjects' understandability time.

For a sample size of 20 (mean values for each diagram) and $\alpha = 0.05$, the Spearman cut-off for accepting H_0 is 0.44 (Briand et al., 1997; CUHK, 2002). Because the computed Spearman's correlation coefficients for

Table 11. Mean of the Understandability time obtained in the experiment.

Diagram	Understandability time (seconds)	Diagram time (seconds)	Understandability
1	110.00	11	153.16
2	95.00	12	86.37
3	222.89	13	88.05
4	186.37	14	136.05
5	153.37	15	175.05
6	149.58	16	140.05
7	154.05	17	108.63
8	140.00	18	154.89
9	131.79	19	84.26
10	85.21	20	85.84

Table 12. Spearman's correlation coefficients between metrics and understandability time.

NEntryA	NExitA	NA	NSS	NCS	NT	NE	NG	McCabe
0.1808	−0.2521	**0.4830**	**0.4999**	0.3352	**0.6049**	0.4261	**0.5535**	0.0773

metrics NA, NSS, NT and NG (see Table 12), are above this cut-off and the p-value < 0.05, the null hypothesis H_0, is rejected.

Given these results, we can conclude that there is a significant correlation between NA, NSS, NT and NG metrics and subjects' understandability time.

7.1.4.2. Principal component analysis

Apart from the correlational analysis, we wished to investigate, by means of Principal Component Analysis (PCA) (Dunteman, 1989), whether the metrics used in the experiment capture different dimensions of structural complexity and size. This means that we wanted to demonstrate the non-redundancy of the metrics in our structural complexity and size metrics suite. Three rotated principal components (PC) were obtained (see Table 13), using an eigenvalue larger than 1.0 as a threshold for component selection. With these three rotated PCs, 80.35% of the data can be explained (see Table 14).

Looking at Table 13, we can observe that the metrics with high loadings for PC1 refer to the the Number of Simple States, Number of Transitions,

Table 13. Rotated components.

	PC1	PC2	PC3
NEntryA	0.059992049	**0.85351867**	0.131003324
NExitA	0.013027005	**0.91429555**	−0.06337288
NA	0.460220531	−0.582532006	0.027029277
NSS	**0.88527947**	−0.052992539	0.329313814
NCS	−0.020393506	0.265248417	**0.80326549**
NT	**0.96915554**	0.005867242	0.139801209
NE	**0.98253363**	0.013137952	−0.041393221
NG	0.134374549	−0.399939488	**0.6509216**
McCabe	**0.86028153**	−0.159305833	−0.432228346

Table 14. Total variation explained by the PCs.

PCs	Eigenvalue	Percentage	Accumulated percentage
PC1	3.66248294	40.6942549	40.6942549
PC2	2.16247593	24.0275103	64.7217652
PC3	1.40736966	15.6374406	**80.3592058**

Number of Events and the Cyclomatic Complexity of McCabe. In the correlational analyses, only two of the metrics of this component show high correlation with the understandability time, NSS and NT.

The second rotated PC seems to capture another dimension as the metrics with high loadings in PC2 refer to actions (NEntryA and NExitA).

The NCS metric and the NG metric shows a high loading on PC3 reflecting apparently another dimension. It should be noted though that the eigenvalue of PC3 is much lower than that of the other two components and that PC3 explains only 15% of the total variation, whereas both PC1 and PC2 explain about 40% and 64% respectively.

Even though the metric NA is not included in any rotated component, it shows a high correlation with the understandability time, in the correlational analysis.

To summarise the results of the PCA, we may conclude that the rotated principal components are difficult to interpret, and it is too premature to decide which of the metrics we proposed are redundant. These results obtained in the PCA confirm what is already known (Briand et al., 1998;

2002), that the results obtained in the PCA are dependent on the data. So further investigation is needed to obtain stronger findings and decide if some of the metrics are redundant.

7.1.5. *Validity evaluation*

We will discuss the various issues that threaten the validity of the empirical study and the way we attempt to alleviate them:

- **Threats to conclusion validity.** The conclusion validity defines the extent to which conclusions are statistically valid. The only issue that could affect the statistical validity of this study is the size of the sample data (20 values), which perhaps is not enough for both a parametric and non-parametric statistic test (Briand et al., 1997). We are aware of this, so we will try to obtain a bigger sample of data through more experimentation.
- **Threats to construct validity.** The construct validity is the degree to which the independent and the dependent variables are accurately measured by the measurement instruments used in the experiment. For the dependent variable we use the understandability time, i.e. the time each subject spent answering the questions related to each diagram, that it is considered the time they need to understand it. It is an objective measure so we consider that the understandability time could be considered a constructively valid measure. The construct validity of the metrics used for the independent variables is guaranteed by the DISTANCE framework (Poels and Dedene, 2000a), used for their theoretical validation (Genero et al., 2002) (see Sec. 6.2).
- **Threats to internal validity.** The internal validity is the degree of confidence in a cause-effect relationship between factors of interest and the observed results. The analysis performed here is correlational in nature. We have demonstrated that several of the metrics investigated had a statistically and practically significant relationship with understandability. Such statistical relationships do not demonstrate *per se* a causal relationship. They only provide empirical evidence of it. Only controlled experiments, where the metrics would be varied in a controlled manner and all other factors would be held constant, could really demonstrate causality. However, such a controlled experiment would be difficult to run since

varying structural complexity and size in a system, while preserving its functionality, is difficult in practice. On the other hand, it is difficult to imagine what alternative explanations for our results could be besides a relationship between structural complexity and size and understandability. The following issues have also been dealt with: differences among subjects, knowledge of the universe of discourse among class diagrams, precision in the time values, learning effects, fatigue effects, persistence effects, subject motivation, plagiarism influence between students, etc.

- **Threats to external validity.** External validity is the degree to which the research results can be generalised to the population under study and other research settings. The greater the external validity, the more the results of an empirical study can be generalised to actual software engineering practice. Two threats to validity have been identified which limit the ability to apply any such generalisation:

  - MATERIALS AND TASKS USED. In the experiment we tried to use statechart diagrams and tasks which can be representative of real cases, but more empirical studies taking "real cases" from software companies must be done in the future.
  - SUBJECTS. To solve the difficulty of obtaining professional subjects, we used teachers and students from advanced software engineering courses. We are aware that more experiments with practitioners and professionals must be carried out in order to be able to generalise these results. However, in this case, the tasks to be performed do not require high levels of industrial experience, so, experiments with students could be appropriate (Basili et al., 1999).

7.1.6. *Presentation and package*

As the diffusion of experimental data is important for the external replication of the experiments (Brooks et al., 1996) we have put all of the material of this experiment onto the website http://alarcos.inf-cr.uclm.es.

7.2. *Replication of the experiment*

In order to corroborate the findings obtain in the experiment previously described we carried out a strict internal replication (Brooks et al., 1996;

Basili et al., 1999) of it. The most important difference between the previous experiment and this replication are:

- The subjects were undergraduate third-year students of computer science, which have had only one course of software engineering, where they learnt how to design OO software using UML. This means that the experience of the subjects is lesser.
- The subjects had to solve the tests alone, in no more than two hours. Any doubt could be solved by the person who monitored the experiment. This fact could have contributed to the control of plagiarism between subjects.

The data obtained in the replication is shown in Table 15.

After performing a correlational analysis (Spearman correlation) between the metrics values (see Table 10) and the subjects' understandability (see Table 15), we obtained the results shown in Table 16.

On comparing the findings of both experiments (see Table 12 and Table 16) we realized that they were similar. This means that the metrics NA, NSS, NG and NT are to some extent correlated with the understandability time of UML statechart diagrams.

Table 15. Mean of the understandability time obtained in the replication.

Diagram	Understandability time (seconds)	Diagram	Understandability time (seconds)
1	129.83	11	185.65
2	124.43	12	115.35
3	261.65	13	93.3
4	195.43	14	128.48
5	129.39	15	181.26
6	134.83	16	162.87
7	169.57	17	149.43
8	135.83	18	166.52
9	155.39	19	108.87
10	108.87	20	99.52

Table 16. Spearman's correlation coefficients between metrics and understandability time (replication).

NyEntrA	NExitA	NA	NSS	NCS	NT	NE	NG	McCabe
−0.04581	−0.34611	**0.51714**	**0.57474**	0.42809	**0.54980**	0.36412	**0.63063**	−0.03260

8. Conclusions

In software engineering, it is widely recognised that not only the structural properties of UML structural diagrams but also that of the UML behavioural diagrams could have a great influence on the quality of the software product which is finally delivered. For that reason, the existence of metrics is crucial, due to the fact that they allow us to evaluate the structural properties of such diagrams in a quantative and objective way. This chapter addresses the quantitative assessment of behavioural diagrams, focusing in particular on UML statechart diagrams.

With the hypothesis that the size and the structural complexity and size of UML statechart diagrams may influence their understandability (and therefore their maintainability), we defined a set of metrics for the structural complexity and size of UML statechart diagrams.

Apart from the definition of a metrics suite, a contribution of this chapter is the methodological approach that was followed to theoretically validate the proposed metrics as structural complexity and size measures and to empirically validate them as understandability indicators.

The theoretical validity of the proposed metrics, which means that they really measure the attribute they purport to measure, was demonstrated through the validation following two approaches: a property-based approach such as Briand et al.'s framework (1996) and a measurement-theory-based approach such as the DISTANCE framework (Poels and Dedene, 2000a). Moreover, the use of DISTANCE guarantees that the metrics can be used as ratio scale measurement instruments.

Our hypothesis was to some extent empirically corroborated by a controlled experiment we carried out and its replication. As a result of all the experimental work, we can conclude that the metrics Number of Activities (NA), Number of Simple States (NSS), Number of Guards (NG) and Number of Transitions (NT) seem to be highly correlated with the understandability of UML statechart diagrams.

Nevertheless, despite the encouraging results obtained we still consider them as preliminaries. Further replication, both internal and external, is of course necessary and also new experiments must be carried out with practitioners who work in software development organisations. Only after performing a family of experiments can we build an adequate body of knowledge to extract useful measurement conclusions regarding the use of these metrics to be applied in real measurement projects as early understandability indicators of the UML statechart diagrams (Basili et al., 1999; Miller, 2000; Shull et al., 2002).

Once we obtain stronger results in this line, we think the metrics we proposed could also be used for allowing OO software modellers a quantitative comparison of design alternatives, and therefore, an objective selection among several statechart diagram alternatives with equivalent semantic content, and predicting external quality characteristics, like maintainability in the initial stages of the OO software lifecycle and a better resource allocation based on these predictions.

Acknowledgements

This research is part of the DOLMEN project (TIC 2000-1673-C06-06), financed by "Subdirección General de Proyectos de Investigación, Ministerio de Ciencia y Tecnología (Spain)" and the MESSENGER project (PCC-03-003-1), financed by "Consejería de Ciencia y Tecnología de la Junta de Comunidades de Castilla-La Mancha (Spain)".

References

Basili, V. and Rombach, H. (1988). The TAME Project: Towards Improvement-Oriented Software Environments. *IEEE Transactions on Software Engineering*, Vol. 14, No. 6, pp. 758–773.

Basili, V. and Weiss, D. (1984). A Methodology for Collecting Valid Software Engineering Data. *IEEE Transactions on Software Engineering*, Vol. 10, No. 6, pp. 728–738.

Basili, V., Shull, F. and Lanubille, F. (1999). Building Knowledge Through Families of Experiments. *IEEE Transactions on Software Engineering*, Vol. 25, No. 4, pp. 456–473.

Boehm, B. (1981). *Software Engineering Economics*. Prentice-Hall.

Briand, L., Morasca, S. and Basili, V. (1996). Property-Based Software Engineering Measurement. *IEEE Transactions on Software Engineering*, Vol. 22, No. 1, pp. 68–85.

Briand, L., Morasca, S. and Basili, V. (1997). Response to: Comments 'Property-Based Software Engineering Measurement': Refining the Additivity Properties. *IEEE Transactions on Software Engineering*, Vol. 22, No. 3, pp. 196–197.

Briand, L., Wüst, J. and Lounis, H. (1998). Replicated Case Studies for Investigating Quality Factors in Object-oriented Designs. *Technical Report ISERN 98-29 (version 3)*, International Software Engineering Research Network.

Briand, L., Arisholm, S., Counsell, F., Houdek, F. and Thévenod-Fosse, P. (1999). Empirical Studies of Object-Oriented Artifacts, Methods, and Processes: State of the Art and Future Directions. *Empirical Software Engineering*, Vol. 4, No. 4, pp. 387–404.

Briand, L. and Wüst, J. (2002). Empirical Studies of Quality Models. To be published in Advances in Computers Academic Press, Ed. Zelkowitz.

Brito e Abreu, F., Poels, G., Sahraoui, H. and Zuse, H. (2000). *Quantitative Approaches in Object-Oriented Software Engineering ECOOP'2000 Workshop Reader, Lecture Notes in Computer Science 1964*, Springer-Verlag, pp. 93–103.

Brito e Abreu, F., Henderson-Sellers, B., Piattini, M., Poels, G. and Sahraoui, H. (2002). *Quantitative Approaches in Object-Oriented Software Engineering. ECOOP'01 Workshop Reader, Lecture Notes in Computer Science 2323*, Springer-Verlag, pp. 174–183.

Brooks, A., Daly, J., Miller, J., Roper, M. and Wood, M. (1996). Replication of Experimental Results in Software Engineering. *Technical report ISERN-96-10*, International Software Engineering Research Network.

Calero, C., Piattini, M. and Genero, M. (2001). Method for Obtaining Correct Metrics. *International Conference on Enterprise and Information Systems (ICEIS'2001)*, pp. 779–784.

Cantone, G. and Donzelli, P. (2000). Production and Maintenance of Goal-oriented Measurement Models. *International Journal of Software Engineering & Knowledge Engineering*, World Scientific Publishing Company, Vol. 10, No. 5, pp. 605–626.

Carbone, M. and Santucci, G. (2002). Fast & Serious: A UML Based Metric for Effort Estimation. *6th International ECOOP Workshop on Quantitative Approaches in Object-Oriented Software Engineering (QAOOSE'2002)*, pp. 35–44.

Cartwright, M. and Shepperd, M. (2000). An Empirical Investigation of an Object-Oriented Software System. *IEEE Transactions on Software Engineering*, Vol. 26, No. 8, pp. 786–796.

CUHK — Chinese University of Hong Kong — (2002). http://department.obg. cuhk.edu.hk/ResearchSupport/Minimum_correlation.asp

Derr, K. (1995). *Applying OMT.* SIGS Books, Prentice Hall, New York.

Dunteman, G. (1989). Principal Component Analysis. *Sage University Paper 07-69*, Thousand Oaks, CA.

Fenton, N. (1994). Software Measurement: A Necessary Scientific Basis. *IEEE Transactions on Software Engineering*, Vol. 20, No. 3, pp. 199–206.

Fenton, N. and Pfleeger, S. (1997). *Software Metrics. A Rigorous and Practical Approach. 2nd edition.* International Thomson Publishing Inc.

Fenton, N. and Neil, M. (2000). *Software Metrics: A Roadmap.* Future of Software Engineering, Ed. Finkelstein, A., *ACM*, pp. 359–370.

Genero, M., Miranda, D. and Piattini, M. (2002). Defining and Validating Metrics for UML Statechart Diagrams. *6th International ECOOP Workshop on Quantitative Approaches in Object-Oriented Software Engineering (QAOOSE'2002)*, pp. 120–136.

Harrison, R., Counsell, S. and Nithi, R. (2001). Experimental Assessment of the Effect of Inheritance on the Maintainability of Object-Oriented Systems. *The Journal of Systems and Software*, Vol. 52, pp. 173–179.

ISO 9126. (2001). *Software Product Evaluation-Quality Characteristics and Guidelines for their Use*, ISO/IEC Standard 9126. Geneva.

Kitchenham, B. and Stell, J. (1997). The Danger of Using Axioms in Software Metrics. *IEE Proc.-Soft. Eng.*, Vol. 144, No. 5–6, pp. 79–285.

Kitchenham, B., Pflegger, S., Pickard, L., Jones, P., Hoaglin, D., El-Emam, K. and Rosenberg, J. (2002). Preliminary Guidelines for Empirical Research in Software Engineering. *IEEE Transactions of Software Engineering*, Vol. 28, No. 8, pp. 721–734.

McCabe, T. (1976). A Complexity Measure. *IEEE Transactions on Software Engineering*, Vol. 2, No. 4, pp. 308–320.

Miller, J. (2000). Applying Meta-Analytical Procedures to Software Engineering Experiments. *Journal of Systems and Software*, Vol. 54, pp. 29–39.

Object Management Group (1999). UML Revision Task Force. OMG Unified Modeling Language Specification, v. 1.3, document ad/99-06-08.

Object Management Group (2001). UML Revision Task Force. OMG Unified Modeling Language Specification, v. 1.4, document formal/01-09-67.

Perry, D., Porter, A. and Votta, L. (2000). Empirical Studies of Software Engineering: A Roadmap. *Future of Software Engineering.* Ed. Finkelstein, A., *ACM*, pp. 345–355.

Poels, G. and Dedene, G. (1997). Comments on Property-Based Software Engineering Measurement: Refining the Additivity Properties. *IEEE Transactions on Software Engineering*, Vol. 23, No. 3, pp. 190–195.

Poels, G. (1999). On the Formal Aspects of the Measurement of Object-Oriented Software Specifications, Ph.D. Thesis, Faculty of Economics and Business Administration. Katholieke Universiteit Leuven, Belgium.

Poels, G. and Dedene, G. (2000a). Distance-Based Software Measurement: Necessary and Sufficient Properties for Software Measures. *Information and Software Technology*. Vol. 42, No. 1, pp. 35–46.

Poels, G. and Dedene, G. (2000b). Measures for Assessing Dynamic Complexity Aspects of Object-Oriented Conceptual Schemes. *Proceedings of 19th International Conference on Conceptual Modelling (ER 2000)*, pp. 499–512.

Rumbaugh, J., Blaha, M., Premerlani, W., Eddy, F. and Lorensen, W. (1991). *Object- Oriented Modelling and Design*. Prentice Hall. USA.

Shull, F., Basili, V., Carver, J. and Maldonado, J. (2002). Replicating Software Engineering Experiments: Addressing the Tacit Knowledge Problem. *Proceedings of 2002 International Symposium on Empirical Software Engineering (ISESE 2002)*, Nara, Japan, IEEE Computer Society, pp. 7–16.

Snoeck, M. (1995). On a Process Algebra Approach for the Construction and Analysis of M.E.R.O.D.E. — based Conceptual Models. Ph.D. Thesis. Katholieke Universiteit Leuven.

Suppes, P., Krantz, M., Luce, R. and Tversky, A. (1989). *Foundations of Measurement*, Vol. 2. Academic Press.

SPSS 11.0 (2001). *Syntax Reference Guide*. Chicago. SPSS Inc.

Van Solingen, R. and Berghout, E. (1999). *The Goal/Question/Metric Method: A Practical Guide for Quality Improvement of Software Development*. McGraw-Hill.

Weyuker, E. (1988). Evaluating software complexity measures. *IEEE Transactions on Software Engineering*, Vol. 14, No. 9, pp. 1357–1365.

Wohlin, C., Runeson, P., Höst, M., Ohlson, M., Regnell, B. and Wesslén, A. (2000). *Experimentation in Software Engineering: An Introduction*. Kluwer Academic Publishers.

Zuse, H. (1998). *A Framework of Software Measurement*. Walter de Gruyter.

Appendix A

LIFT

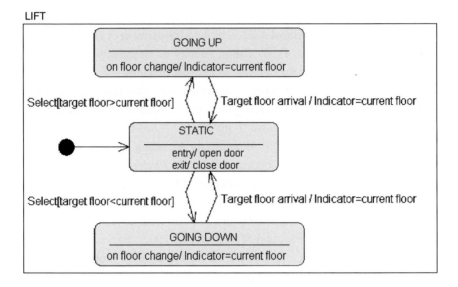

START TIME: _____

Answer the following questions:

- If you are in the state GOING UP and the event *Target floor arrival* happens, which state do you get to?
- Which event should happen to reach the state GOING UP from the state STATIC?
- Which events should happen (at least) and in which order to go from the GOING UP state to the GOING DOWN state?
- Starting at the initial state, which state do you get to if the following events sequence happens?

(1) Select[target floor < current floor]
(2) Target floor arrival
(3) Select[target floor < current floor]

FINISH TIME: _____

Chapter 8

METRICS FOR SOFTWARE PROCESS MODELS

FÉLIX GARCÍA*, FRANCISCO RUIZ[†] and MARIO PIATTINI[‡]

Alarcos Research Group
Department of Computer Science
Paseo de la Universidad, 4 – Ciudad Real – 13071, Spain
*Felix.Garcia@uclm.es
[†]Francisco.RuizG@uclm.es
[‡]Mario.Piattini@uclm.es

1. Introduction

Research into the software process has acquired great importance over the last few years due to the growing interest of software companies in improving their quality. Software processes have an important influence on the quality of the final software product, and for this reason companies are becoming more and more concerned about software process improvement, when looking to improve their final products. Software applications are very complex products, and this fact is directly related to their development and maintenance processes.

The software process is therefore a process, with special characteristics stemming from the particular complexity of the software products obtained. To support software process evaluation and improvement, a great variety of initiatives have arisen establishing reference frameworks: CMM (SEI, 1995), CMMI (SEI, 2002), the ISO 15504 (ISO/IEC 1998) standard.

Process improvement has also been incorporated into the new family of ISO 9000:2000 (ISO/IEC 2000a; 2000b) standards that promote the adoption of a focus based on processes when developing, implementing or improving a quality management system. Among the above-mentioned improvement initiatives, CMMI (Capability Maturity Model Integration) stands out as being especially important. Within the context of CMMI, the company should continuously understand, control and improve its processes, in order to reach the aims of each level of maturity. As a result of effective and efficient processes, a company will, in return, receive high quality products that satisfy both the needs of the client and the company itself.

Successful management of the software process is necessary in order to satisfy the final quality, cost, and time of the marketing requirements of software products. In order to carry out such management, four key responsibilities need to be assumed (Florac and Carleton, 1999) — **Definition**, **Measurement**, **Control** and **Improvement** of the process. Taking these responsibilities into account, it is very important to consider the integrated management of the following aspects in order to be able to promote process improvement:

- **Process Modelling.** Given the particular complexity of software processes, due to the high diversity of elements that have to be considered when managing them, it is necessary to carry out effectively a definition process of the software process. Software processes are defined for different reasons (human understanding, communication, process improvement, process management, etc.) and can be defined at different levels of abstraction — generic vs tailored, prescriptive vs descriptive, etc. (El Emam, 2001). Moreover, process modelling is a fundamental factor necessary for their measurement and consequently, as support for their evaluation and improvement.
- **Process Evaluation.** In order to promote software process improvement, it is very important to establish beforehand a framework for analysis (with the aim of determining its strong and weak points). An effective framework for the measurement of the software processes and products of a company must be provided. The other key aspect to be considered is the importance of defining and validating software process metrics, in order to evaluate their quality. The step previous to this is the process evaluation, and this goal requires the definition of metrics related to

the different elements involved in software processes. Due to the great diversity of elements involved in software processes, the establishment of a common terminology for the definition, calculation and exploitation of metrics is fundamental for the integrated and effective management of the measurement process.

In this chapter, a set of representative metrics for software process models is presented. These metrics have been formally and empirically validated obtaining important conclusions about the influence of the metrics proposed in the complexity, and hence, in the maintainability of the software process models. The proposed metrics are included in a conceptual framework for the integrated measurement of the software process. This framework incorporates the elements necessary to facilitate the definition and evaluation of software processes.

Firstly, we present a general view of the conceptual framework. In Sec. 4, the fundamentals of software process modelling are described. In the following section, a generic metamodel for the integration of measurement is presented. It has been defined and incorporated into the conceptual architecture, aiming to establish the needed reference for integrated measurement in an organisation. In Sec. 5, a set of representative metrics for the evaluation of software process models, are presented. Sections 6 and 7 present the formal and empirical validation of the proposed metrics, respectively. Finally, some conclusions and further lines of work are outlined.

2. Conceptual Framework for the Modelling and Measurement of Software Processes

In order for a company to carry out integrated management of the software processes, it is very important to establish a rigorous base for the:

- **Definition** of the process models, using singular terminology and precise and well-defined semantics.
- **Integrated management of measurement** in the company, using a measurement metamodel that will be the framework of reference for the creation of specific measurement models (database, design, analysis result or work product, or process model measurements).

A conceptual architecture with four levels of abstraction has been defined in order to integrate these both important aspects of a software process. This architecture is based on the MOF (Meta Object Facility) standard for object-oriented metamodelling (OMG, 2002a), proposed by the Object Management Group (OMG). The aim of MOF is to specify and manage metadata on different levels of abstraction. MOF describes an abstract modelling language for the definition of metamodels. In Fig. 1, the MOF standard conceptual architecture and its application to the framework proposed for the integrated measurement of the software process is as shown:

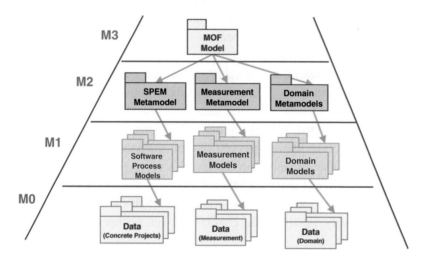

Fig. 1. MOF conceptual levels and their application for integrated measurement.

The levels included in the conceptual architecture are:

- **Meta-MetaModel Level (M3)**. In the higher conceptual level (M3), an abstract language for the definition of metamodels is found. This is the MOF language, which is basically composed of two structures — MOF class and MOF association (these are the main elements for us, although others do exist such as: package, type of data, etc.). With these levels, it is possible to integrate different domains and for this reason, according to our objective, we integrate software process modelling and software process measurement by using the MOF language to represent the metamodels which are in level M2.

- **Metamodel Level (M2).** In the M2 level, generic metamodels useful for the creation of specific models should be included. In our framework, the generic metamodels required are:

  - *Software Process Metamodel*, to define specific process models. SPEM (OMG, 2002b) has been chosen as a software process metamodel due to its significant industrial support. This metamodel contains the constructors needed to define any specific software process model. SPEM makes the software process integrated management easier because the concepts of the different models are grouped under a common terminology. This metamodel is described in Sec. 4.
  - *Measurement Metamodel*, in order to define specific measurement models. This metamodel is described in detail in Sec. 5.
  - *Domain Metamodels*, for the representation of relevant entities (from the measurement point of view) related with the software process in each specific project.

  All of the concepts in level M2 are instances of MOF class or MOF association. For example, the SPEM concepts like "Activity" or "Work Product", concepts of the measurement metamodel like "Metric", "Indicator", "Measurement Unit", and concepts of the relational metamodel (domain) like "Table", "Attribute", "Primary Key" are instances of MOF class. Relationships "Activity precedes Activity", "Work Product precedes Work Product", "Metric has a Measurement Unit" or "Table is composed for Attributes" are instances of MOF association.

- **Model Level (M1).** At this level specific models (for the definition of software processes, their measurement and other necessary domain models) will be included. From the definition point of view, at this level the company will include its process models, for example, the models for the software processes of development, maintenance, evaluation or improvement. From the measurement point of view, this level will include the specific measurement models used by the company. Finally, from the domain point of view we could define entities related with the software process, like for example the artefacts consumed or produced (relational databases, UML class diagrams, etc.). Integrated measurement is possible because we could include specific measurement models for the relational (Calero et al., 2001), object-relational (Piattini, 2001), active

(Díaz et al., 2001) database models and specific models for measuring software artifacts such as UML class diagrams (Genero et al., 2001) or state transition diagrams (Genero et al., 2002). Moreover, at this level the company could also dispose of measurement models for the defined process models themselves. In this sense, a collection of metrics for software process models is described in Sec. 5.

- **Data Level (M0).** The lower level includes the results of the enactment of the models defined at level M1. According to our framework these results belong to the enactment of a: **process model**, for example, a model for evaluation and improvement (García et al., 2002), or maintenance model (Ruiz et al., 2001) for a specific software project. At this level, the results of the enactment of a specific process model will be registered; **measurement model**, according to which the values obtained following the application of a specific measurement model will be registered. For example, the values of the measurement of a relational database or of the measurement of UML class diagrams; and **domain model** data, which represent any specific entity, related with the software process (a relational database of a bank) and which is a candidate for measurement.

With this architecture, it is possible to perform integrated management of the software process improvement, since process definition and its measurement are systematically integrated. In order to provide the technical support, a technical environment is also necessary. The proposed environment is shown in Fig. 2.

As we can observe in Fig. 2, the technical environment is composed of two tools:

- **Metamod** (García et al., 2001), as a means of support to the conceptual architecture proposed, and which allows for the definition of metamodels (based on the MOF language constructors) and of models (based on the constructors of their metamodels). These metadata are stored in a repository as XMI documents.
- **Gen-Metric** (García et al., 2003), which is an extensible tool for the definition, calculation and visualisation of software metrics. This tool for the integrated management of the measurement process supports the definition and management of software metrics based on ISO 15939 (see

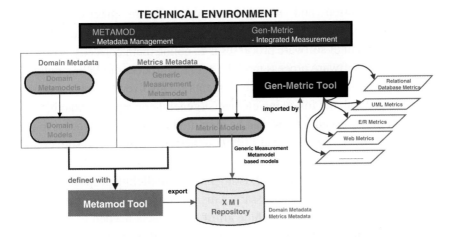

Fig. 2. Technical support for integrated measurement.

Sec. 5). For the management of the measurement process, the tool can import information on the domain, measurement and process models and their corresponding metamodels, which are represented in XMI document form (OMG, 2002c).

The **XMI repository** constitutes the key element for the integrated management of the measurement process. The metadata are defined and exported in XMI with the Metamod tool. The information of the repository is imported by GenMetric for the management of the metrics needed, and with GenMetric, the user can build metric models (based on the generic metamodel). These models are exported to the repository. This repository is managed by a repository manager (Ruiz et al., 2002) which provides the MOF-based metadata import and export services needed.

3. Fundamental Elements of Software Process Modelling

In order to deal with the complexity of software processes, it is necessary to know all of the elements involved. The software process may be defined as the conjunction of coherent policies, organisational structures, technologies, procedures and artifacts which are necessary in order to conceive, develop, package and maintain a software product (Derniame et al., 1999).

The definition and management of software processes in an organisation is not a trivial task. One of the basic elements for the successful management of software processes is to define them correctly, based on the notion of software process model. From the process modelling point of view, it is necessary to know which elements are involved before processing them. In general, the following elements (general concepts, although, with different notations and terms) can be identified in a software process in the different PMLs (Derniame et al., 1999) — **activity**, **product**, **resource** and **organisations** and **roles**.

Faced with the diversity of existing process modeling proposals, a process metamodel becomes necessary. This metamodel can serve as a common reference, and should include all of the aspects needed to define, as semantically as possible, the way in which the software is developed and maintained. With this goal in mind, the Object Management Group recently proposed the SPEM (Software Process Engineering Metamodel Specification) metamodel (OMG, 2002b) that constitutes a language for the creation of specific process models in a company. This language is within the conceptual framework of the OMG four level architecture based on the MOF standard (OMG, 2002a). It allows the effective management of the different concepts related to software processes on different levels of abstraction. This metamodel is described in more detail in Sec. 3.1.

3.1. *Software Process Engineering Metamodel (SPEM)*

The SPEM metamodel specifies the minimal set of elements needed to describe any specific process of software development, without including constructors for specific areas or disciplines, making SPEM a generic metamodel. The main objective of this specification is to make the already existing diverse terminology in the languages of software process modelling more homogeneous, since the same concepts are sometimes referred to by different names.

The conceptual model of SPEM is based on the idea that a software development process consists of the collaboration between abstract and active entities (referred to as process roles), which carry out operations (called activities) on tangible entities (called work products). The basis of software processes consists of the interaction or collaboration of multiple roles through the exchange of work products and triggering the execution or enactment of certain activities. The aim of a process is to bring a set of work products to a well-defined state.

The SPEM specification is composed of a set of packages in which each of the elements is described. All of these packages are constructed through the SPEM_Foundation package, a sub-set of UML 1.4, and the SPEM_Extensions_Package, which adds the constructors and semantics needed for the software process engineering.

SPEM is basically structured in 5 packages:

- **Basic elements.** In this package, the basic elements needed to describe processes are described. They are external description, which contains a description of the elements of the model that can be understood by the reader, and guidance, which is associated with each model element and provides more detailed information for the process performers.
- **Dependences.** This package contains the following dependences defined in SPEM: *Categorises*, which is a relation that goes from a particular package to a process element corresponding to another package. It provides a means for associating multiple categories to the process elements; *Impacts* that relates work products, and indicates that one work product could invalidate another; *Import*, which has the same semantics as the Import element of ULM, with the difference being that all of the elements have public visibility in SPEM; *Precedes*, which is a relationship between activities or between work definitions and it indicates "beginning-beginning", "end-beginning" or "end-end" dependences between these elements depending on the value of their kind of attribute; *Refers to* that relates process elements and indicates whether or not they are included in the same process component; and *Trace* which is a relationship between Work Definitions and it has the same semantics as the Trace relation in UML.
- **Process structure.** The main structural elements with which a process description is constructed are described in this package. In Fig. 3, the components of this package are represented.

   The main elements of this package are:

   - *Work Product* or *Artifact*, which is anything that is produced, consumed or modified by a process. It could be a document, a model, source code, etc.

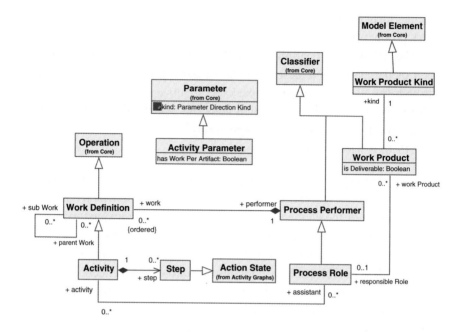

Fig. 3. SPEM structure process package.

- *Work Definition*, which is a non-abstract operation that describes the work carried out in a process. They have explicit inputs and exits referred to via *Activity Parameter* constructor.
- *Activity*, which is the main subclass of *Work Definition* and describes a part of work carried out by a *Process Role* such as tasks, operations and actions that a particular role carries out or helps. An activity can be made up of a set of atomic elements called *Steps*.
- *Process Performer*, which describes the one responsible for carrying out a set of *Work Definitions* that make up a process.
- *Process Role*, that is a subclass of *Process Performer* and it describes the responsibilities associated to *Work Products* and defines the roles that are carried out and helps in specific activities.

- **Process components.** This package contains the elements needed to divide one or more process descriptions into self-contained parts to which configuration management processes or version controls can be applied. Its main elements are — *Package*, a container of model elements; *Process Components*, part of a description of a process that is internally consistent and could be reused along with other process components to make up a complete process; *Process*, a component of process which differs form the rest in that it is not included in other components, and *Discipline*, a package specialisation that divides the activities of a process according to a common subject.

- **Process life cycle.** This package includes the process definition elements that help to define how the processes will be executed. They describe or restrict the behaviour of the process to be carried out and they are used to help plan, execute and monitor the process. With these elements the order of the execution process is established and it is possible to define the iterations and phases of the process.

SPEM does not have a graphical notation by itself, but basic UML diagrams can be used to present different perspectives of a software process model. In particular, the following UML notations are useful — class diagram, package diagram, activity diagram, use case diagram and sequence diagram. Figure 4 shows an example of a simplified software process model, which belongs to the Rational Unified Process (Jacobson et al., 1999). For the graphical representation of the model the Activity Diagram notation and the stereotypes, which represent the SPEM constructors, have been used.

As we can see in Fig. 4, using UML Activity diagrams it is possible to represent a view of the software process in which the different activities, their precedence relationships, the work products consumed or produced and the responsible roles are included.

Consequently, SPEM constitutes the reference metamodel for the definition of software process models, which facilitates the integrated management of the software processes defined.

4. Generic Metamodel for Software Measurement

A fundamental element to take into consideration when establishing a framework for process improvement is the possibility of defining objective indicators of the processes that allow a software company to efficiently evaluate and improve its processes at any given moment. A measurement process framework must be established in order to do so.

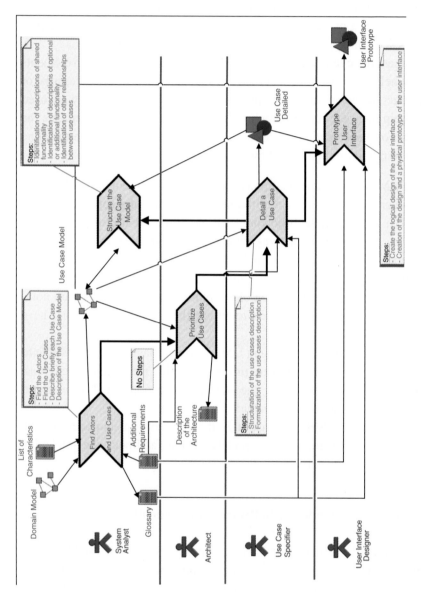

Fig. 4. Example of a software process model represented with SPEM.

A good base for developing a measurement process is the one provided by CMMi (SEI, 2002). In CMMi, a new key process area called "Measurement and Analysis" is included. The aim of this area is to develop and establish a measurement capacity that can be used to support the company's information needs, and this implies broadening the concepts included in the CMM model. It gives support to the rest of the process areas by providing the companies with a framework when aligning objectives and measurement needs with a focus on measurement based on providing objective results that are useful for carrying out correctional decisions and actions. This focus is consistent with the idea of Goal-Question-Metric (Basili and Rombach, 1988) and the ISO 15939 (ISO/IEC, 2000c) standard.

According to CMMi, the first step in the measurement process is to identify the measurement objectives so that, in a second step, a measurement and analysis process can be implemented. This requires the measurement to be integrated in the different work processes of a company. It is very important for a company wishing to implement an effective measurement process to be able to define specific measurement models that, being supported by an integrated measurement tool, allow the appropriate and necessary automation for process evaluation.

Most of the problems associated with collecting data on a measurement process are mainly due to poor definition of the software measures being applied. Therefore, it is important not only to gather the values pertaining to the measurement process, but also to represent in an appropriate way the metadata associated to this data. In Kitchenham et al. (2001), a method for the specification of measurement models is defined with the aim of capturing the definitions and relationships between software measurements. The proposed framework is made up of three levels of abstraction for measurement, starting with a generic measurement model and moving up to automation of the gathering of metric values on a project level. This idea of abstraction is fundamental to be able to integrate effectively the measurement process into the organisation.

Therefore, it is very convenient to introduce a generic metamodel for measurement, making it possible to derive specific measurement models that make up the base for assessment and improvement processes in an organisation. In Fig. 5, our proposal for a measurement metamodel based on the ISO 15939 (ISO/IEC, 2000c) standard is represented in UML.

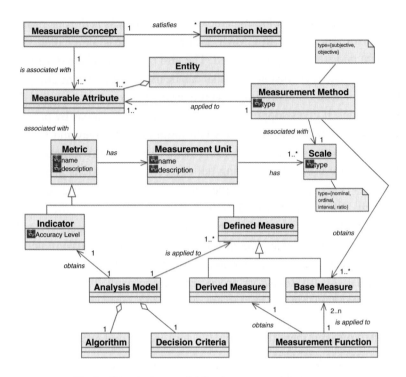

Fig. 5. Generic metamodel for the measurement process.

As can be observed in Fig. 5, from the measurement point of view, the elements on which properties can be measured are "**Entities**". An entity is an object (for example, a process, product, project or resource) that can be characterised through the measurement of its "**Measurable attributes**" which describe properties or characteristics of entities, which can be distinguished quantitatively or qualitatively by human or automatic means. The aim of attributes is to satisfy specific information needs such as, *"the need to compare software development productivity with respect to a determined value"*. This abstract relation between attributes and information needs is represented by the element called "**Measurable concept**", that, in this case, would be *"productivity ratio of software development"*. As measurable attributes, attributes of the developed product size or of development effort could be used.

All measurable attributes are associated to a metric, which is an abstraction of the different types of measurements used to quantify and to make decisions concerning the entities. All metrics are associated to a unit of measure (for example, code lines), which at the same time belong to a determined scale. According to the standard, the four scales distinguished are nominal, ordinal, interval and ratio, although other classifications can be established as in (Kitchenham et al., 2001). The three types of metrics are:

- **Base measurement**, defined in function of an attribute and the method needed to quantify it (a measurement is a variable to which a value is assigned).
- **Derived measurement**, a defined measurement in function of two or more values of base measurements.
- **Indicator**, a measurement that provides an estimate or assessment of specific attributes derived from a model with respect to information needs. The indicators are the base for analysis and decision-making. These measurements are the ones that are presented to the users in charge of the measurement process.

The procedures for calculating each of the metric types are:

- The values of the base measurements are reached with "**Measurement methods**" that consist of a logical sequence of operations, generically described, used to quantify an attribute with respect to a specific scale. These operations can imply activities such as, counting occurrences or observing the passing of time. The same measurement method can be applied to multiple attributes.
- The derived measurements are obtained by applying a "**Measurement function**", which is an algorithm or calculation carried out to combine two or more base measurements. The scale and unit of the derived measurement depend on the scales and units of the base measurements.
- The indicators are obtained with an "**Analysis model**". An analysis model produces estimates and assessments relevant to the defined information needs. It consists of an algorithm or calculation that combines one or more base measurements and/or derivates with determined decision-making criteria. All decision-making criteria is composed of a series of limit values or used objects for determining the need to research, or to describe the confidence level with regard to a determined result. These criteria help to interpret the measurement results.

Using this reference metamodel, it is possible to measure any element of a process or data model. Taking into account that our main objective is software process improvement, and therefore, evaluation, it is necessary to establish the relationship between the main elements of the software process metamodel and the main elements of the software measurement metamodel. This relationship is represented in Fig. 6.

As we can see in Fig. 6, any software process model is enacted in specific software projects. As a result of carrying out a software project, certain work products are produced and all the software project requirements to satisfy some information needs. The main candidate elements to be measured in order to evaluate the software process are:

- **The Software process model.** It could be useful to research if the model of software processes has an influence on its final quality. For this reason with the framework proposed it is possible to define metrics related to the constructors of the software process metamodel. For example, if we apply the measurement metamodel to the elements of the SPEM model, we could measure important elements like the class *Activity*, and the classes *Work Product* and *Process Role*. These elements of the model have a set of measurable attributes, such as for an activity: "*the number of activities with which there is a precede type dependence*". This attribute would be calculated with a metric to satisfy an information need like

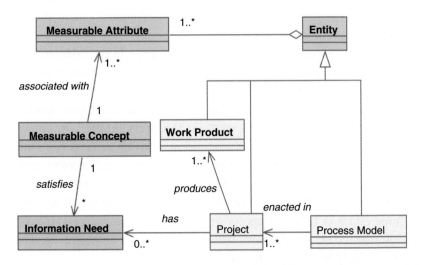

Fig. 6. Relation between the software process metamodel and the measurement metamodel.

"Evaluate the software process coupling" and, in this case, the unit of measure would be of *"Ratio"* type. This issue will be looked at in the following section.

- The **Work product**. This is a fundamental factor in the quality of the software process. Work Products are the results of the process (final or intermediate) and their measurement is fundamental in order to evaluate the software processes. With the framework proposed it is possible to measure the quality attributes related to the artifacts or work products by defining the metamodels related to the different work products. For example, if we have to evaluate the quality of a UML class diagram we have to incorporate into the framework, the necessary UML metamodel and metrics.

By using the framework proposed, the work of an assessment and improvement process is facilitated, since the fulfillment of the software processes carried out in a specific organisation is registered quantitatively.

5. Proposal of Metrics for Software Process Models

In the literature dealing with this subject explicit metrics on software process models have not been defined as research on software process evaluation is focused on the collection of project data to obtain throughput, efficiency and productivity metrics.

The study of the possible influence of the complexity of software process models on their execution (enactment) could be very useful. For this reason, the first step is to define a collection of metrics in order to characterise the software process model. The main objective to be achieved is the development of an empirical study to demonstrate the influence of the metrics proposed (which are applied to the attributes of software process models) with their structural complexity, taking into account that a software process model with a high degree of complexity will be much more difficult to change, decreasing its maintanibility. This affirmation is based on the theoretical basis for developing quantitative models relating to structural properties and external quality attributes provided by Briand et al. (1998). This basis could be applied to the software process in the same way as it is applied to software artefacts. Software process models have a hardly maintainable effect on the execution of projects (more expensive in resources and schedule) and on the final quality of the software products obtained.

5.1. Metrics definition

The metrics have been defined according to the SPEM terminology, but they can be directly applied to other process modeling languages. The metrics proposed could be classified as **model level metrics**, if they evaluate the characteristics of a software process model, or as fundamental **element** (activity, process role and work product) **metrics**, if they describe the characteristics of a model element. For this reason, they will be described separately.

5.1.1. Model level metrics

Model level metrics are applied in order to measure the structural complexity of the overall software process model. These metrics are represented in Table 1. Their formal and empirical validation is described in Sec. 6.

5.1.2. Fundamental element level metrics

The main elements of a software process model are the activities to be performed, the work products consumed and/or produced by the activities and the roles responsible for performing the activities. It is also fundamental to evaluate the relationships between these fundamental elements. For this reason, we have defined metrics for the elements — **activity, work product** and **process role**. The formal and empirical validation of these metrics is described in Sec. 6.

5.1.2.1. Activity metrics

The metrics for the process constructor **Activity** are defined in order to measure the structural complexity of a specific activity in the software process model. These metrics are represented in Table 2.

Table 1. Definition of software process model level metrics.

Metrics	Definition
NA(PM)	Number of **Activities** of the software process model
NWP(PM)	Number of **Work Products** of the software process model
NPR(PM)	Number of **Roles** which participate in the process
NDWPIn(PM)	Number of input dependences of the **Work Products** with the **Activities** in the process
NDWPOut(PM)	Number of output dependences of the **Work Products** with the **Activities** in the process
NDWP(PM)	Number of dependences between **Work Products** and **Activities** $NDWP(PM) = NDWPIn(MP) + NDWPOut(MP)$
NDA(PM)	Number of precedence dependences between **Activities**
NCA(PM)	Activity Coupling in the process model $$NCA(PM) = \frac{NA(PM)}{NDA(PM)}$$
RDWPIn(PM)	Proportion of **input dependences** of Work Products with Activities of the **total number of dependences** of Work Products with Activities $$RDWPIn(PM) = \frac{NDWPIn(PM)}{NDWP(PM)}$$
RDWPOut(PM)	Proportion of **output dependences** of Work Products with Activities of the **total number of dependences** of Work Products with Activities $$RDWPOut(PM) = \frac{NDWPOut(PM)}{NDWP(PM)}$$
RWPA(PM)	Average of **Work Products** and **Activities** $$RWPA(PM) = \frac{NWP(PM)}{NA(PM)}$$
RRPA(PM)	Average of **Process Roles** and **Activities** $$RRPA(MP) = \frac{NRP(MP)}{NA(MP)}$$

5.1.2.2. Work product metrics

Work product metrics are defined in order to measure the structural complexity of a specific work product in the software process model. These metrics are represented in Table 3.

Table 2. Activity metrics.

Metrics	Definition
NWPIn(A)	Number of **Work Products** which are **input** of the Activity
NWPOut(A)	Number of **Work Products** which are **output** of the Activity
NWPInOut(A)	Number of **Work Products** which are **input/output** of the Activity
NWP(A)	Total Number of **Work Products** related to an Activity $NWP(A) = NWPIn(A) + NWPOut(A) - NWPInOut(A)$
RWPIn(A)	Proportion of **Input Work Products** of the total number of Work Products in activity A $RWPIn(A) = \dfrac{NWPIn(A)}{NWP(A)}$
RWPOut(A)	Proportion of **Output Work Products** with of the total number of Work Products in activity A $RWPOut(A) = \dfrac{NWPOut(A)}{NWP(A)}$
RWPInOut(A)	Proportion of **Input-Output Work Products** of the total number of Work Products in activity A $RWPInOut(A) = \dfrac{NWPInOut(A)}{NWP(A)}$
NR(A)	Number of responsible **Roles** of an Activity
NPD(A)	Number of **Activities** which are **predecessors** of Activity A
NSD(A)	Number of **Activities** which are **successors** of Activity A
ND(A)	Total number of **dependences** of activity A $ND(A) = NPD(A) + NSD(A)$
PR(A)	Proportion of **Predecessors Activities** of the total number of dependences in activity A $PR(A) = \dfrac{NPD(A)}{ND(A)}$
PS(A)	Proportion of **Successors Activities** of the total number of dependences in activity A $PS(A) = \dfrac{NSD(A)}{ND(A)}$

5.1.2.3. Process role metrics

Process role metrics are defined in order to measure the structural complexity of a specific process role in the software process model. These metrics are represented in Table 4.

Table 3. Work product metrics.

Metrics	Definition
NAWPIn(WP)	Number of **Activities** in which the work product is consumed (input)
NAWPOut(WP)	Number of **Activities** in which the work product is produced (output)
NAWPInOut(WP)	Number of **Activities** in which the work product is modified (input/output)
NAWP(WP)	Number of **Activities** related with the Work Product $$NAWP(WP) = NAWPIn(WP) + NAWPOut(WP)$$ $$-NAWPInOut$$
RDWPA(WP)	Proportion of activities related with the work product of the total number of activities in the model $$RDWPA(WP) = \frac{NAWP(WP)}{NA(PM)}$$

Table 4. Process role metrics.

Metrics	Definition
NARP(R)	Number of **Activities** for which role R is responsible
RRPR(R)	Level of **Responsibility** of the process role R. Average of the activities in which role R is responsible and the total number of activities in the model $$RRPR(A) = \frac{NARP(R)}{NA(PM)}$$

Table 5. Values of model level metrics.

Metric	Value	Metric	Value
NA(PM)	5	NDA(PM)	4
NWP(PM)	8	NCA(PM)	$5/4 = 1.25$
NPR(PM)	4	RDWPIn(PM)	$13/18 = 0.722$
NDWPIn(PM)	13	RDWPOut(PM)	$5/18 = 0.278$
NDWPOut(PM)	5	RWPA(PM)	$8/5 = 1.6$
NDWP(PM)	18	RRPA(PM)	$4/5 = 0.8$

5.1.3. *Example of calculation*

In Tables 5, 6 and 7 the values of the metrics proposed shown are applied to the software process model represented in Fig. 4.

Table 6. Metrics of the activity "Detail a Use Case".

Metric	Value	Metric	Value
NWPIn(A)	3	NR(A)	1
NWPOut(A)	1	NPD(A)	1
NWPInOut(A)	0	NSD(A)	2
NWP(A)	4	ND(A)	3
RWPIn(A)	$3/4 = 0.75$	PR(A)	$1/3 = 0.333$
RWPOut(A)	$1/4 = 0.25$	PS(A)	$2/3 = 0.666$

Table 7. Examples of metrics related to work products and process roles.

Work product "Use Case Model" Metrics	Value	Process role "System Analyst" Metrics	Value
NAWPIn(WP)	4	NARP(R)	2
NAWPOut(WP)	2	RRPR(R)	$2/5 = 0.4$
NAWPInOut(WP)	1		
NAWP(WP)	$4 + 2 - 1 = 5$		
RDWPA(WP)	$5/5 = 1$		

Table 8. Theoretical validation of the software process model level metrics.

Metrics	Type	Briand et al. (1996)	Poels and Dedene (1999; 2000a)
NA	Base	Size	Ratio
NWP	Base	Size	Ratio
NPR	Base	Size	Ratio
NDA	Base	Coupling	Ratio
NDWP	Derived	Complexity	Ratio
NDWPIn	Base	Size	Ratio
NDWPOut	Base	Size	Ratio

6. Theoretical Validation of the Proposed Metrics

For the theoretical validation of metrics defined for measuring the structural complexity of software process models and their fundamental elements (activity, work product and process role) we have followed

Table 9. Theoretical validation of the activity level metrics.

Metrics	Type	Briand et al. (1996)	Poels and Dedene (2000)
NWP	Derived	Coupling	Ratio
NWPIn	Base	Coupling	Ratio
NWPOut	Base	Coupling	Ratio
NWPInOut	Base	Coupling	Ratio
NR	Base	Coupling	Ratio
ND	Derived	Coupling	Ratio
NPD	Base	Coupling	Ratio
NSD	Base	Coupling	Ratio

Table 10. Theoretical validation of the work product level metrics.

Metrics	Type	Briand et al. (1996)	Poels and Dedene (2000)
NAWP	Derived	Coupling	Ratio
NAWPIn	Base	Coupling	Ratio
NAWPOut	Base	Coupling	Ratio
NAWPInOut	Base	Coupling	Ratio

Table 11. Theoretical validation of the process role level metrics.

Metric	Type	Briand et al. (1996)	Poels and Dedene (2000)
NARP	Derived	Coupling	Ratio

Briand et al.'s framework (1996) as a property-based framework (which is explained in more detail in Chapter 5), and Poels and Dedene's framework (2000) as measurement theory-based frameworks (which is further explained in Chapter 4). In Tables 8–11, the results of the theoretical validation according to the frameworks followed are summarised.

7. Empirical Validation of the Proposed Metrics

In order to validate in practice the influence of the software process model level metrics proposed we have carried out two controlled experiments, which have allowed us to obtain an initial validation of these metrics. In this section, we summarise the results and conclusions of these experiments.

7.1. *First experiment*

In this section, we describe the first experiment we have carried out to validate empirically the proposed measures as early maintainability indicators. We have followed some suggestions provided by Wohlin et al. (2000), Perry et al. (2000) and Briand et al. (1999) on how to perform controlled experiments. To describe the experiment we use (with only minor changes) the format proposed by Wohlin et al. (2000) comprising the following main tasks — definition, planning, operation, analysis and interpretation, validity evaluation and presentation and package.

7.1.1. *Definition*

Using the GQM template (Basili and Rombach, 1988) for goal definition, the goal of the experiment is defined as follows:

Analyse	Software Process Models (SPM) structural complexity metrics
For the purpose of	Evaluating with respect to the possibility of using them as software process model maintainability indicators
From the point of view of	Software Process Analysts
In the context of	Undergraduate Computer Science students and professors of the Software Engineering area in the Department of Computer Science at the University of Castilla-La Mancha

7.1.2. *Planning*

- **Context selection.** The context of the experiment is a group of undergraduate students and professors of the software engineering area, and hence the experiment is run off-line (not in an industrial software development environment). The subjects consisted of ten professors and ten students enrolled in the final-year of computer science in the Department of Computer Science at the University of Castilla-La Mancha in Spain. All the professors belong to the software engineering area.

The experiment is specific since it is focused on SPM structural complexity metrics. The ability to generalise from this specific context is discussed in further detail below when looking at threats to the experiment. The experiment addresses a real problem, i.e. what indicators can be used for the maintainability of SPM? With this end in view it investigates the correlation between SPM structural complexity metrics and maintainability sub-characteristics.

- **Selection of subjects.** The subjects are chosen for convenience. The subjects are undergraduate students and professors who have wide experience and knowledge in software product modelling (UML, databases, etc), but they have no experience or knowledge of conceptual modelling of SPM.

- **Variable selection.** The independent variable is SPM **structural complexity**. The dependent variables are three maintainability sub-characteristics — **understandability, analysability** and **modifiability**.

- **Instrumentation.** The objects were 18 SPM. The independent variable was measured through the metrics proposed at process model level (see Sec. 5.1.1). The dependent variables were measured according to the subject's ratings.

- **Hypothesis formulation.** We wish to test the following hypotheses:

  - *Null hypothesis, H_0*: There is no significant correlation between the structural complexity metrics (NA, NWP, NPR, NDA, NDWP, NDWPIn, NDWPOut, NCA, RDWPIn, RDWPOut, RWPA, RRPA) and the subject's rating of three maintainability sub-characteristics, such as understandability, analysability and modifiability.

  - *Alternative hypothesis, H_1*: There is a significant correlation between the structural complexity metrics (NA, NWP, NPR, NDA, NDWP, NDWPIn, NDWPOut, NCA, RDWPIn, RDWPOut, RWPA, RRPA) and the subject's rating of three maintainability sub-characteristics, such as understandability, analysability and modifiability.

- **Experiment design.** We selected a within-subject design experiment, i.e. all the tests (experimental tasks) had to be solved by each of the subjects. The tests were put in a **different order** for each subject.

7.1.3. *Operation*

- **Preparation.** Subjects were given an intensive training session before the experiment took place. However, the subjects were not aware of what aspects we intended to study. Neither were they aware of the actual hypothesis stated. We prepared the material to be handed to the subjects, consisting of eighteen SPM. These models were related to different universes of discourse but they were general enough to be understood by the subjects. The structural complexity of each diagram is different, because as Table 12 shows, the values of the metrics are different for each diagram.

  Each model had a test enclosed, which included the description of three maintainability sub-characteristics — understandability, analysability and modifiability. Each subject had to rate each sub-characteristic using a scale consisting of seven linguistic labels. For example for understandability we proposed the following linguistic labels shown in Table 13. We chose seven linguistic labels because we considered they were enough to cover all the possible categories of our maintainability variables.

- **Execution.** The subjects were given all the materials described in the previous paragraph. We explained to them how to carry out the tests. We allowed one week to do the experiment, i.e. each subject had to carry out the test alone, and could use unlimited time to solve it. We collected all the data, including subjects' rating obtained from the responses of the experiment and the metric values of the different SPM.

- **Data validation.** We collected all the tests, checking if they were complete. As all of them were complete we consider their subjective evaluation reliable.

7.1.4. *Analysis and interpretation*

First, we summarised the data collected. We had the metric values calculated for each SPM, and we calculated the median of the subjects' rating for each maintainability sub-characteristic. By so doing we obtained the data we wanted to analyse to test the hypotheses stated above. We applied the Kolmogorov-Smirnov test to ascertain if the distribution of the data collected was normal or not. As the data were non-normal we decided to use

Table 12. Metric values for each software process model.

Mod	NA	NWP	NPR	NDWPIn	NDWPOut	NDWP	NDA	NCA	RDWPIn	RDWPOut	RWPA	RRPA
1	6	6	3	5	6	11	6	1.000	0.455	0.545	1.000	0.500
2	5	6	4	5	5	10	4	1.250	0.500	0.500	1.200	0.800
3	2	13	2	12	3	15	1	2.000	0.800	0.200	6.500	1.000
4	9	25	9	25	21	46	11	0.818	0.543	0.457	2.778	1.000
5	5	6	4	5	5	10	8	0.625	0.500	0.500	1.200	0.800
6	4	11	4	14	9	23	3	1.333	0.609	0.391	2.750	1.000
7	8	17	1	15	11	26	9	0.889	0.577	0.423	2.125	0.125
8	5	8	4	13	5	18	4	1.250	0.722	0.278	1.600	0.800
9	7	12	1	12	11	23	6	1.167	0.522	0.478	1.714	0.143
10	24	37	10	72	40	112	24	1.000	0.643	0.357	1.542	0.417
11	7	12	5	12	11	23	6	1.167	0.522	0.478	1.714	0.714
12	2	8	3	6	4	10	1	2.000	0.600	0.400	4.000	1.500
13	3	6	1	8	3	11	4	0.750	0.727	0.273	2.000	0.333
14	3	5	7	5	3	8	2	1.500	0.625	0.375	1.667	2.333
15	4	9	1	9	7	16	6	0.667	0.563	0.438	2.250	0.250
16	8	6	4	9	9	18	7	1.143	0.500	0.500	0.750	0.500
17	4	24	1	20	11	31	3	1.333	0.645	0.355	6.000	0.250
18	5	21	3	21	11	32	4	1.250	0.656	0.344	4.200	0.600

Table 13. Linguistic labels for understandability.

Extremely difficult to understand	Very difficult to understand	A bit difficult to understand	Neither difficult nor easy to understand	Quite easy to understand	Very easy to understand	Extremely easy to understand

Table 14. Spearman's correlation between the metrics and understandability, analysability and modifiability.

	NA	NWP	NPR	NDWPIn	NDWPOut	NDWP
Underst.	0.629	0.756	0.149	0.841	0.802	0.888
Analis.	0.612	0.789	0.042	0.830	0.855	0.892
Modif.	0.675	0.784	0.148	0.871	0.858	0.931
	NDA	**NCA**	**RDWPIn**	**RDWPOut**	**RWPA**	**RRPA**
Underst.	0.481	−0.201	0.220	−0.220	0.189	−0.385
Analis.	0.498	−0.254	0.131	−0.131	0.227	−0.454
Modif.	0.532	−0.243	0.145	−0.145	0.173	−0.412

a non-parametric test like Spearman's correlation coefficient, with a level of significance $\alpha = 0.05$, which means the level of confidence is 95%.

Using Spearman's correlation coefficient, each of the metrics was correlated separately to the median of the subject's rating of understandability, analysability and modifiability (see Table 14).

For a sample size of 18 (median values for each SPM) and $\alpha = 0.05$, the Spearman cutoff for accepting H_0 is 0.4684 (Briand et al., 1995). Because the computed Spearman's correlation coefficients (Table 14) are above the cutoff, the null hypothesis H_0, is rejected. Analysing Table 14 we can conclude that there is a significant correlation (rejecting the null hypothesis) between the structural complexity of the SPM and the metrics (NA, NWP, NDWPIn, NDWPOut, NDWP y NDA) because the correlation coefficient is greater than 0.4684. The metric RRPA seems to be less correlated with the three maintainability sub-characteristics with respect to the prior metrics, although it has a correlation value near to the cutoff. The metrics NPR, NCA, RDWPIn, RDWPOut and RWPA do not seem to be correlated with the maintainability.

7.1.5. *Validity evaluation*

We will discuss the empirical study's various threats to validity and the way we attempted to alleviate them:

- **Threats to conclusion validity.** The only issue that could affect the statistical validity of this study is the size of the sample data (360 values: 18 models and 20 subjects), which is perhaps not enough for both parametric and non-parametric statistic tests (Briand et al., 1995). We are aware of this, so we will consider the results of this experiment only as preliminary findings.
- **Threats to construct validity.** The dependent variables are three maintainability sub-characteristics — understandability, analysability and modifiability. We proposed subjective metrics for them (using linguistic variables), based on the judgement of the subjects. The construct validity of the metrics used for the independent variables is guaranteed by Poels and Dedene's framework (Poels and Dedene, 2000) used to define and validate them.
- **Threats to internal validity.** The following issues have been dealt with:

  - *Differences among subjects.* Using a within-subjects design, error variance due to differences among subjects is reduced. In this experiment, professors and students had approximately the same degree of experience in modelling software products and they had a minimum knowledge about process modelling, which did not influence the results because they have product modelling skills and knowledge.
  - *Knowledge of the universe of discourse among SPMs.* The SPMs were from different universes of discourse but general and well-known enough to be familiar to the subjects. Consequently, knowledge of the domain does not affect the internal validity.
  - *Accuracy of subject responses.* Subjects assumed responsibility for rating each maintainability sub-characteristic. As they have wide experience in product modelling by mapping this experience to the process modelling, we think their responses could be considered valid. However, we are aware that not all of them have exactly the same degree of experience, and if the subjects have more experience minor inaccuracies could be introduced by subjects.

- *Learning effects.* The subjects were given the test in a different order, to cancel out learning effects. Subjects were required to answer in the order in which the tests appeared.
- *Fatigue effects.* On average, the experiment lasted for less than one hour (this fact was corroborated summing up the total time for each subject), so fatigue was not very relevant. Also, the different order in the tests helped to cancel out these effects.
- *Persistence effects.* In order to avoid persistence effects, the experiment was run with subjects who had never done a similar experiment.
- *Subject motivation.* All the professors who were involved in this experiment have participated voluntarily, in order to help us in our research. We motivated students to participate in the experiment, explaining to them that similar tasks to the experimental ones could be done in exams or practice and it could be useful in their professional career.
- *Other factors.* Plagiarism and influence among students could not really be controlled. Students were told that talking to each other was forbidden, but they did the experiment alone without any supervision, so we had to trust them as far as that was concerned. We are conscious that this aspect to some extent could threaten the validity of the experiment, but at that moment it was impossible to gather all the subjects together.

- **Threats to external validity.** External validity is the degree to which the results of the research can be generalised to the population under study and other research settings. The greater the external validity, the more the results of an empirical study can be generalised to actual software engineering practice. Two threats to validity have been identified which limit the possibility of applying any such generalisation:

  - *Materials and tasks used.* In the experiment we have used SPMs which are representative of real cases. With regard to the tasks, the judgement of the subjects is to some extent subjective, and does not represent a real task. Therefore, more empirical studies taking "real cases" from software companies must be done.
  - *Subjects.* To solve the difficulty of obtaining professional subjects, we used professors and advanced students from software engineering courses. We are aware that more experiments with practitioners and

professionals must be carried out in order to be able to generalise these results. However, in this case, the tasks to be performed do not require high levels of industrial experience, so, experiments with students could be appropriate (Basili et al., 1999).

7.2. Second experiment

In order to confirm the results obtained in the first experiment we replicated this experiment under the same conditions. As the majority of the steps are identical to those of the first experiment we will only point out those issues which are different. The subjects were fifteen professors and ten research technicians of the Alarcos research group of computer science in the Department of Computer Science at the University of Castilla-La Mancha in Spain. All the professors belong to the software engineering area.

We included a new dependent variable measured by the time that the subjects spent to completely understand the SPM before answering the subjective questions. We called this time "understandability time". Understandability time comprises the time taken to understand the class diagram. Our assumption here is that the faster a class diagram can be understood, the easier it is to maintain.

We wish to test the following hypotheses:

- *Null hypothesis, H_0*: There is no significant correlation between structural complexity metrics (NA, NWP, NPR, NDA, NDWP, NDWPIn, NDWPOut, NCA, RDWPIn, RDWPOut, RWPA, RRPA) and understandability time.
- *Alternative hypothesis, H_1*: There is a significant correlation between structural complexity metrics (NA, NWP, NPR, NDA, NDWP, NDWPIn, NDWPOut, NCA, RDWPIn, RDWPOut, RWPA, RRPA) and understandability time.

The material we gave to the subjects was the same material provided in the first experiment, consisting of a guide explaining SPEM notation and the same eighteen SPM diagrams of different application domains. We collected all the data including the **understandability** time obtained from the responses of the tests and the metrics values which were already calculated for analysis of the results of the first experiment.

Once the data was collected, we checked to see if the tests were complete. They were. We calculated the mean of the understandability time and the median of the subjects' ratings about understandability, analysability and modifiability of the SPM. Thus, we obtained the data we wanted to analyse to test the hypotheses stated above. We applied the Kolmogorov-Smirnov test to ascertain if the distribution of the data collected was normal. As the data were non-normal we decided to use a non-parametric test like Spearman's correlation coefficient, with a level of significance $\alpha = 0.05$, correlating each of the metrics separately with understandability time and subjects' ratings (see Table 15).

The Spearman cutoff for accepting H_0 is 0.4684 (the sample size is the same as the first experiment) because the computed Spearman's correlation coefficients (Table 15) are above the cutoff, the null hypothesis H_0 is rejected with respect to the influence of some metrics in the sub-characteristics of maintainability. Analysing Table 15 we can conclude that there is a significant correlation (rejecting the null hypothesis) between the structural complexity of the SPM and the metrics (NA, NWP, NDWPIn, NDWPOut, NDWP y NDA) because the correlation coefficient is greater than 0.4684. The metric RRPA is correlated with analysability and it seems to be less correlated other two maintainability sub-characteristics respect

Table 15. Spearman's correlation between the metrics and understandability, analysability and modifiability.

	NA	NWP	NPR	NDWPIn	NDWPOut	NDWP
Underst	**0.684**	**0.724**	0.174	**0.775**	**0.819**	**0.852**
Analis	**0.602**	**0.778**	−0.012	**0.802**	**0.854**	**0.878**
Modif.	**0.698**	**0.750**	0.175	**0.847**	**0.874**	**0.917**
Underst Time	0.182	−0.007	0.189	−0.121	−0.103	−0.132
	NDA	**NCA**	**RDWPIn**	**RDWPOut**	**RWPA**	**RRPA**
Underst	**0.508**	−0.181	0.075	−0.075	0.105	−0.369
Analis	**0.503**	−0.275	0.108	−0.108	0.225	**−0.506**
Modif.	**0.558**	−0.269	0.099	−0.099	0.128	−0.415
Underst Time	0.176	−0.085	−0.276	0.276	−0.193	0.254

to the prior metrics, although it has a correlation value near to the cutoff. The metrics NPR, NCA, RDWPIn, RDWPOut y RWPA do not seem to be correlated with maintainability. These results confirm the results obtained in the first experiment.

According to the correlation between the metrics proposed and the understandability time the results show that it does not exist. With these results we do not think that time is a meaningful factor to be measured in subjective experiments because it is not a real indicator. We cannot demonstrate that the subjects completely understood the diagram in the times indicated.

7.3. *Comparison of results*

An overall analysis of the obtained results (see Tables 14 and 15) leads us to conclude that the metrics NA, NWP, NDWPIn, NDWPOut, NDWP and NDA are to some extent correlated with the three maintainability sub-characteristics we considered. The metric RRPA seems to be less correlated with the three maintainability sub-characteristics with respect to the prior metrics, although it has a correlation value near to the cutoff with respect to understandability and modifiability and seems to be correlated with analysability. The metrics NPR, NCA, RDWPIn, RDWPOut and RWPA do not seem to be correlated with maintainability, although this preliminary result may be caused by the design of the experiment.

We believe it is too early to consider these results as definitive. As previously stated, further empirical validation is needed, including internal and external replication of these experiments, and also new experiments must be carried out in which the subjects demonstrate that they have correctly understood the models and that they can modify them. Besides it is necessary to apply new experiments with practitioners who work in software development organisations. As Basili et al. (1999) remark, after performing a family of experiments you can build the cumulative knowledge to extract useful measurement conclusions to be applied in real measurement projects. Moreover, data related to "real projects" is also needed for gathering real evidence that these metrics can be used as early SPM maintainability indicators.

8. Conclusions and Further Work

This chapter has looked at measurement of the software process as support for their improvement. In order to support the integrated measurement of the different elements of the software process a framework, in which the measurement and the modelling of software processes are integrated, has been developed. The SPEM metamodel is used for the modelling of processes under a common terminology, and a metamodel based on the ISO 15939 standard, facilitating the management of an integrated measurement process to promote improvement in a company's processes, has been defined as an integrated framework for measurement. This framework is necessary due to the great diversity of elements to manage in order to evaluate and improve software processes. The conceptual framework is supported by the tools Metamod, for the management of metadata in different abstraction levels according to the MOF standard, and GenMETRIC, a generic and extensible tool for the definition, calculation and results visualisation of software metrics.

With the proposed framework, any company dedicated to the development and/or maintenance of software can effectively define and evaluate its processes as a step prior to promoting their improvement. Furthermore, as the framework is based on the MOF standard, the simple extension and modification of its elements is possible, with the incorporation and modification of the necessary metamodels, since all of them are represented using the common terminology provided by the MOF model.

As part of the integrated framework, and due to the lack of proposals in relation to this topic, a set of representative metrics for the evaluation of the structural complexity of software process models has been defined. These metrics are focused on the main elements included in a model of software processes, and may provide the quantitative base necessary to evaluate the changes in the software processes in companies with high maturity levels, which are applying continuous improvement actions (Pfleeger, 1996). The metrics proposed have been theoretically validated using the frameworks of Briand et al. (1996) and Poels and Dedene (2000). Besides, in order to demonstrate the practical utility of the metrics proposed, one experiment has been performed and replicated. This experiment and its replica have allowed us to draw preliminary conclusions about the influence of the met- rics proposed at model level in the maintainability of the software pro- cess models through three of its sub-characteristics (understandability, analysability and modifiability). As a result of these experiments performed we could conclude that the metrics NA, NWP, NDWPIn, NDWPOut, NDWP and NDA are good maintainability indicators. However, we can- not say the same about the metrics NPR, NCA, RDWPIn, RDWPOut and RWPA.

Although the results obtained in these experiments are good, we cannot consider them to be definitive results. It is necessary to elaborate new, more objective experiments in subjects by answering questions related with the models and modifying them could enable us to make a better evaluation of their maintainability. Besides, it is necessary to further develop study cases with the metrics proposed.

With these considerations in mind, we propose as future research lines:

- Refinement of the conceptual and technological framework proposed in which possible improvements of the modelling and measurement metamodels of the software process and of the support tools could be incorporated.
- Development of an objective experiment in order to confirm the conclu- sions obtained regarding the influence of the metrics in the maintainabil- ity of the software process models.
- Development of case studies in which we evaluate the metrics proposed using software process models of a specific company.
- Consideration of other views related with the modelling of software pro- cesses, like for example, roles and their responsibilities in work products, in order to define and validate new possible metrics.

Acknowledgements

This work has been partially funded by the TAMANSI project financed by "Consejería de Ciencia y Tecnología, Junta de Comunidades de Castilla- La Mancha" of Spain (project reference PBC-02-001) and by the MAS project partially supported by "Dirección General de Investigación of the Ministerio de Ciencia y Tecnología" (TIC 2003-02737-C02-02).

References

Basili, V. and Rombach H. (1988). The TAME Project: Towards Improvement-Oriented Software Environments. *IEEE Transactions on Software Engineering*, Vol. 14, No. 6, pp. 728–738.

Basili, V., Shull, F. and Lanubile, F. (1999). Building Knowledge Through Families of Experiments. *IEEE Transactions on Software Engineering*, Vol. 25, No. 4, pp. 435–437.

Briand, L., El Emam, K. and Morasca, S. (1995). Theoretical and Empirical Validation of Software Product Measures. *Technical Report ISERN-95-03*, International Software Engineering Research Network.

Briand, L., Morasca, S. and Basili, V. (1996). Property-Based Software Engineering Measurement. *IEEE Transactions on Software Engineering*, Vol. 22, No. 1, pp. 68–86.

Briand, L., Wüst, J. and Lounis, H. A. (1998). Comprehensive Investigation of Quality Factors in Object-Oriented Designs: An Industrial Case Study. *Technical Report ISERN-98-29*, International Software Engineering Research Network.

Briand, L., Arisholm, S., Counsell, F., Houdek, F. and Thévenod-Fosse, P. (1999). Empirical Studies of Object-Oriented Artefacts, Methods, and Processes: State of the Art and Future Directions, *Empirical Software Engineering*, Vol. 4, No. 4, pp. 387–404.

Calero, C., Piattini, M. and Genero, M. (2001). Empirical Validation of Referential Metrics. Information Software and Technology. Special Issue on Controlled Experiments in Software Technology, Vol. 43, No. 15, pp. 949–958.

Derniame, J. C., Kaba, B. A. and Wastell, D. (1999). *Software Process: Principles, Methodology and Technology. Lecture Notes in Computer Science 1500*, Springer.

Díaz, O., Piattini, M. and Calero, C. (2001). Measuring Triggering-Interaction Complexity on Active Databases. Information Systems Journal. Elsevier Science, Vol. 26, No. 1, pp. 15–34.

El Emam, K. (2001). Software Engineering Process. In Guide to the Software Engineering Body of Knowledge. IEEE — Trial Version 1.00. Chapter 9. May.

Florac, W. A. and Carleton, A. D. (1999). Measuring the Software Process. Statistical Process Control for Software Process Improvement. SEI Series in Software Engineering. Addison Wesley.

García. F., Ruiz. F., Piattini. M. and Polo. M. (2002). *Enterprise Information Systems IV*. Chapter: Conceptual Architecture for the Assessment and Improvement of Software Maintenance. Kluwer. The Netherlands, pp. 219–226.

García, F., Ruiz, F., Cruz, J. A. and Piattini, M. (2003). Integrated Measurement for the Evaluation and Improvement of Software Processes. *9th European Workshop on Software Process Technology (EWSPT'9). Lecture Notes in Computer Science (LNCS 2786)*. Helsinki (Finland), 1–2 September, pp. 94–111.

Genero, M., Olivas, J., Piattini, M., and Romero, F. (2001a). Using Metrics to Predict OO Information Systems Maintainability. *13th International Conference on Advanced Information Systems Engineering (CAiSE'01)*, Eds. Dittrich, K., Geppert, A. and Norrie, M. C., *Lecture Notes in Computer Science*, 2068, Interlaken, Switzerland, pp. 388–401.

Genero, M., Miranda, D. and Piattini, M. (2002). Defining and Validating Metrics for UML Statechart Diagrams. *Proceedings of the 6th International ECOOP Workshop on Quantitative Approaches in Object-Oriented Software Engineering (QAOOSE)*, pp. 120–136.

ISO/IEC (1998). ISO IEC 15504 TR2:1998, part 2: A reference model for processes and process capability.

ISO/IEC (2000a). International Organization for Standardization (ISO). Quality management systems — Fundamentals and vocabulary. ISO 9000:2000. See http://www.iso.ch/iso/en/iso9000-14000/iso9000/selection_use/iso9000family.html

ISO/IEC (2000b). International Organization for Standardization (ISO). 2000. Quality management systems — Requirements ISO 9001:2000.

ISO/IEC (2000c). ISO IEC 15939, Information Technology — Software Measurement Process, Committee Draft, December.

Jacobson, I. Booch, G. and Rumbaugh, J. (1999). *The Unified Software Development Process*. Addison Wesley.

Kitchenham, B. A., Hughes, R. T. and Linkman, S. G. (2001). Modeling Software Measurement Data. *IEEE Transactions on Software Engineering*, Vol. 27, No. 9, pp. 788–804.

OMG (2002a). Meta Object Facility (MOF) Specification; version 1.4. Object Management Group. April. In http://www.omg.org/technology/documents/formal/mof.htm.

OMG (2002b). Software Process Engineering Metamodel Specification; adopted specification, version 1.0. Object Management Group. November. Available in http://cgi.omg.org/cgi-bin/doc?ptc/02-05-03.

OMG (2002c). OMG XML Metadata Interchange (XMI) Specification; version 1.2. Object Management Group. January. In http://www.omg.org/technology/documents/formal/xmi.htm.

Perry D., Porter, A. and Votta, L. (2000). *Future of Software Engineering.* Chapter: Empirical Studies of Software Engineering: A Roadmap. Ed. Finkelstein, A., *ACM*, pp. 345–355.

Pfleeger, S. L. (1996). *Software Measurement.* Chapter: Integrating Process and Measurement. Ed. Melton, A. London. International Thomson Computer Press, pp. 53–74.

Piattini, M., Calero, C., Sahraoui, H. and Lonis, H. (2001). Object-Relational Database Metrics. *L'object.* HERMES Science Publications, Paris, Vol. 7, No. 4.

Poels, G. and Dedene, G. (2000). Distance-Based Software Measurement: Necessary and Sufficient Properties for Software Measures, *Information and Software Technology*, Vol. 42, No. 1, pp. 35–46.

Ruiz, F., Piattini, M. and Polo, M. (2001). A Conceptual Architecture Proposal for Software Maintenance. *Proceedings of the International Symposium on Systems Integration (ISSI, Intersymp'2001).* Baden-Baden, Germany, VIII:1–8.

Ruiz, F., Piattini, M., García, F. and Polo, M. (2002). An XMI-based Repository for Software Process Metamodeling. *4th International Conference on Product Focused Software Process Improvement (PROFES'2002). Lecture Notes in Computer Science (LNCS 2559),* Eds. Markku, O. Seija Komi-Sirviö. Springer. Rovaniemi (Finland). December, pp. 546–558.

SEI (1995). Software Engineering Institute (SEI). The Capability Maturity Model: Guidelines for Improving the Software Process. In http://www.sei.cmu.edu/cmm/cmm.html.

SEI (2002). Software Engineering Institute (SEI). Capability Maturity Model Integration (CMMISM), version 1.1. In http://www.sei.cmu/cmmi/cmmi.html.

Wohlin, C., Runeson, P., Höst, M., Ohlson, M., Regnell, B. and Wesslén, A. (2000). *Experimentation in Software Engineering: An Introduction.* Kluwer Academic Publishers.

INDEX

analysability, 121, 122, 297, 304, 305, 307

behavior, 165
behavioural diagrams, 237, 267
Briand *et al.*'s framework, 194, 250, 267, 295

case studies, 103
chunking, 163, 164, 168, 178, 183, 201
class diagram, 99
class diagram quality, 100, 161
class-scope metrics, 214
CM fitness, 38
CM quality, 21
cognitive complexity, 162, 163, 213
Cognitive Complexity Model, 163
cognitive techniques, 163, 168, 177
completeness, 5, 21, 22, 24, 29, 43
completeness measure, 24, 45
concept map, 27–30, 32, 45
conceptual model quality, 2, 8–10
conceptual modelling quality, 3, 4, 6, 10, 13
conclusion validity, 128, 230, 264, 301
construct validity, 128, 228, 264, 301
controlled experiment, 221
correlational analysis, 127, 134, 138, 261

datawarehouse, 207–210, 214, 221, 222, 231
datawarehouse conceptual models, 212
datawarehouse models, 209

defects, 88, 89
descriptive dictionary, 32, 33, 35, 37, 38, 41
descriptive quality, 6
diagram-scope metrics, 215
DISTANCE framework, 108, 112, 215, 252, 253, 267

element level metrics, 290
empirical strategies, 103
empirical validation, 101, 103, 104, 117, 150, 203, 221, 257, 295
estimation of system effort, 78
experiments, 103
external validity, 130, 151, 229, 265, 302

feasible completeness, 5, 22
feasible validity, 5
fitness, 38, 41, 46
fitness measure, 41, 42, 44, 46
function points, 75, 76, 78
Fuzzy Deformable Prototypes, 145, 151
Fuzzy Prototypical Knowledge Discovery, 142

heuristics, 87, 88

incompleteness, 88
incompressibility, 88
inferential quality, 6
internal validity, 129, 229, 264, 301

laboratory packages, 152

maintainability, 100, 117, 118, 120, 122,
    140–142, 162, 213, 222, 223, 246, 289,
    296, 297, 304, 305, 307
measurement theory-based approaches,
    103
metrics for "chunking", 178, 183
metrics for "tracing", 185
metrics for project estimation, 74
metrics for requirements engineering, 84
model completeness, 20
model level metrics, 290
modelling language, 6
modelling process, 6
modifiability, 121, 122, 135, 136, 297,
    304, 305, 307
multidimensional modelling, 210

Object Constraint Language, 161
OCL characteristics, 165
OCL expression, 162, 164, 166, 177, 201

perceived semantic quality, 5
perceptual quality, 6
physical quality, 5
pragmatic quality, 6
prediction, 141
prediction models, 152
principal component analysis, 126, 133,
    137, 262
process evaluation, 274
process modelling, 274, 279
process models, 289
property-based approaches, 101
property-based framework, 193

quality frameworks, 2

requirements specification, 85, 94

semantic quality, 5
size, 118, 120–122, 140, 240, 242, 245,
    246, 248, 259, 267
size and complexity, 75, 83
size metrics, 248
social quality, 6
software process models, 275, 287, 289
star-scope metrics, 214
statechart diagram, 238, 239, 245–247
statechart diagrams maintainability, 243
structural complexity, 105, 106, 117, 118,
    120–122, 139, 140, 149, 151, 213, 242,
    245, 246, 248, 259, 267, 289, 294, 296,
    297, 303, 306
structural complexity metrics, 131
structural diagrams, 237
syntactic quality, 5

theoretical validation, 101, 108, 150, 163,
    193, 201, 215, 221, 244, 250, 294, 295
tracing, 163, 164, 168, 185, 201
type of quality, 3, 4

understandability, 121, 122, 135, 136,
    138, 140, 162, 177, 203, 246, 258, 259,
    267, 297, 303–305, 307
use case points, 78
use case relationships, 71, 74
use cases diagrams, 86
use cases metrics, 59, 60, 91, 93, 94
use cases quality, 85

verification of requirements, 85